Everyday
Diabetes
Meals

Everyday
Diabetes
Meals

Cooking for One or Two

Laura Cipullo, RD, CDE, CEDRD, CDN
& Lisa Mikus, RD, CNSC, CDN

Robert
ROSE

For complete cataloguing information, see page 278.

Disclaimer

This book is a general guide only and should never be a substitute for the skill, knowledge and experience of a qualified medical professional dealing with the facts, circumstances and symptoms of a particular case.

The nutritional, medical and health information presented in this book is based on the research, training and professional experience of the authors, and is true and complete to the best of their knowledge. However, this book is intended only as an informative guide for those wishing to know more about health, nutrition, and medicine; it is not intended to replace or countermand the advice given by the reader's personal physician. Because each person and situation is unique, the authors and the publisher urge the reader to check with a qualified health-care professional before using any procedure where there is a question as to its appropriateness. The authors and the publisher are not responsible for any adverse effects or consequences resulting from the use of the information in this book. It is the responsibility of the reader to consult a physician or other qualified health-care professional regarding his or her personal care.

This book contains references to products that may not be available everywhere. The intent of the information provided is to be helpful; however, there is no guarantee of results associated with the information provided. Use of brand names is for educational purposes only and does not imply endorsement.

The recipes in this book have been carefully tested by our kitchen and our tasters. To the best of our knowledge, they are safe and nutritious for ordinary use and users. For those people with food or other allergies, or who have special food requirements or health issues, please read the suggested contents of each recipe carefully and determine whether or not they may create a problem for you. All recipes are used at the risk of the consumer. We cannot be responsible for any hazards, loss or damage that may occur as a result of any recipe use. For those with special needs, allergies, requirements or health problems, in the event of any doubt, please contact your medical adviser prior to the use of any recipe.

Design and production: Alicia McCarthy & Kevin Cockburn / PageWave Graphics Inc.
Managing editor: Sue Sumeraj
Copy editor: Kelly Jones
Recipe editor: Jennifer MacKenzie
Proofreader: Sue Sumeraj
Indexer: Gillian Watts
Photographer: Colin Erricson
Associate photographer: Matt Johannsson
Food stylist: Michael Elliott
Prop stylist: Charlene Erricson

Cover image: Angel-Hair Pasta with Shrimp, Sun-Dried Tomatoes and Peppers (page 160)

Background pattern © istockphoto.com/uncle-rico

Published by Robert Rose Inc.
120 Eglinton Avenue East, Suite 800, Toronto, Ontario, Canada M4P 1E2
Tel: (416) 322-6552 Fax: (416) 322-6936
www.robertrose.ca

Printed and bound in Canada
3 4 5 6 7 8 9 MI 25 24 23 22 21 20 19 18

*Dedicated to our clients and
all who are affected by diabetes,
especially those who are making
meals for just one or two people!*

CONTENTS

Introduction

EMBRACE DIABETES. We know you didn't choose to have diabetes. If you have been diagnosed with diabetes in any form, focus on acceptance first. Then prepare yourself for a delicious life made easy with these 150 recipes created specifically for you or two in *Everyday Diabetes Meals*. As you turn the pages of this book, you will learn:

- The many faces of diabetes
- The complications associated with diabetes and when to screen for them
- The connection between inflammation, obesity and diabetes
- The secret sauce for managing blood sugar
- When to eat saturated fat versus unsaturated fat
- The latest buzz on everything from clean eating to gluten-free foods
- How to prepare 150 recipes portioned and tailored to manage your blood sugar, including breakfast, lunch and dinner recipes with 45 to 60 grams of carbohydrates, and sweet and savory snack recipes with 15 to 30 grams of carbohydrates.

In the United States, diabetes affects 29 million people and is the seventh leading cause of death. In Canada, 11 million Canadians live with diabetes or prediabetes. Perhaps it affects you or your partner, directly or indirectly. Maybe your mother has type 2 diabetes and you fear that you will as well. Have you had gestational diabetes? Do you need help in preventing the further development of type 2 diabetes? Were you diagnosed with type 1 diabetes at 12 years old and you now need a quick refresher on the disease? Are you looking for a diabetes cookbook adapted to meet your single lifestyle? If so, this cookbook was made for you.

■ ■ ■

We have learned that living with diabetes takes planning and effort. This lifestyle pursuit can seem daunting, but you are not alone and we know you will find your everyday living much easier with this cookbook.

■ ■ ■

Registered dietitian Lisa Mikus and I have both been affected by diabetes. In fact, both our families are genetically predisposed to diabetes. We have learned that living with diabetes takes planning and effort. This lifestyle pursuit can seem daunting, but you are not alone and we know you will find your everyday living much easier with this cookbook. Simply enjoy our 150 recipes made for just one or two servings to ease any nutrition anxiety. We have done all of the work for you. Each recipe has been created to fall within a 45-gram to 60-gram carbohydrate range. If you follow a diabetes-friendly diet that adheres to these carbohydrate counts, such as the recipes in this book, you may:

■ ■ ■

Each recipe has been created to fall within a 45-gram to 60-gram carbohydrate range.

■ ■ ■

- Eliminate or decrease your risk of insulin resistance
- Eliminate or decrease your hypoglycemic and/or hyperglycemic episodes
- Decrease the risk for health issues associated with diabetes
- Decrease time spent preparing meals
- Eliminate or decrease food waste
- Decrease your food shopping bill
- Decrease your waist circumference

These recipes can also:

- Improve your blood sugar management
- Improve your overall wellness
- Improve your mindfulness
- Improve your cooking skills
- Improve your sleep
- Increase your knowledge of diabetes and dispel diet myths
- Improve your quality of life

What are you waiting for? Let's get started!

— *Laura Cipullo*

CHAPTER 1

Diabetes Deconstructed

FIRST, LET'S DECONSTRUCT the many types of diabetes. Diabetes is not a singular diagnosis. There are many different forms of diabetes and many different reasons one may develop diabetes. This disease does not discriminate. You can be any age or gender, or even seemingly healthy when you receive this lifetime diagnosis. Most people have heard of type 1 and type 2 diabetes. Type 1 was formerly known as juvenile-onset diabetes or insulin-dependent diabetes, and type 2 was called adult-onset diabetes. These names no longer ring true. Bear in mind that sometimes a medical doctor cannot determine which type of diabetes a person may have at the time of diagnosis or onset. This is especially true for adults. If you happen to find yourself in this situation, you are not alone and it does not mean your doctor is incompetent.

What Is Type 1 Diabetes?

The first classification of diabetes, now called type 1 diabetes, is a disease in which the pancreas does not produce insulin, a result of an autoimmune beta-cell destruction. Type 1 diabetes, specifically immune-mediated diabetes, accounts for 5% to 10% of diabetes cases.

DID YOU KNOW?

The Diabetic Ketoacidosis Connection

One-third of children presenting with diabetic ketoacidosis will be diagnosed with type 1 diabetes. The acute onset of diabetic ketoacidosis plus a random blood glucose level greater than or equal to 200mg/dL (11.1mmol/L) can confirm type 1 diabetes.

Deconstructing Terms Related to Diabetes

- **Beta cells:** Insulin-producing cells found in the pancreas.
- **Diabetic ketoacidosis:** A condition caused by the body's action of breaking down fat due to a lack of insulin in the blood, which produces a buildup of ketone acids (fat by-products).
- **Insulin:** A natural hormone that manages blood sugar by transporting sugar from the bloodstream into cells to create energy.
- **Insulin resistance:** A condition that occurs when the body is not responding well to insulin; the pancreas continues to pump insulin into the bloodstream in high levels in an effort to transport sugar into the cells (both insulin and blood sugar levels will be elevated).
- **Macrophages:** Large white blood cells that are part of the immune system; their function is to rid the body of foreign particles and infections. Macrophages are found in the liver, spleen and connective tissue.

A person with type 1 diabetes would have autoimmune markers in their blood, including islet cell autoantibodies and autoantibodies to insulin, glutamic acid decarboxylase (GAD), tyrosine phosphatase 1A-2 and others. The presence of one or more of these autoimmune markers is sufficient to make the diagnosis of type 1 diabetes. Keep in mind, the rate of beta cell destruction can vary in each person. This will affect when type 1 diabetes manifests in physical symptoms. It's important to note that infection and/or stress can increase the speed of beta cell destruction.

Eventually, when little or no insulin is secreted, low levels of plasma C peptide occur, which can be determined by a blood test. Type 1 diabetes can now be diagnosed at any age, typically between the ages of 6 months and 80 years.

Within the type 1 diabetes classification, there is a form of diabetes called idiopathic type 1 diabetes, which is less understood and has no known cause. For example, a person may present with ketoacidosis, yet no autoantibodies to the beta cells are present in his or her system.

What Is Type 2 Diabetes?

Type 2 diabetes makes up the majority of diabetes diagnoses — a whopping 90% to 95% of all cases. This type of diabetes is a disease in which your pancreas doesn't produce enough insulin or your body doesn't use the insulin it does produce. In either case, glucose builds up in your bloodstream instead of being absorbed and converted into energy. It is of utmost importance to understand what it is and how to live easily with this medical condition.

This form of diabetes is common with individuals who have a greater fat distribution around the belly area. People with type 2 diabetes may fit into the classification of overweight or obese, based on their body mass index (BMI), but this is not an exclusive association. Thin people can have type 2 diabetes, too! In fact, 86 million American adults have prediabetes.

As the body becomes incrementally more resistant to insulin, the pancreas eventually stops producing insulin altogether. Consequently, blood glucose gradually elevates over time without you realizing. Many people have no idea they have type 2 diabetes. When the pancreas stops producing insulin, an individual needs to self-administer the drug, just like someone with type 1 diabetes.

There are very simple tests available to screen for prediabetes, or impaired glucose tolerance. Screening is of utmost importance if you have one or more risk factors, such as a family history of diabetes, polycystic ovary syndrome, gestational diabetes or family history of diabetes. Keep in mind, the American Diabetes Association recommends that all adults should be screened at age 45 and at minimum every 3 years after (the Canadian Diabetes Association recommends age 40). Why? Because you can prevent prediabetes from unfolding into full-blown diabetes. Facts like these should be reason enough to use this book as your meal guide whether you have diabetes, are at risk or just want to live a healthy lifestyle.

What about Prediabetes?

Prediabetes is also known as insulin resistance or impaired glucose tolerance. You are considered to have prediabetes when your blood sugar is greater than normal but not as high as someone with diabetes. See Getting to Know the Terms and Values for Diabetes, page 15, for prediabetes criteria.

Be a Prediabetes Sleuth

Have your medical doctor check your liver function, specifically your levels of alanine aminotransferase (ALT), to identify the presence of a fatty liver. A fatty liver, impaired glucose metabolism and high levels of triglycerides are indicators of insulin resistance. Insulin resistance may be the cause of the fatty liver.

Take Action

It is time to make lifestyle changes, if you haven't already. Whether you have been identified as having prediabetes or perhaps are at risk for diabetes (including but not limited to being older than 45 years of age, having a BMI greater than or equal to 23 to 25, and/or having a first-degree relative with diabetes), it may be worth your while to become proactive.

If you are at high risk of diabetes, specifically with impaired fasting glucose and/or impaired glucose tolerance, you can decrease your risk by about 58% with lifestyle modifications — as proven by the Diabetes Prevention Program through the National Institute of Diabetes and Digestive and Kidney Disease. Nutrition and fitness are the keys to prevention. The aim of your efforts is to decrease your weight by 7% of your current body weight (if warranted) and achieve a moderately active lifestyle with 150 minutes of exercise each week, plus two 30-minute sessions each week of weight resistance (such as lifting weights or using weight machines).

In a Nutshell: Goals of Diabetes Prevention

- Focus on the quality of fats in your diet — follow a more Mediterranean-style diet, increase monounsaturated fats.
- Increase your intake of foods high in fiber and antioxidants, such as nuts and berries.
- Perform resistance training and endurance exercise weekly.
- Avoid smoking.
- Consider metformin medication if your BMI is greater than or equal to 35.

What Is Gestational Diabetes?

The third classification of diabetes is gestational diabetes mellitus (GDM). This is elevated blood sugar diagnosed in the second or third trimester of pregnancy. All women with risks factors, such as obesity, are now tested for undiagnosed diabetes on their first prenatal visit. If diagnosed at the first prenatal visit or even in the first trimester, this will be classified as type 2 diabetes (it is not diagnosed as gestational diabetes during this time because diabetes was likely present before pregnancy).

If no risk factors are present, testing occurs for the first time between 24 and 28 weeks' gestation, and a diagnosis would be called gestational diabetes. There are two approaches to testing. The first approach is a one-step test, which includes a 75-gram oral glucose tolerance test (OGTT), administered while you are fasting. The second approach is two steps. A 1-hour, 50-gram OGTT is administered while you are in

DID YOU KNOW?

Gestational Diabetes after Pregnancy

Women with a history of gestational diabetes should be screened for diabetes at 6 to 12 weeks postpartum and every 3 years thereafter. Women should be screened for both prediabetes and diabetes.

Feeding the Mommy-to-Be

Nutrition should be the first approach used when you are diagnosed with gestational diabetes. Medical nutrition therapy alone can potentially manage a pregnant mom's blood sugar until delivery. As of spring 2016, the American Diabetes Association refrains from endorsing one specific diet to treat gestational diabetes mellitus (GDM). Before 2005, the organization favored a restricted carbohydrate diet, one that included no more than 40% of calories as carbohydrate. This was due to positive outcomes including improved postprandial (1 hour after meal time) blood sugar when following this diet.

However, there was and still is concern regarding the benefit versus risk to the fetus. Mom is likely to compensate for her decreased carbohydrate intake by increasing her fat intake. The increase in free fatty acids and triglycerides can negatively affect the fetus and the fetus's future health status. There is potential risk for these babies to become obese or to develop glucose intolerance or metabolic syndrome. Furthermore, an increase in dietary fat could potentially increase insulin resistance in Mom's fatty tissues (adipose tissue).

What's a mom to do? Studies have confirmed that diets (such as the Choosing Healthy Options in Carbohydrate Energy, or CHOICE diet) that range between 55% and 70% of complex carbohydrates (including lower–glycemic index carbohydrates) and that are overall lower in fat, at 25% or less, may reduce insulin resistance and inflammation in women with GDM.

This means moms can eat wholesome grains such as barley, buckwheat and oats, but they will need to avoid highly processed foods. The goal of the higher-carbohydrate diet is to balance after-meal blood sugar, reduce the need for insulin, decrease low-density lipoprotein (LDL, or "bad") cholesterol and even improve insulin sensitivity, all while keeping the baby in utero healthy. Woohoo! Carbs are not catastrophic, evil, bad or harmful. It is just a matter of focusing on less processed, more wholesome carbohydrate choices.

the non-fasted state. If the results of this "glucose challenge" are greater than or equal to 140 mg/dL (7.8 mmol/L) in the non-fasted state, then a 3-hour, 100-gram OGTT in the fasted state will be administered. Two elevated glucose levels are considered to be consistent with the diagnosis of gestational diabetes.

What Is the Fourth Classification?

The fourth classification encompasses diabetes resulting from many different causes.

Chemical-Induced Diabetes

This category includes drug- or chemical-induced diabetes. For example, you may develop diabetes from steroid treatments, since steroids elevate blood sugar. Says author Laura Cipullo: "I personally observed this happening to many patients who were undergoing treatments for cancer when I was a young registered dietitian on the oncology floor."

Monogenic Diabetes Syndrome

The fourth classification also includes monogenic diabetes syndrome, which is broken down into two groups: neonatal diabetes and maturity-onset diabetes of the young (MODY). In neonatal diabetes, which onsets within the first 6 months of life, there are genetic and autosomal defects that cause beta cell dysfunction. In MODY, which onsets within the first 24 years of life, the young person shows symptoms of having inherited an autosomal dominant defect from a parent. This type of diabetes is more rare than type 1 or 2 diabetes. Monogenic diabetes can be determined by genetic testing.

Cystic Fibrosis–Related Diabetes

Cystic fibrosis–related diabetes (CFRD) also falls into the fourth classification. Diabetes is the most common disease associated with individuals diagnosed with cystic fibrosis (CF). Within this disease state, not enough insulin is produced, which is further aggravated by the insulin resistance associated with infection and inflammation. All children with cystic fibrosis should have yearly screenings for diabetes from age 10 onward. Individuals with CFRD have different nutrition considerations and should always seek care and guidance from their physician, not this book.

Getting to Know the Terms and Values for Diabetes

The jumble of numbers and complicated terms may sometimes make you feel like you need a degree in mathematics to understand diabetes. There are so many numbers to know, such as your HgA1c (A1c), your fasting glucose numbers and your cholesterol values. There may be numbers to log when tracking your progress, such as your pre- and post-meal blood sugars. Numbers are needed to determine how many grams of carbohydrates you need and, if necessary, what type and how many units of insulin you need.

Below is a chart to help you navigate some of these numbers and terms. To be diagnosed with diabetes, the medical doctor should always do a second test to confirm diagnosis. The second test should be a repeat of the initial test you received or one of the tests below. Two positive test results confirms a diagnosis of diabetes. Being educated about the disease will help increase your self-efficacy and overall self-care when living with diabetes. Use this chart as a reference when a medical doctor discusses diabetes with you.

■ ■ ■

Being educated about the disease will help increase your self-efficacy and overall self-care when living with diabetes.

■ ■ ■

Blood Test Levels for Diagnosis of Diabetes and Prediabetes

	A1c* (percent) (for adults only)	Fasting plasma glucose (no food or drink 8 hours beforehand)	2-hour fasting plasma glucose after consuming a 75-gram load	With symptoms of hyperglycemia and random plasma glucose or hyperglycemia crisis
Diabetes	>/= 6.5	>/= 126 mg/dL (7.0 mmol/L)	>/= 200 mg/dL (11.1 mmol/L)	>/= 200 mg/dL (11.1 mmol/L)
Prediabetes (impaired fasting glucose)	5.7–6.4 (6.0–6.4 in Canada)	100–125 mg/dL (6.1–6.9 mmol/L)	140–199 mg/dL (7.8–11.0 mmol/L)	n/a
Normal	</= 5.6 (5.9 in Canada)	</= 99 mg/dL (6.0 mmol/L)	</= 139 mg/dL (7.7 mmol/L)	n/a

*A1c should be performed by a laboratory employing the National Glycohemoglobin Standardization Program (NGSP).

What's the Fuss with Hemoglobin A1c Numbers?

It seems many clients show up in our office with concerns of "prediabetes" and/or "unmanaged" blood sugar based on their A1c values. But is this truly reflective of their blood sugar? It depends.

First, it's important to understand a few facts about the A1c test. Your HgA1c is also known as A1c. It is reflective of your average blood sugar levels over the previous 2 to 3 months. It is a quick and easy test, but it provides only an average number. This means you could have high and low blood sugar that averages out to an ideal number. In our practice, we ask all clients with a diagnosis of diabetes to check their blood sugar before and after meals to get a more accurate read on their blood sugar management.

Second, when using A1c for screening diabetes, the American Diabetes Association now endorses the very strict criteria set by the National Glycohemoglobin Standardization Program (NGSP). These criteria are set to help decrease variants in the A1c test, but the test still remains imperfect. Different forms of hemoglobin, such as HbC or fetal hemoglobin, can affect your A1c. The A1c blood test is not an accurate reflection of blood sugar in someone who has sickle-cell anemia, someone who is pregnant or someone who has had recent blood loss. While this is a great tool for screening, keep in mind the results are an average. Remember to have your test done through a lab that carries the NGSP certification.

The Heart of the Matter

Heart disease is the macrovascular disease correlated with diabetes. In fact, statistics from the American Heart Association (AHA) declare that adults with diabetes are more than two to four times more likely to have heart disease or stroke than an adult without diabetes. The good news is the AHA also lists type 2 diabetes as one of several controllable risk factors associated with heart disease.

Risk factors for heart disease include hypertension, high levels of low-density lipoprotein (LDL, or "bad") cholesterol/low levels of high-density lipoprotein (HDL, or "good") cholesterol, high triglycerides, having a body mass index greater than or equal to 25, especially with a larger waist circumference (greater than 40 inches/102 cm for men and greater than 35 inches/88 cm for women), being physically inactive, smoking cigarettes and high blood sugar. You can decrease the complications of cardiovascular disease when you are able to have tight glucose management (a smaller range of blood glucose levels) for at least 10 years and with the help of medication. The best scenario would be to make lifestyle changes to prevent cardiovascular disease from developing.

The Blood Sugar Connection to Eye, Nerve and Kidney Health

"Blood glucose management," "blood sugar self-management" and "optimal glycemic control" are common terms you are likely to hear when researching diabetes. Why is there so much emphasis on blood sugar management? Most people have heard of diabetes-related macrovascular complications, previously discussed as cardiovascular disease, but there are also microvascular diseases caused by diabetes, such as retinopathy, neuropathy and nephropathy (kidney disease). Tighter blood sugar control has been shown to be beneficial in preventing these microvascular complications.

The longer you've had diabetes with dysregulated blood sugar, the greater your chances of developing microvascular complications. This means your diabetes team may eventually include an ophthalmologist, possibly a neurologist, a nephrologist and a podiatrist (to check for neuropathy in the feet and for Charcot joint). Again, do not view this as a failure, but rather as a piece of information to increase your awareness about the complications of diabetes and empower you to care for yourself.

Keep in mind, it may be beneficial to manage your blood sugar within a tighter range at a higher blood glucose level rather than managing it within a wider range with many highs and lows. The greater the range, the more likely you are to have complications such as hyperglycemia and hypoglycemia. Although lower blood sugar numbers may be recommended, be realistic in your goal setting. Work with your registered dietitian and/or diabetes educator to set reasonable blood sugar target ranges rather than unrealistic definitive numbers.

■ ■ ■

The longer you've had diabetes with dysregulated blood sugar, the greater your chances of developing microvascular complications.

■ ■ ■

Be Your Own Advocate

In order to prevent complications from diabetes, it is recommended that you undergo screening for microvascular complications. Use the table on page 18 as a reference guide to ensure you are doing your best to stay proactive and educated on this topic. Refer annually to the American Diabetes Association's Standards of Medical Care in Diabetes or the Canadian Diabetes Association's Clinical Practice Guidelines; the American Diabetes Association's position statement is updated about every 5 years. Always contact your physician for guidance and medical advice. Refer to the table to make sure you are receiving the recommended screens for microvascular disease.

Screening for Microvascular Disease

	Dilated eye exam for retinopathy	Urinary albumin test and established glomerular filtration rate (GFR) test for nephropathy	10-g Semmes Weinstein monofilament test and other tests for neuropathy (such as nerve conduction studies, electromyography)
Type 1 diabetes without microvascular complications	At diagnosis and every 5 years	Yearly after first 5 years	Yearly after first 5 years
Type 1 diabetes with microvascular complications	Every year	Yearly after first 5 years	Every year
Type 2 diabetes without microvascular complications	At diagnosis and every 2 years	Every year	At diagnosis and every year
Type 2 diabetes with microvascular complications	Every year	Every year	Every year

Inflammation, Obesity and Diabetes

Which came first: the chicken or the egg? The Atherosclerosis Risk in Communities (ARIC) study identified that low-grade inflammation is associated with and likely to precede cardio-vascular disease and diabetes, regardless of body size. There is a good possibility that inflammation comes first as a result of fat mass (not body weight), followed by insulin resistance, leptin resistance and obesity. (Just like insulin resistance, leptin resistance occurs when the body does not recognize the presence of the fullness hormone, leptin.) This cascades into gaining more weight and type 2 diabetes.

Insulin resistance as it relates to the immune system was first recognized when studying sepsis, also known as the body's response to serious infection. In fact, many inflammatory states, such as hepatitis C and arthritis, are associated with insulin resistance.

Fatty tissue is now recognized as one of the largest endocrine organs. Fat cells can produce tumor necrosis factor (TNF)-α, a pro-inflammatory cytokine called interleukin-6 (IL-6), leptin, resistin and adiponectin. While adiponectin

Normal-Weight Obese Syndrome

Maybe you have heard the slang term "skinny fat" or heard someone identify another person as a "thin fat" person. The title is referring to a person who appears thin yet is not fit, with a high lean body mass. There is a medically accepted syndrome name to replace this slang. It is called normal-weight obese syndrome. It refers to an individual who appears/qualifies as "normal weight" but who has a higher fat mass (greater than or equal to 30%). Individuals meeting these criteria have higher levels of inflammation than individuals who qualify as normal weight. In other words, it should not be assumed that all thin people are healthy or without risk for insulin resistance. Rather, a person with a fat mass greater than 30% of body weight is likely to have inflammation and thus likely to have insulin resistance with risk of diabetes. Perhaps "obese" should be redefined as a percentage of fat mass rather than total body weight or scale weight.

and leptin may increase insulin sensitivity, the fat cells' macrophages increasingly produce inflammatory agents (such as tumor necrosis factor), which can inhibit insulin signaling, thereby decreasing insulin sensitivity. In other words, storing extra body fat can cause inflammation and trigger insulin resistance, the precursors to type 2 diabetes.

Despite the need for more information regarding inflammation as it is related to obesity and diabetes, there are four things you can do to positively affect your health. First, eat cruciferous vegetables (specifically broccoli, cabbage, cauliflower, bok choy, kale and Brussels sprouts). Second, practice mindfulness, specifically self-compassion. The intake of cruciferous vegetables and self-compassion are both associated with lower levels of the pro-inflammatory markers TNF and IL-6.

Third, lose weight if needed. Fourth, supplement or increase your intake of vitamin D if you are deficient. Researchers from the Fred Hutchinson Cancer Research Center studied more than 200 overweight postmenopausal women with vitamin D levels less than 32 ng/mL. Women who lost between 5% and 10% of their baseline weight by following a diet, engaging in regular physical activity and supplementing vitamin D at 2000 IUs daily for 12 months showed a significant decrease in inflammation compared to the blinded placebo group.

The vitamin D study participants showed a 37% reduction in interleukin-6, as compared to those in the placebo group, who saw a 17.2% reduction in IL-6. Ask your medical doctor to test your vitamin D levels. If you are deficient, have the doctor recommend an appropriate dose for your state of health (if you cannot raise your vitamin D levels through diet; see table, page 20).

■ ■ ■

Storing extra body fat can cause inflammation and trigger insulin resistance, the precursors to type 2 diabetes.

■ ■ ■

Top Five Foods High in Vitamin D

Food source	Amount	IUs per serving
Cod liver oil	1 tbsp (15 mL)	1,360
Swordfish (cooked)	3 oz (90 g)	566
Sockeye salmon (cooked)	3 oz (90 g)	447
Tuna, chunk light (canned, drained)	3 oz (90 g)	154
Vitamin D–fortified milk (nonfat, reduced-fat and whole)	1 cup (250 mL)	115–124

Adapted from the National Institutes of Health Office of Dietary Supplements Selected Food Sources of Vitamin D.

Eat Cruciferous Vegetables to Decrease Inflammation

- **Broccoli:** See Pasta Salad with Grilled Chicken (page 108), Orange-Glazed Tofu with Sautéed Vegetables (page 134) and Chinese Five-Spice Tempeh (page 136).
- **Cabbage:** See Chinese Five-Spice Tempeh (page 136), Stir-Fried Peppered Shrimp with Cockles (page 154), Chinese Chicken Salad (page 174), Small-Batch Sauerkraut (page 234) and Slow Cooker Corned Beef, Potatoes and Cabbage (page 242).
- **Cauliflower:** See Fried Cauliflower Rice with Shrimp (page 162).
- **Kale:** See Kale Salad with Pine Nuts, Endive and Champagne Vinaigrette (page 106), Macro Bowl (page 124), Grilled Shrimp and Kale Caesar (page 152), Beet and Goat Cheese Salad (page 210) and Pumpkin Beef Stew (page 236).
- **Brussels sprouts:** See CABB Salad (Chicken, Apple, Brussels Sprouts and Bacon) (page 112) and Shredded Brussels Sprouts with Cranberries (page 209).

Now that we have deconstructed diabetes and you have a great foundation, see chapter 2 for some lip-smackin' food, fitness and lifestyle talk.

The Everyday Diabetes Non-Diet Starts Now

IMAGINE: YOU EAT ALL FOODS, all recipes are diabetes-friendly and you never have to count carbohydrates again. Welcome to your new world. *Everyday Diabetes Meals* includes 150 recipes made to meet your needs! Whether it's time to eat breakfast, hit the beach or celebrate your favorite holiday, you will always have a recipe at your fingertips to prepare simply, savor and satisfy every desire. This is your time to finally live stress-free. As you turn the pages of this chapter, you will understand why we have created these nutritious meals — including everything from traditional eggs and bacon to childhood favorites like s'mores — with easy education on lifestyle behaviors to help you live every day with diabetes, healthfully. Welcome to your "everyday diabetes" guide to food, fitness, sleep and mindfulness. Hello to the new you!

Fortunately, there is a plethora of high-quality research about diabetes to help you make educated health-care decisions. This research supports many different ways to eat, behave and even lose weight while living healthfully with diabetes. The great news is that the American Diabetes Association shares this stance: "One diet does not fit all."

To clarify, your new approach to life is:

1. There is no perfect diet.
2. You can do this.
3. It is a matter of confidence in lifestyle skills.
4. Flexibility is a must, especially around food choices.

Let's prep for wellness!

Living the Single-Serve Lifestyle

One of the best parts of this book is the variety of recipes for just one or two people, tailored to manage your blood sugar and hormones (such as insulin) whether you're living with or preventing diabetes. Yes, this cookbook was created specifically for singles and couples living with diabetes. Honestly, the majority of our own clients are singles or couples, and they have asked for single-serving recipes to prevent food waste, decrease meal-prep time and avoid the confusion of portion distortion. Most important, people don't want to be consumed

---

DID YOU KNOW?

DPP Research

The Diabetes Prevention Program (DPP), through the National Institute of Diabetes and Digestive and Kidney Disease, and ancillary research specifically exploring the psychological and behavioral outcomes in the DPP, found that self-efficacy/self-confidence in skills and flexible dietary-restraint skills are key in your success at preventing diabetes and/or living healthfully with diabetes.

What Are Self-Confidence in Lifestyle Skills and Flexible Dietary Restraint?

Self-confidence can be increased by teaching skills that apply to daily living, such as the ability to follow dietary guidelines, setting small achievable goals, self-monitoring and balancing food intake, learning stimulus control, managing stress and high-risk situations, and problem-solving. Flexible dietary restraint is the ability to choose the diet plan that works best for you and to find your way through day-to-day living rather than adhering to a specific, rigid diet plan.

A 7% weight loss was one of the best predictors of preventing diabetes, with every 2-lb (1 kg) weight loss associated with a 16% decrease in risk of developing diabetes, as evidenced by the Diabetes Prevention Program (DPP). When studying the behaviors of the DPP participants, flexible dietary restraint was the most important behavior to predict successful weight outcomes. Individuals who self-monitored their own weight and food intake were 4.3 times more successful in achieving their weight loss goals, compared to those who didn't self-monitor. They balanced their food choices and total intake rather than engaging in a black-and-white mindset of success and failure. If they overate, rather than feeling like a failure, the participants were able to move forward and balance their intake in other ways. There was no expectation that their diet had to be perfect. Use the success of these self-monitoring participants to guide your approach to live flexibly and recognize that all foods fit.

■ ■ ■

With 29 million people living with diabetes and 86 million people with prediabetes in the United States alone, the message is loud and clear: we need nutrition solutions for blood glucose management and overall wellness.

■ ■ ■

with counting carbohydrates or blood sugar management — which are nutrition cornerstones for individuals with diabetes. And with 29 million people living with diabetes and 86 million people with prediabetes in the United States alone, the message is loud and clear: we need nutrition solutions for blood glucose management and overall wellness.

The recipes in this book require no extra thought. Every recipe serves just one or two people and uses carbohydrate counting to portion each serving. The majority of the recipes use nutrient-dense foods, such as whole grains, dark green vegetables and Mediterranean fats, like olive oil. The recipes are devised to help manage your blood sugar at breakfast, lunch, dinner and snack time, and we've even included holiday single-serve recipes! Translation: this means everyone can enjoy these recipes, even if they don't have diabetes. Let's all join together to prevent diabetes and prevent it from interfering with the quality of your life.

What Is a Single Serving?

Most recipes in this book range between 45 to 60 grams of carbohydrate per serving. This single serving is based on an age-old approach to managing blood sugar known as carbohydrate counting. The concept is to determine how many carbohydrates your body needs throughout the day (using 45% to 60% of calories as carbohydrates) and to divide that total by your meal and snack times. This typically results in meals with an average of 45 to 60 grams of carbohydrates and snacks with about 15 to 30 grams of carbohydrates. This has become the standard starting point when learning to count carbohydrates. The remainder of calories through protein and fat are flexible, allowing each individual to make dietary choices and live with less dietary constraint.

Everyday Diabetes Meals uses the lower range of the recommended range for calories as carbohydrates (45%), which is consistent with research supporting a Mediterranean diet. The Mediterranean diet is lower in carbohydrates and higher in unsaturated fat than the average diet, and is associated with weight loss and reduced A1c and fasting glucose. Research has shown that lower-carbohydrate diets with higher-unsaturated-fat profiles achieved greater improvements in lipid (fat) profiles in the blood, blood glucose stability and reductions in the need for diabetes medication when compared to low-fat, high-carbohydrate diets.

Just as the Mediterranean diet differs among the 21 countries that border the Mediterranean Sea, *Everyday Diabetes* recipes allow for personal preference and embrace the concept of flexible dietary restraint. *Everyday Diabetes* recipes are based on 45% of calories as carbohydrate, leaving each individual with options to manage overall calorie intake by choosing how much protein and fat to eat each day. Forty-five percent of a 1,600-calorie daily dietary intake equates to 180 grams of total carbohydrate a day. Based on a 2,000-calorie daily dietary intake, this equals 225 grams of carbohydrate a day. Spreading out those carbohydrates throughout the day could look like this:

Spreading Carbs Throughout the Day

	1600-calorie daily intake (grams of carbohydrate)	2000-calorie daily intake (grams of carbohydrate)
Breakfast	45	60
Lunch	45	60
Snack	25	25
Dinner	45	60
Snack	20	20
Total carbohydrates	180 grams spread over day	225 grams spread over day

Ideally, you should determine your individual caloric, macronutrient and medical-nutrition therapy needs with your registered dietitian and/or certified diabetes educator. These recipes are a great starting point to help you spread out your carbohydrates evenly throughout the day, which supports the American Diabetes Association's recommendations to follow a consistent carbohydrate intake daily.

Consistent Carbohydrates Throughout the Day

The recipes in *Everyday Diabetes Meals* are all less than or equal to 45 to 60 grams of carbohydrates for the main dishes, and less than or equal to 15 to 30 grams for snacks. Some of the recipes use simple sugars — yes, even granulated sugar — because we believe that all foods fit. At the end of the day, it doesn't matter if refined sugar came from honey, agave nectar or white table sugar. What matters is that your sugar intake is moderated, evenly spread out throughout the day and paired with protein and fat to keep the meal or snack's glycemic load within a narrow range.

The glycemic load is the entire meal's effect on your blood sugar — rather than just the glycemic index, which is the potential effect of one food on your blood sugar. All 150 recipes help to balance your blood sugar by providing a balanced range of carbohydrates at breakfast, lunch and dinner. Most recipes contain all three macronutrients (proteins, carbohydrates and fats), allowing for slower digestion, more steady absorption and extended release of sugar into the bloodstream. This prevents quick spikes in blood sugar and helps you to feel fuller longer.

There's no need to worry if a recipe contains more than 60 grams of carbohydrates per serving. This just means that there are at least 6 grams of fiber in that particular recipe. In this case, you take half of the total grams of fiber and subtract it from the total grams of carbohydrate; this gives you the number of total carbohydrates that are actually going to be absorbed. A math degree is not necessary here. Just know that all main dish recipes are less than or between 45 and 60 grams of absorbable carbohydrates. Plus, the nutrition facts are provided for each recipe, empowering you with the ability to make the best choices for your personal needs.

Having a Choice

The recipes in this book do not provide any additional information on the grams of protein or grams of fat. Why? Because the philosophy here is about learning to have flexibility with your food choices. As we discussed at the beginning of this chapter, one of the most important parts of living with diabetes is being flexible about dietary behaviors. This book allows you the opportunity to make your own choices. Carbohydrates easily and quickly affect both insulin and blood sugar. That is why we have chosen to help you portion this specific nutrient — the protein and fat elements are up to you! The overarching goal is to balance your blood sugar. How individuals may choose to do this will vary slightly, hence no "one diet fits all" approach.

There are no formal or rigid restrictions; however, being educated about nutrition allows you to make better choices for yourself. The recipes include all foods — carbohydrates, fats and proteins. Lean proteins and fats, which are associated with satiety, weight management and decreased risk for cardiovascular disease, are used most often in *Everyday Diabetes Meals*. The box on page 26 will help you make choices about which proteins and fats to favor in your daily intake.

■ ■ ■
One of the most important parts of living with diabetes is being flexible about dietary behaviors. This book allows you the opportunity to make your own choices.
■ ■ ■

No Perfect Diet

As registered dietitians, we are well aware that there is an overwhelming amount of nutrition information out there — and that it changes daily. This can be quite frustrating and confusing for you, the consumer. For instance, think about the fat dilemma. Remember the era of bagels and fat-free cookies and desserts during the 1980s and 1990s? At one time, it was recommended that you eat a low-fat diet, and all fats were seemingly demonized. As a result of this dietary recommendation, people went carb crazy and included very-low-fat, highly processed foods in their diets to replace their usual fat intake. Consequently, portions increased along with average body weight and the prevalence of diabetes.

The next wave of diets pulled a complete one-eighty by focusing on carbohydrate-free foods and favoring all types of fats. Think: the Atkins diet in the early 1970s and then again in the 1990s. Such extreme dietary restrictions can result in weight loss by severely cutting calories. Yet at the time, it was unclear if the public at large would be able to follow a low-carbohydrate intake in the long term (meaning longer than 2 years) or how a high amount of dietary fats would affect the cardiovascular system down the road. The public was willing to risk their health for the glory of weight loss.

From 1980 to 1994, the Nurses' Health Study analyzed the dietary consumption of saturated fat versus unsaturated fat of more than 80,000 women. The results indicated that replacing 5% of energy from saturated fat would reduce the risk of cardiovascular disease by 42%.

The Lean Protein and Favored Fats Cheat Sheet

Use this cheat sheet as your new guide for grocery shopping, recipe modifications and meal planning. It will make following *Everyday Diabetes Meals* simple! It is ideal for recipes to contain sources of both or at least one favored fat: monounsaturated fatty acids (MUFAs) and omega-3 fatty acids.

Lean Proteins

- Fish and seafood (monkfish, tilapia, shrimp)
- White meat (skinless chicken, turkey)
- Lean grass-fed beef (sirloin, round, tenderloin/filet mignon)
- Vegetable protein (tofu, lentils and dried beans, such as lima beans, black beans, pinto beans or split peas)

Healthy Fats

Omega-3 Fatty Acids

ALA: Eat daily

- Canola oil
- Chia seeds
- Ground flax seeds
- Hemp seeds
- Pumpkin seeds
- Walnuts

EPA and DHA: Eat twice weekly

- Bass
- Bluefish
- Cod
- Mackerel
- Salmon
- Sardines
- Trout
- Tuna (chunk light canned in water, no added salt)

MUFAs: Eat Daily

- Olives
- Avocados
- Nuts (such as almonds, cashews and pecans) and peanuts
- Hummus (when possible, choose hummus without tahini)
- Oils (such as olive oil, canola oil and peanut oil)

Saturated Fat

- Limit or eliminate saturated fat.
- Choose foods with labels showing 2 grams or less of saturated fat per serving.
- If butter is used, there should be no added salt; preferably, choose olive oil instead.
- Avoid trans fat (partially hydrogenated oils).
- Remove all visible fat.
- Choose lean proteins that are low in saturated fat.
- Choose a variety of dairy fat.
- Choose harder cheeses and use small quantities.

Dietitians and other health professionals who were reading similar research released in 1997 and in the early 2000s had evidence to substantiate that a higher amount of dietary fat (monounsaturated fats), as seen in the Mediterranean diet, improved glycemia and lipid levels (the amount of glucose and fat) in the blood. After this message was relayed to the masses, people subsequently followed "branded" diets lower in carbohydrates and with higher percentages of unsaturated fat. Think: Zone and South Beach diets.

The latest trend is "fat is good, sugar is bad." This completely opposes what we learned 20 years ago and what media outlets and health reporters relayed to the public just 5 years ago. To make things clear, read this message: all fat is not bad, all sugar is not bad. No one food is bad or good. Further, there are health benefits to all foods — at a minimum, all foods provide energy! However, regularly consuming large quantities of artificial foods and/or food products that include trans fats, chemicals and fake sugars will cause some level of inflammation, and inflammation contributes to the development of disease.

The Facts on Fat

Fat is no longer taboo. Unsaturated fats — especially mono-unsaturated fats and polyunsaturated fats, and specifically omega-3 fatty acids — play an important role in heart health by increasing high-density lipoprotein (HDL, or "good") cholesterol, decreasing triglycerides, thinning the blood and preventing inflammation. The current recommendation is to eat fat, specifically monounsaturated fatty acids (MUFAs) such as olive oil, canola oil and olives, among other foods. It is also recommended to eat fish twice a week for the anti-inflammatory properties of the polyunsaturated fatty acids (PUFAs), specifically docosahexaenoic acid (DHA), which new research suggests may positively affect the metabolites caused by high blood sugar and may help prevent a fatty liver. Research has associated alpha-linolenic acid (ALA) and eicosapentaenoic acid (EPA), two polyunsaturated fats, with improved outcomes related to diabetes and glucose management. The focus on MUFAs and PUFAs is not really new. If you look at the research, there are studies from the late 1990s associating these fats with heart health.

So go ahead and savor fat without feeling guilty. This is not a green light to eat this macronutrient in excess. As a guideline, enjoy a diet high in MUFAs and low in saturated fat, with 30% to 45% total calories as fat.

DID YOU KNOW?

Potential Short-Term Benefits

It's important to recognize that it is challenging to adapt branded diets to your lifestyle on a long-term basis because they ban specific foods and/or food groups. However, these diets may be effective for short-term weight loss and possibly disease prevention.

DID YOU KNOW?

Fat Intake Balance

Gram for gram, carbohydrates are less caloric than fats. When increasing your intake of fats, determine how to incorporate this macronutrient without affecting your total caloric intake. You may need to eat smaller portions of fats or decrease your portions of carbohydrates and proteins to stay in your calorie range.

- **Carbohydrates:** 4 calories per gram
- **Proteins:** 4 calories per gram
- **Fats:** 9 calories per gram

Although unsaturated fats are encouraged, saturated fats remain controversial. Mark Bittman's op-ed article "Butter Is Back," which appeared in the *New York Times*, suggests focusing on real food rather than fake and processed food. He argues that it is better to eat real butter, with naturally occurring saturated fat, rather than margarine that contains trans fats created through hydrogenating unsaturated fats.

Yes, we should eat real food rather than fake food. Yet some questions regarding fat still remain. First, are trans fats equivalent in health effects to saturated fats? Second, are saturated fats equivalent to unsaturated fats? People want to know whether to eat real butter and real dairy — and what to think about coconut and palm oils. As mentioned earlier, anything in excess has the potential to become harmful, and the opposite is true as well.

Before we answer the above questions, recognize that all dietary fats contain multiple chains of different types of fats. For example, when you eat MUFAs, you are also eating saturated fats. If you study the table below, you will see that

Average Nutrient Composition of Nuts (per 3.5 oz/100 g)

Nut	Energy (kJ)	Fat (g)	SFA (g)	MUFA (g)	PUFA (g)	LA (g)	ALA (g)	Protein (g)	Fiber (g)	Folate (µg)	PS (mg)
Almonds	2418	50.6	3.9	32.2	12.2	12.2	0.00	21.3	8.8	29	120
Brazil nuts (dried)	2743	66.4	15.1	24.5	20.6	20.5	0.05	14.3	8.5	22	NR
Cashews	2314	46.4	9.2	27.3	7.8	7.7	0.15	18.2	5.9	25	158
Hazelnuts	2629	60.8	4.5	45.7	7.9	7.8	0.09	15.0	10.4	113	96
Macadamias	3004	75.8	12.1	58.9	1.5	1.3	0.21	7.9	6.0	11	116
Peanuts	2220	49.2	6.8	24.4	15.6	15.6	0.00	25.8	8.5	145	220
Pecans	2889	72.0	6.2	40.8	21.6	20.6	1.00	9.2	8.4	22	102
Pine nuts (dried)	2816	68.4	4.9	18.8	34.1	33.2	0.16	13.7	3.7	34	141
Pistachios	2332	44.4	5.4	23.3	13.5	13.2	0.25	20.6	9.0	51	214
Walnuts	2738	65.2	6.1	8.9	47.2	38.1	9.08	15.2	6.4	98	72

* Data is for raw nuts, except where specified.
** SFA, saturated fatty acids; MUFA, monounsaturated fatty acids; PUFA, polyunsaturated fatty acids; LA, linoleic acid; ALA, α-linolenic acid; PS, plant sterols; NR, not reported.

Adapted from "Health Benefits of Nut Consumption," U.S. National Library of Medicine, National Institutes of Health.

3.5 ounces (100 grams) of almonds contains 3.9 grams of saturated fatty acids, 12.2 grams of polyunsaturated fatty acids and 32.2 grams of monounsaturated fatty acids.

Fats are composed of many different types of fatty acids. Fatty acids can be further divided by their carbon-chain lengths. Most dietary fatty acids range from 12 to 22 carbons. For example, the saturated fat lauric acid is a 12-carbon chain, and stearic acid, also a saturated fat, is an 18-carbon chain.

Trans fat is found naturally in some foods, but is mostly found in processed and hydrogenated foods. Remember the ban on hydrogenated oils and partially hydrogenated palm oil? In 2015, the U.S. Food and Drug Administration (FDA) decided that all food manufacturers must remove partially hydrogenated oils from their products within the next 3 years. Hydrogenated and partially hydrogenated oils are trans fats used in packaged goods like crackers and cookies to make these products shelf-stable for long periods of time. In order to make foods shelf-stable, food scientists add hydrogen to an unsaturated fat, which creates a trans fat. For example, if a food scientist adds hydrogen to vegetable oil, it becomes a "hydrogenated oil" or a "partially hydrogenated oil" and solid at room temperature — turning into margarine!

When researchers compared margarine that has trans fat and hydrogenated oil to naturally occurring saturated fat, specifically lauric acid, they found that the saturated fat produced more favorable lipid profiles. Lauric acid, which is found in coconut and palm oils, produced a beneficial increase in high-density lipoprotein (HDL, or "good") cholesterol versus the trans fat. HDL cholesterol transports excessive cholesterol circulating in the blood to your liver so it can be excreted. High levels of HDL cholesterol have been associated with a lower risk of heart attack and stroke. This suggests that saturated fat, when compared to trans fats, may be favorable in the prevention of cardiovascular disease. Several research studies have found consistent results favoring saturated fats over trans fats.

■ ■ ■

High levels of HDL cholesterol have been associated with a lower risk of heart attack and stroke. This suggests that saturated fat, when compared to trans fats, may be favorable in the prevention of cardiovascular disease.

■ ■ ■

The Final Fat Verdict

If the choice is butter or margarine, choose butter. If the choice is butter or coconut oil, choose coconut oil. If the choice is coconut oil or olive oil and/or canola oil, choose the latter. Do not replace saturated fats with refined carbohydrates or trans fats. Refer to the table on page 30 for a quick guide to what types of fats and oils to eat and how often to eat them.

Everyday Diabetes Fats and Oils Guide

Frequency	Type of fat	Food choices
Every day	Monounsaturated fatty acids and polyunsaturated fatty acids in the form of omega-3 fatty acids	Olive oil, canola oil, rapeseed oil, fish oils (salmon, trout, krill), flaxseed oil, walnut oil
Most days	Saturated fat in the form of tropical oils	Coconut oil and palm oil
Some days	Saturated fat	Butter
Few days, if ever*	Artificial trans fats processed through hydrogenation	Hydrogenated and partially hydrogenated oils (such as hydrogenated palm oil or partially hydrogenated vegetable oil)

* In June 2015, the U.S. Food and Drug Administration ruled that all artificial trans fats must be removed from processed foods by 2019.

Sweet Snacks and Butter Pats

The oils used in the recipes in this book are typically olive oil or canola oil. Avocado and nut butters are fats we favor as well. We incorporated complex carbohydrates such as whole oats and buckwheat flour into our recipes. The recipes do include sugar in different forms, such as honey, pure maple syrup and just plain old white granulated sugar. There are sweet snacks, butter pats and full fats. Sometimes plant milk is used and sometimes cow's milk, or even goat's milk, may be recommended for taste, texture and/or a way to keep the carbohydrates within range. If you and your registered dietitian decide you should use low-fat dairy, you can easily swap out the full-fat milk or 2% Greek yogurt for a skim or 1% fat option.

Just be sure to check your blood glucose before your meal and then 2 hours after to learn how your body handled the glycemic load of that meal. You may find you can have fat-free milk in your buckwheat pancake mix but you need to use a full-fat dairy yogurt when you eat it alone or with a specific carbohydrate, such as grapes.

Remember, every person is different. Many factors vary from individual to individual, such as rate of digestion and absorption of food, rate of stomach emptying, the amount of insulin needed for 45 grams of carbohydrates and overall daily caloric intake. These factors may also change on a daily basis. This is why you need flexibility regarding your food and nutrition choices. Do not compare yourself to your friend. Read and respect your own body.

■ ■ ■

Be sure to check your blood glucose before your meal and then 2 hours after to learn how your body handled the glycemic load of that meal.

■ ■ ■

Goals of Medical Nutrition Therapy for Adults with Diabetes

Consult a registered dietitian to help you with these goals.

1. Emphasize eating patterns with a variety of nutrient-dense foods in appropriate portion sizes, specifically to:
   - Achieve and maintain body weight goals.
   - Attain reasonable blood sugar, blood pressure and lipid goals.
   - Delay or prevent complications of diabetes.
2. Live life healthfully based on personal and cultural preferences, and identify your level of readiness and access to health-promoting foods.
3. Maintain pleasure in eating all foods, avoiding judgmental messages about food choices.
4. Identify and create tools for healthy eating with diabetes rather than focusing on individual macronutrients.

Adapted from "Goals of Medical Nutrition Therapy for Adults with Diabetes" by the American Diabetes Association's Diabetes Care.

DID YOU KNOW?

How to Test Your Blood Sugar Using a Glucometer

1. Wash and dry your hands with warm water to help the blood flow.
2. Choose a spot on a fingertip (don't check from the same finger every time).
3. Follow the manufacturer's instructions to prepare the lancing device.
4. Collect a drop of blood from the side of your fingertip and hold the test strip against it until it has been absorbed.
5. Record the results in your logbook.
6. Discard the used lancet properly.

Adapted from Accu-Chek's Glucometer Guidelines.

Principles of Everyday Diabetes

1. Choose Rather than Cheat

Diabetes is not a game. There is no cheating on a diet. This is your lifestyle and you need to make food decisions every time you eat. Sometimes you choose to eat foods because they keep you full and prevent blood sugar highs and/or lows. Other times you may opt to eat a food because it tastes so darn good. Most important is that you make an educated choice and realize that perfect self-care doesn't exist. Do your best and accept that emotional health is just as important as physical health. Make choices to improve your quality of life.

2. Your Body Is Your Teacher

Ultimately, no single registered dietitian, certified diabetes educator or research study can tell you definitively what the best foods are for you. Rather, listen to your body, as it will signal you, but be aware that these signals may change over time. Test your blood sugar before you eat and then

2 hours after. Work on the breakfast meal for 3 days, collecting enough data to compare, followed by lunch and dinner on the subsequent days. Be sure to track what time of the day you eat, your fasting blood sugar, the food you eat and your 2-hour post-meal blood sugar. Compare your food choices to see how they affect your blood sugar. You will learn what and when to eat to improve your blood sugar range.

3. You Are More Than a Number

Oh, this has so many meanings! You are not just a number on a scale. You are more than your A1c and your daily blood glucose levels. You are more than your diagnosis of type 1 or type 2 diabetes. You may be affected by diabetes on a daily basis in both positive and negative ways, but please, oh please, recognize that your self-worth is tied to your incredible inner strength and character traits. You are determined, sensitive, anxious, curious and so much more.

4. Practice Self-Care: Just Like Brushing Your Teeth!

Whether or not they have diabetes, all individuals need to practice self-care. This encompasses nutrition, fitness, mindfulness and sleep. Everyone needs to learn coping skills to deal with life's challenges. Exercise, blood sugar self-monitoring and making food decisions are all forms of self-care that you need to practice daily. You may not want to do these things, but you will feel so much better afterward. Granted, not everyone must be diligent with checking blood sugar, but we can assure you that they have something else to contend with. If you are feeling rebellious or even overwhelmed, recognize that self-care is just a thing we all do, just like brushing your teeth.

Let's Get Physical

Whether you have prediabetes or diabetes, are an adult or a child, the recommendation is the same — to exercise! Children are encouraged to exercise for 60 minutes daily, with 3 of the days including bone-strengthening activities such as light weights with higher repetitions. Adults see benefits with 150 minutes of moderately intense cardio over a week-long period. This can translate to 50 minutes every other day or 30 minutes 5 days a week. Try not to skip physical activity for more than 2 consecutive days. Ideally, adults should aim for a weight-resistance regimen twice a week, as long as there are no contraindications present, such as hypertension or retinopathy.

■ ■ ■

Exercise, blood sugar self-monitoring and making food decisions are all forms of self-care that you need to practice daily.

■ ■ ■

How Exercise Helps

You know you are supposed to exercise, but why? Exercise benefits your body by making your muscles more sensitive to insulin and by improving your body's cardiovascular health. Specifically, your muscles use sugar in two ways. The first way involves the hormone insulin. When you are at rest or after a meal, insulin will help transport sugar to muscle cells to store sugar as glycogen. During exercise, and hours after exercise, muscle contractions increase insulin's active uptake of sugar from your blood. Simultaneously, muscles also break down glycogen — their sugar stores — during exercise to help maintain an even blood sugar and supply the body with an energy source. Go ahead and flex those muscles again and again; know that you are helping to decrease your blood sugar!

Before You Move

Exercise is a lifestyle factor that must be part of your everyday routine. Before you start a fitness routine, be sure to speak with your medical team in order to understand any contraindications or limits to your movement. While aerobic exercise typically lowers blood sugar and improves insulin sensitivity, anaerobic exercise actually has the potential to increase your blood sugar. For example, if during a cardio class your rate of breathing interferes with your ability to talk, you are likely moving into the anaerobic phase of exercise. If you identify with this description, make an action plan with your certified diabetes educator and consider working with a certified personal trainer who specializes in diabetes. These professionals can help you find the best plan to forecast, balance and treat your blood sugar.

Preventing Hypoglycemia (Low Blood Sugar)

In general, always check your blood glucose before exercising. If your blood sugar is less than 100 mg/dL (5.6 mmol/L), you may need to add a carbohydrate snack or use an insulin pump to decrease your insulin. Make sure to bring your glucometer to your activity and check your blood glucose every 45 minutes. If you use a newer insulin pump, such as the MiniMed, your pump may have a feature that alerts you when your blood sugar is elevated or low. This feature is a glucose-sensing feature known as a continuous glucose monitoring system.

Keep snacks such as juice, fruit or glucose tabs on hand to treat low blood sugar. Medications that help release insulin from the pancreas may need to be adjusted when exercising. If you exercise daily, you may need to decrease the dose of your medication overall. When you exercise occasionally,

■ ■ ■

Before you start a fitness routine, be sure to speak with your medical team in order to understand any contraindications or limits to your movement.

■ ■ ■

DID YOU KNOW?

Steps to Take If You Are Hypoglycemic

1. Consume 15 grams of simple carbohydrates, such as 2 tablespoons (30 mL) raisins, three to four 15-gram glucose tablets, or 1/2 cup (125 mL) juice.
2. Recheck your blood sugar 15 minutes after consuming the carbohydrate.
3. If you continue to experience symptoms of hypoglycemia, repeat the above steps.
4. When your blood sugar returns to its normal range, make sure you eat a meal or snack to help continue stabilizing your blood sugar.

perhaps once a week, you may have to decrease your insulin dosage in the short term or perhaps add an extra carbohydrate snack between 3 and 12 hours later. If you are someone with type 2 diabetes who plans to or already exercises vigorously, you may experience increased insulin sensitivity into the next day and may need to adjust medications and snacks accordingly.

Individuals with type 1 and 2 diabetes who are treated with insulin may need to decrease their units of insulin before the meal, before the activity, during the activity and before the first meal following the activity.

Though this may sound intimidating, exercise can improve diabetes-related blood sugar management and help decrease the risks of cardiovascular disease. If you are nervous about starting an exercise routine, find a friend who can exercise with you. Let this friend know your fears and educate them on an action plan for low blood sugar. This may help you feel more confident in starting your exercise regimen.

There is more blood sugar predictability when you exercise at the same time every day and do the same activity. You may find this helpful in identifying how your blood sugar responds to movement and medication. Remember: the effects of exercise can last 2 to 72 hours after exercise and may lead to hypoglycemia while sleeping. Be proactive and make a plan to check your blood sugar often and throughout the night when starting physical activity.

Physical Activity versus Exercise

Did you know that physical activity is not synonymous with exercise? Physical activity is defined as bodily movement produced by the contraction of skeletal muscle that significantly increases calorie consumption. Exercise is physical activity specifically done with the intention of developing physical fitness (cardiovascular conditioning, strength and flexibility training). In reality, don't worry about these definitions and nuances. This book uses the terms interchangeably. The main message is to move more! Start by walking for 5 minutes or adding a 5-minute weight routine to your day. If this seems intimidating, grab a dusting rag or garden shovel. Gardening, house cleaning, vacuuming, folding laundry, going up and down stairs and walking are all forms of movement that improve insulin sensitivity. What are you waiting for? Grab your sneakers and feel good!

Does Yoga Count?

Short bouts of activity from as little as 2 minutes to 15 minutes can improve blood glucose, but not everyone can easily engage in aerobic activity or resistance training. Furthermore, exercise such as high-intensity interval training and circuit training may be contraindicated for individuals with hypertension, retinopathy or even neuropathy. If you have never exercised or are dealing with decreased muscle strength or slower cognitive processing related to aging, you may need different forms of movement to increase flexibility, maintain balance and increase muscle strength. Balance training, yoga and other forms of movement, such as tai chi, may be less intimidating. These movements may not significantly improve glycemic control, but they do prove beneficial in other ways.

There is less convincing evidence suggesting that yoga supports improved A1c outcomes, high-density lipoprotein (HDL, or "good") cholesterol, triglycerides and blood pressure. Yet participating in yoga and tai chi, for example, helps with stress management and relaxation. Tai chi also reduces the risk of falls and decreases neuropathic symptoms. Just remember: some movement is better than none. If you are sticking to the American Diabetes Association's Standards of Care as the Holy Grail of movement, yoga cannot replace aerobic or muscle-strengthening activities. In this case, yoga must be done in addition to the recommended 150 minutes of weekly aerobic activity and the two 30-minute sessions of resistance training.

Further research on the benefits of yoga and diabetes is needed, especially since there are so many forms of yoga, varying in intensity and temperature.

> ■ ■ ■
>
> **Balance training, yoga and other forms of movement, such as tai chi, may not significantly improve glycemic control, but they do prove beneficial in other ways.**
>
> ■ ■ ■

Sweet Dreams and Everyday Diabetes

Sweet dreams ain't so easy anymore, especially when you are restless during the night and wake with high blood sugar in the morning. Our circadian body clock is located in the brain and dictates the cycles of wakefulness and sleep over 24 hours. The light and dark cycle, known as the diurnal cycle, affects sleep: light acts as a stimulant for wakefulness and dark for rest.

What Type of Sleeper Are You?

- **Ideal sleeper:** You sleep between 7 and 9 hours during the dark cycle of the light-dark diurnal rhythm.
- **Sleep restricted:** You experience a reduced amount of total sleep, typically between 5 and 8 hours of sleep per night.
- **Sleep fragmented:** Your sleep periods are fragmented by periods of wakefulness throughout the night.
- **Sleep deprived:** You experience total sleep loss.

Sleep is divided into two distinct categories. These are called rapid eye movement (REM) and non-rapid eye movement (NREM). Our brains manage the flip-flop and back-and-forth between the dream state of REM and NREM. These systems cycle with help from our hormones, particularly the counterregulatory hormones — and in particular growth hormone and cortisol. These same hormones greatly affect the hormone everyone associates with diabetes: insulin!

Counterregulatory Hormones

- **Cortisol:** Under normal metabolic conditions, this hormone, known as the stress hormone, signals the body, specifically fat and muscle cells, to be resistant to the action of insulin and to make glucose (via gluconeogenesis). However, under long-term stress, cortisol causes insulin resistance by signaling the continuous production of glucose and increasing appetite, which can lead to weight gain.
- **Epinephrine:** Secreted by the adrenal glands, epinephrine signals the liver and kidneys to produce more glucose and it reduces insulin secretion. It is known as the fight-or-flight hormone.
- **Glucagon:** Glucagon, made by islet cells (alpha cells) in the pancreas, controls the production of glucose and another fuel, ketones, in the liver. Glucagon is released overnight and between meals to maintain the body's sugar and fuel balance. It signals the liver to break down its starch or glycogen stores and helps to form new glucose units and ketone units from other substances. It also promotes the breakdown of fat in fat cells.
- **Growth hormone:** Growth hormone is similar to cortisol. Under normal metabolic conditions, this hormone signals the body, specifically fat and muscle cells, to be resistant to the action of insulin and to make glucose via gluconeogenesis. High levels of growth hormone cause insulin resistance.

Three Sleep Disorders and Diabetes

There are three common sleep disorders that affect sleep duration and are associated with type 2 diabetes and weight gain: insomnia, restless legs syndrome and obstructive sleep apnea (OSA). Insomnia is defined as difficulty falling asleep and staying asleep and waking too early at least 3 times a week for at least 3 months. Restless legs syndrome is the urge or need to move your legs in order to decrease uneasy sensations felt during inactivity, like during sleep. Obstructive sleep apnea is a disorder that causes you to cease breathing for 10 seconds or longer during sleep. OSA decreases airflow and oxygen and can negatively affect your blood sugar management in both type 1 and 2 diabetes. Snoring, holding your breath and sleepiness are potential signs of OSA. Serious cardiac complications can occur from OSA as well. Inform your doctor about your symptoms and ask whether a sleep study is warranted. You may need a continuous positive airway pressure (CPAP) machine.

Sleepless Nights and Shift Work

What do sleep and diabetes have to do with each other? First of all, people who work the night shift are at greater risk for cardiovascular disease and type 2 diabetes. The greater the number of years working the night shift, the greater the risk of developing these diseases. Currently, researchers are making connections between sleep disruptions, night shift work and a person's chronotype, which involves one's tendency toward being an "early bird" or a "night owl." Data gathered from the Nurses' Health Study II looked at time of work and chronotype. Results indicate that your 24-hour body clock, sleep disruption and metabolism are specifically linked. When your 24-hour body clock is dysregulated through sleep disruption and/or disregard of your internal biological clock, you are at greater risk for disease in general. For example: early birds had a reduced risk of type 2 diabetes when not exposed to night shift work, and early birds' diabetes risk increased when they worked longer durations of night shift work.

■ ■ ■

People who work the night shift are at greater risk for cardiovascular disease and type 2 diabetes. The greater the number of years working the night shift, the greater the risk of developing these diseases.

■ ■ ■

Effect of Sleep Disruptions

While you may know many adults who have difficulty sleeping, children with type 1 diabetes are recognized as having less deep sleep throughout the night. Such sleep disruptions affect metabolism and cardiovascular disease, especially in adolescents with type 1 diabetes. Both the length of time it takes to fall asleep and sleep duration are associated with a higher A1c. As well, the lighter the sleep, the higher the A1c. Insulin sensitivity decreases after just 1 night of sleep restriction.

More research is needed to determine the specific cause of these disruptions. Further exploration is also needed to investigate the complex relationships among diet, medication, sleep disruption, blood sugar and hormones. Does diet or medication induce an elevated or low blood sugar, causing the sleep disruption? Or is this issue more closely related to growth hormone, cortisol and the body clock? What we do know is that adequate sleep of 7 to 9 hours a night is the goal for all people, regardless of diabetes or type of diabetes.

If you have elevated blood sugar in the morning or just feel tired all of the time, assess your sleep patterns and talk with your endocrinologist. Your doctor or certified diabetes educator may suggest participating in a sleep study or wearing a glucosensor during the night (see page 58 for more information on glucosensors).

The Positive Effects of Mindfulness on Diabetes

Just like physical health, your mental health affects your blood glucose management as well as your quality of life. Did you know that anxiety, depression, stressful social experiences and diabetes complications are the four cornerstones affecting your emotional well-being as it specifically relates to diabetes? People with diabetes are 20% more likely to experience anxiety. Twenty-five percent of people with diabetes will experience depression, and more than 70% will experience a heart attack or complication from diabetes. The good news is that mindfulness, a nonjudgmental awareness in the present moment, is being studied as an effective tool in handling stress by decreasing counterregulatory hormones.

This form of meditation can be applied to eating, walking down the street or more formally through a self-practiced body scan or a sitting mediation. Mindfulness can be accessible to anyone at any time or any place. You can improve your blood sugar management using this form of mediation — even without focusing on losing weight! Twenty-eight veterans who participated in the Mind-STRIDE study experienced a drop in A1c levels — from an average of 8.3 to 7.3 after the 3-month training.

The University of Massachusetts Medical School Center for Mindfulness reports a 35% reduction in the number of medical symptoms and a 40% reduction in psychological symptoms when using Mindfulness-Based Stress Reduction (MBSR). Jon Kabat Zinn's 8-week MBSR program resulted in improved glycemia regardless of weight change. This program was developed in 1979 at the Stress Reduction and Relaxation Program at the University of Massachusetts Medical School to help individuals manage stress caused by their medical issues.

The formal program involves 2.5-hour weekly sessions for 8 weeks with a 1-day retreat wherein participants learn about mindfulness, meditation and hatha yoga. Though a small study, it warrants the need for more research on mindfulness in relation to diabetes. More recently, Brown University released new results associating everyday

> When life gives you lemons, make lemonade. When living with diabetes every day, make life a moving meditation.

mindfulness with diabetes. These results showed that those who practiced mindfulness were 20% less likely to have diabetes and that those with high scores on the Mindfulness Attention Awareness Scale were 35% more likely to have a glucose level less than 100 mg/dL (5.5 mmol/L).

For more information on mindfulness, visit the Mindfulness Meditation Institute at www.mindfulnessmeditationinstitute.org and the Center for Mindfulness at www.umassmed.edu/cfm.

Steps for Mindfulness

Mindfulness can be applied to eating, cooking, gardening and even walking. Here is a simple mindful-eating exercise to begin your journey of living every day with diabetes, mindfully. Try to do this before your next meal and then as often as possible.

1. Breathe

Your first step is to breathe deeply before and after meals. Separate the chaos of the day from the experience of eating. Sit down without phone, computer or TV screen and take five deep breaths. Bring your attention to your breath. On a long, stretched-out inhale through your nose, fill your belly, ribs and chest. Exhale through your nose, first releasing the air from your chest, then ribs and then belly. Stretch your exhale like taffy and constrict the back of your throat. Repeat five times. If you feel ready for more, try a yoga breath such as a ujjayi breath; find out more information about this at www.yogajournal.com or www.chopra.com. Consider apps like Headspace and Calm, which can guide you through meditations of various lengths.

2. Test Sugar

Test your blood sugar. Log your blood sugar and the food you're about to eat, plus any thoughts, feelings or behaviors. Return your attention to your breath.

3. Eat Mindfully

Next, eat mindfully. Eat with intention. Use all five senses — taste, touch, look at, listen to and smell your food. Before you even pick up your food, just notice it; notice how your mind and body react to its presence. Observe the color, the smell, sounds and textures. Next, bring the food to your mouth and truly taste it. Make this an eating experience. Notice where you taste the food in your mouth. What side are you chewing on? What is your heart rate like now? Repeat this intentional act for about five bites and then proceed with your meal either in silence or socializing.

Three Types of Meditation

- **Focus/object meditation:** A concentrative practice on a specific external object, which focuses our attention and prevents distraction.

- **Transcendental meditation:** A concentrative practice that includes the use of mantras (sounds or phrases used repetitively) to focus attention.

- **Mindful meditation/ mindfulness:** A practice focused on cultivating a nonjudgmental present-moment awareness of the inner and outer worlds; the focus is on the breath and self-observation to allow for self-transformation.

While it is extremely challenging to be mindful during social meals, make an effort to check in with yourself one-third and two-thirds of the way through your meal. Do this by taking a few mouthfuls of food in silence. When you finally feel both physically sated and psychologically satisfied, take a few more breaths to just notice without judgment how you feel, what you are thinking and if you have any sensations. Log these observations.

4. Test and Treat

Check your blood sugar 2 hours after your meal to identify if it is within your personal range. Log your blood sugar and how the meal has energized you. This is a good way to identify what meals and snacks work with your body in terms of blood sugar management and staying full. If your blood sugar is higher than your goal range, you can take a brisk walk, but not too fast — the movement needs to be aerobic. Hydrate with water. And meditate: it works!

We hope you will take each lifestyle factor into consideration as you experience life with *Everyday Diabetes Meals*. Cheers to ease, health and an increased quality of life, especially surrounding mealtimes!

21 Questions Answered for Everyday Diabetes

SO MANY DIABETES AND NUTRITION MYTHS lead to unanswered questions. We know face time with your doctor can be limited and online information can be misleading or flat-out inaccurate. *Everyday Diabetes Meals* makes living with diabetes easy and healthy. For chapter 3, we have compiled the top trending diabetes questions with answers from the experts. This chapter will prove the best resource for you and your friends' 21 questions! Read it, use it as a reference and clear up the confusion with these evidence-based answers.

Question 1: Should I Follow a Gluten-Free Diet if I Have Type 1 or 2 Diabetes?

The Celiac Disease Foundation estimates that 6% of the population with type 1 diabetes also has celiac disease. If you have been formally diagnosed with both diabetes and the autoimmune disorder celiac disease, you should follow a gluten-free diet.

But What Is Gluten?

When late-night host Jimmy Fallon and his reporters asked New Yorkers a question similar to "What is gluten and why are you on a gluten-free diet?" most were stumped. Let's prevent this naïveté from happening to you.

Celiac and gluten expert Gigi Stewart, editor of *Food Solutions Magazine* and author of GlutenFreeGigi.com, says: "The term 'gluten' is used rather generically to refer to specific proteins that cause small intestine damage to individuals with celiac disease. In science, gluten is actually a group of storage proteins called prolamins. These storage proteins exist in grains to nourish the plant. In wheat [and rye], that protein is gliadin. True gluten (the type that negatively impacts those with celiac disease) is a complex mixture of two primary proteins — gliadin and glutenin. Gliadin and glutenin proteins are, in general, difficult to digest. All prolamins are not necessarily something individuals with celiac disease must avoid. For example, the prolamin zein in corn does not cause small intestine damage to individuals with celiac disease."

DID YOU KNOW?

Celiac Disease Family Connection

If someone in your family has celiac disease, you too can get screened, as most autoimmune diseases involve a genetic component. Always work with a registered dietitian and certified diabetes educator to manage your lifestyle living with both diagnoses.

The gluten-free diet is much easier to follow now that there are Food and Drug Administration regulations for voluntary labeling of gluten-free foods. Gluten-free can be identified as "gluten free," "no gluten," "free of gluten" or "without gluten." This labeling means the food product has a gluten limit of less than 20 parts per million (ppm). This standard is used internationally because most individuals with type 1 diabetes and celiac disease can tolerate this amount of gluten. Gigi Stewart's advice is to read labels carefully with the knowledge that wheat is the main offender. Wheat should be listed on food labels with an allergen alert or a caution statement near the ingredients.

Stewart also tells her readers to "remember BROW: Barley, Rye, Oats and Wheat" when following a gluten-free diet. These grains contain gluten and should be avoided. The exception is oats, which may or may not contain gluten. Stewart says: "Oats are not inherently a gluten-containing grain, but many oats are contaminated with gluten in the field or a facility unless there is purity protocol mandating the oats to be grown gluten-free."

DID YOU KNOW?

Naturally Gluten-Free

Pure forms of corn, potato, rice, soy, amaranth, quinoa, buckwheat and bean flour are all naturally gluten-free.

DID YOU KNOW?

Gluten-Free Recommendations

The U.S. Academy of Nutrition and Dietetics and Health Canada recommend gluten-free diets for individuals diagnosed with celiac disease. The general recommendation is to eliminate all wheat, barley and rye from the diet. Be sure to work with a registered dietitian to prevent vitamin deficiencies and identify hidden sources of proteins derived from both gluten and gliadin.

Possible Hidden and/or Contaminated Sources of Dietary Gluten and Prolamins

- Additives, stabilizers, thickeners, flavorings, extracts and emulsifiers
- Hydrolyzed textured vegetable proteins
- Some ground spices (for example, contaminated coriander and mace)
- Grain alcohol
- Some prescription and over-the-counter medications
- Certain multivitamins
- Toothpastes, lip balms and mouthwash
- Adhesives on stamps and envelopes

Celiac or Gluten Sensitivity or Wheat Allergy

Why would someone need a gluten-free diet when there is no evidence that this diet is advantageous for weight loss? Like type 1 diabetes, celiac disease is also an autoimmune disease whereby gluten and gliadin proteins cause damage to the small intestine, resulting in inflammation, atrophy of the villi (a gradual loss of function of the fingerlike projections that protrude into the small intestine to increase the surface area to aid in maximum absorption), poor absorption of nutrients and pain. Celiac disease is not the same as gluten intolerance, gluten sensitivity or a wheat allergy. They are very different things. While they all can cause abdominal pain and fatigue, only celiac disease can cause long-term damage to the small intestine.

Individuals with gluten sensitivity share many of the same symptoms as those with celiac disease, such as headaches, joint pain and gastrointestinal (GI) issues (including but not limited to diarrhea), yet they do not incur the same level of damage to the villi in the small intestine. There are no autoantibodies found in the blood, as there are with a person with celiac disease. However, when a person with gluten sensitivity removes gluten from their diet, the headaches, joint pain and intestinal distress are eliminated. Gluten sensitivity is now a clinically recognized term.

Wheat allergy causes systemic effects, such as itchy eyes and sneezing, in addition to GI distress. As with other allergies, you can be tested by measuring antibody levels in your blood.

For more information on celiac disease, gluten sensitivity and wheat allergy, visit www.beyondceliac.org.

■ ■ ■

Celiac disease is not the same as gluten intolerance, gluten sensitivity or a wheat allergy. They are very different things.

■ ■ ■

Diagnosing Celiac Disease

Up to 6% of individuals with type 1 diabetes have celiac disease (also known as gluten-sensitive enteropathy, or GSE). If you have type 1 diabetes, talk with your physician about the need to screen for celiac disease. Most important: you must be eating gluten-containing foods at the time of screening and diagnosis. If you are not eating gluten, antibodies may not be present and you may not have an inflamed intestine, resulting in a false negative test result.

If you suspect you have celiac disease, ask your doctor to screen for antibodies. Says Gigi Stewart: "Depending on the physician, some antibodies tested are: tTG (anti-tissue transglutaminase), EmA (anti-endomysium), DGP (anti-deamidated gliadin peptides), IgA (immunoglobulin gamma A) and IgG (immunoglobulin gamma G). The most sensitive of these tests for detecting celiac disease, as well as the most commonly used, is the tTG-IgA test. This test detects celiac disease in patients (who are still eating gluten) about 98% of the time, which shows very high accuracy."

A positive test would then warrant diagnosis by obtaining an intestinal biopsy through a procedure known as an upper gastrointestinal endoscopy. If negative, the doctor may do a genetic test.

DID YOU KNOW?

Nutrient Deficiencies

Celiac disease can cause some nutrient deficiencies in your body. If you are diagnosed with celiac disease, ask your doctor to screen for lactose intolerance and deficiencies such as iron, zinc, B_{12}, folate, calcium, magnesium and fat-soluble vitamins. Consistent supplement use for about 6 to 12 months may help if deficiencies are found. Any lactose intolerance will reverse once the gastrointestinal lining is healed.

Symptoms of Celiac Disease

- Failure to thrive
- Diarrhea or constipation
- Abdominal pain
- Dermatitis herpetiformis (a pruritic papular rash)
- Iron-deficiency anemia
- Osteopenia/osteoporosis
- Short stature
- Dental enamel hypoplasia
- Arthritis and arthralgia
- Chronic hepatitis/ hypertransaminasemia (chronic levels of elevated blood liver transaminase enzymes, causing injury to the liver)
- Neurological problems

Question 2: Is Sugar Bad?

The short answer is: Sugar is not bad, as no food can be good or bad. The terms "good" and "bad" relate to morals and values. All food provides nutrition in the form of energy, with different amounts of nutrients. This message is consistent with the American Diabetes Association's medical nutrition guidelines — specifically the third guideline, which recommends that we maintain pleasure in eating all foods, avoiding judgmental messages about food choices. The goal is to remove guilt from food choices and help you learn to manage your diabetes by eating a variety of foods, regardless of nutritional value.

A more specific question may be: Is sugar safe for someone diagnosed with diabetes? Sugar has definitely received a bad reputation in the past few years. However, did you realize that sugar is a carbohydrate? Anything that is a carbohydrate is sugar. This means table (granulated) sugar, honey, agave nectar, fruits, vegetables, low-fat dairy, fat-free dairy, grains and beans all metabolize to sugar.

If you have diabetes, you still need sugar. Your brain uses sugar as its primary source of energy. The brain can also use the by-products of fat, known as ketones, but this is not typically encouraged, as ketones are not the brain's preferred energy source. Your muscles also need sugar for quick energy when exercising for longer durations (running, cycling, hiking). The Academy of Nutrition and Dietetics and the Canadian Diabetes Association both state that the brain needs 130 grams of carbohydrates every day. In fact, research from the *Journal of the American Dietetic Association* gives the green light for sucrose, a form of sugar, as long as it ranges between 10% and 35% of total daily calories and replaces

> ■ ■ ■
>
> **The goal is to remove guilt from food choices and help you learn to manage your diabetes by eating a variety of foods, regardless of nutritional value.**
>
> ■ ■ ■

calories in the diet. In other words, do not add more calories if you want sugar; instead, make them a small part of your daily intake that would have otherwise been provided by more wholesome complex carbohydrates.

Eating in the Middle

Are you confused about the dietary messages or myths you have read in magazines or heard on the news? While there is excellent research available, do you ever wonder how it's possible that the results of research sometimes seem contradictory? Think about this: there is a vast amount of research and — depending on what authors or journalists stumble upon or seek out — you can usually find something to support your own bias. Further, research that focuses on a specific nutrient is typically testing an excessive quantity of said nutrient. Usually one group in a study will be provided with a disproportionate amount of the nutrient, and the control group will have a neutral, or "normal," amount. For example, the Alpha-Tocopherol, Beta-Carotene Cancer Prevention Study uncovered a potentially higher incidence of lung cancer among men who received synthetic beta-carotene in their study. Dietary beta-carotene in the forms of fruits and vegetables can be cancer-protective, but beta-carotene can have negative effects when taken in high doses through a synthetic supplement.

To summarize, don't eat any one food in excess, eat a variety of real foods for maximum disease-preventing benefits, and be careful about over-supplementation with vitamins and minerals.

Whether studies are evaluating high-carbohydrate versus low-carbohydrate intake, high-fat versus low-fat intake, and/or supplementation versus no supplementation, there is an absolute need to read and evaluate the research. The value of clinical judgment and comparison to a multitude of high-quality studies must be considered when relaying health information. When the media reports diet and health outcomes to the public at large, it usually only represents the findings of one study and it summarizes the information into one flashy, eye-catching sound bite.

Nothing in life is this simple or straightforward. Do yourself a favor: whenever you hear a blanket statement regarding health or wellness, recognize that it isn't directed at you personally. Someone on TV cannot know your exact nutrition needs, just as no one can know exactly how many units of insulin your body needs. What is communicated to the public is that anything that is in excess or at insufficient levels is likely to have negative consequences on your mental and/or physical health.

This is where the "gray zone" comes in. When talking nutrition, your everyday diet should be in the middle of the extremes. Get rid of the black-and-white diet mindset and move to the middle. Leave room for flexibility. You can eat kale and you can eat cupcakes. This doesn't mean just eat kale all the time. That would be just as unbalanced and unhealthful as eating only cupcakes all the time. Eat in the middle! All 150 recipes in this cookbook fall into this everyday gray zone.

What does 10% to 35% calories as refined sugar look like in an average day? Below are two examples of what this potentially could equate to in 1 day's worth of calories.

Calorie Breakdown

Total Daily Intake	Carbohydrate	Protein	Fat	Refined Sugar
2,000 calories	45% calories as carbohydrate (10% calories as refined sugar and 35% calories as complex carbs)	20% calories as protein	35% calories as fat	200 calories as refined sugar
2,000 calories	50% calories as carbohydrate (25% calories as refined sugar and 25% calories as complex carbs)	20% calories as protein	30% calories as fat	500 calories as refined sugar

While including up to 35% daily calories of refined sugar may not harm your overall diabetes blood glucose management, it is still our recommendation to limit your intake of refined carbohydrates due to the lack of fiber, vitamins and minerals — along with the risk of inflammation and other metabolic affects. Of course, combine any carbohydrates with proteins and fats in the meal to prevent a rapid increase in blood sugar.

The research specifically documents that energy in this range and form does not have a negative effect on glycemic or lipid outcomes. The answer is clear: sugar is safe — even pure refined (granulated) sugar in small amounts. Nothing in excess is ever beneficial to our health, but deprivation or elimination of one food is not necessary.

Question 3: Why Do I Become Hypoglycemic a Day after I Exercise?

Regardless of the classification of diabetes, you may experience low blood sugar. In particular, certain medications can compound the increased insulin sensitivity resulting from exercise. Specifically, long-acting sulfonylureas — such as chlorpropamide, glyburide (glibenclamide) and long-acting glipizide — are associated with more episodes of hypoglycemia. The medication glyburide lasts 24 hours and could potentially impair the glucagon response (the ability to release stored sugars) to counter hypoglycemia.

Medications may need to be decreased or adjusted when you begin to exercise more regularly. In fact, improved insulin action and decreased blood sugar can last from 2 to 72 hours after the activity. This is, in part, why the recommendation is to exercise at least every other day, never skipping 2 days in a row, to allow for the lasting effect of improved insulin activity. If you have type 1 diabetes, you may need to lower your insulin dose. Always check your blood sugar before exercising and about every 45 minutes to 1 hour during exercise; of course, always check it again before you go to bed. Refer to page 32 for more information on diabetes and exercise.

Question 4: Is Clean Eating for Me?

Is clean eating a way of life or a diet? It seems that every resource refers to clean eating as something different. We turned to the expert advice of Laura Iu, registered dietitian nutritionist, clinical dietitian and blogger at www.DoWhatIuLove.com, to demystify this undefined term. Iu says: "Surprisingly, a clean diet or the term 'clean eating' has no official universal definition, leaving room for interpretation by all." The definition that resonates the best with Iu as well as with us is: "Avoiding or limiting processed and refined foods and foods that contain a lot of additives, and instead eating more whole foods and focusing on plant-based foods" — as defined by Diabetes Self Management, a publisher that focuses on providing authoritative, reliable health information to people living with diabetes.

Some articles and websites outline following certain diets, like the Paleo diet, as part of the clean eating "approach." While the Paleo diet advocates for the consumption of more whole foods, it is more restrictive than clean eating and can even potentially cause deficiencies of certain micronutrients, like vitamin D and calcium. The Paleo diet prohibits all grains, beans, legumes and dairy products, while clean eating does not. On the Paleo diet, a package of whole wheat crackers would be off-limits. Only flour made from quinoa, almonds or coconuts is allowed, and wheat and wheat products are prohibited.

Iu highlights: "A clean eater would read the ingredient list to ensure the crackers were organic, made from all whole ingredients (millet, brown rice, flax seeds) with minimal processing, and no added sugars or additives." In our private practice, clients who identify as clean eaters typically focus on organic, hormone-free, antibiotic-free produce, dairy, poultry and meat. The clean-eating approach includes a variety of whole foods, providing for all macronutrients and micronutrients.

Iu tells us: "The most important thing to understand is that clean eating is not an all-or-nothing type of thinking about food. The potential danger with clean eating is when you start to label clean foods as 'good,' and less-wholesome foods as 'bad.'" Labeling food as "bad," "unhealthy" or "junk food" can lead you to feel you are bad, unhealthy or junky when eating said food. These behaviors and thoughts may contribute to

■ ■ ■

While the Paleo diet advocates for the consumption of more whole foods, it is more restrictive than clean eating and can even potentially cause deficiencies of certain micronutrients, like vitamin D and calcium.

■ ■ ■

the development of an eating disorder informally known as orthorexia nervosa (it is not yet recognized as a clinical diagnosis by the American Psychiatric Association's Diagnostic and Statistical Manual of Mental Disorders, or the DSM-5). According to the National Eating Disorder Association: "Those who have an 'unhealthy obsession' with otherwise-healthy eating may be suffering from 'orthorexia nervosa,' a term which literally means 'fixation on righteous eating.' Orthorexia starts out as an innocent attempt to eat more healthfully, but orthorexics become fixated on food quality and purity."

Says Iu: "It is unique in that a person can become obsessed over the quality rather than the quantity of food so much so that a high-fiber bread, such as whole wheat bread, would be off-limits if it was not certified organic."

We do not encourage extreme eating. Remember, eat in the middle. In terms of diabetes management, Iu adds that "processed and refined foods aren't the enemy. You can eat foods that come from a bag, jar or box as long as you account for the carbohydrates as part of your overall meal plan."

While there is no evidence to specifically support "clean eating," research has linked a diet high in fruits and vegetables and low in processed foods with improved blood glucose control. You can healthfully adapt aspects of clean eating to your lifestyle as long as you have balance and variety — and remember to eat kale and cupcakes!

Question 5: What Is Sustainable Living?

Whether or not you have diabetes, it is in planet Earth's favor to live sustainably. A sustainable lifestyle and green living go hand in hand. This lifestyle encompasses the full spectrum, from the food you eat and the products you buy to the materials used to build your home.

This type of living starts with sustainable agriculture and farming as defined by the U.S. Farm Bill of 1990: "An integrated system of plant and animal production practices having a site-specific application that will, over the long-term:

- Satisfy human food and fiber needs.
- Enhance environmental quality and the natural resource base upon which the agricultural economy depends.
- Make the most efficient use of nonrenewable resources and on-farm resources and integrate, where appropriate, natural biological cycles and controls.
- Sustain the economic viability of farm operations.
- Enhance the quality of life for farmers and society as a whole."

Buying local products, produce, meat, poultry, eggs and dairy are especially consistent with these values. Hot words associated with sustainability include "organic," "hormone-free," "antibiotic-free," "grass-fed" and "pasture-raised."

Buying a share in community-sourced agriculture (CSA) is one of the easiest ways to start living a "greener" lifestyle without having to make an intentional weekly decision about sustainable food. Typically, you pay a local farm community a monthly fee, which provides you with food on a weekly basis and ensures that the food is fresh, seasonal and likely organic.

If CSA isn't for you, consider buying local and in-season produce. Instead of buying berries from South America, eat local and in-season. Visit www.fruitsandveggiesmorematters.org to find in-season produce. Depending on where you live, hardier vegetables like kale and cabbage can grow in the cooler seasons while berries and herbs will be ready in the spring. In summer, peppers, zucchini and lettuce are ready for picking. In the fall, apples, corn and pumpkins are typically plentiful.

If you have diabetes, one can surmise it may be beneficial to adopt some of these practices, as sustainable eating

Top 10 Reasons to Eat Sustainably

Grace Communications Foundation shares its top 10 reasons to eat sustainably at www.SustainableTable.org. Below is an adapted version of the list. Refer to their website for the documented resources and footnotes supporting the list.

1. Sustainable foods taste better since they are local, picked closer to peak ripeness (providing intense flavors) and sold immediately (not shipped across the country).

2. Sustainable foods are healthier and more nutrient-dense (see points 3 to 6)

3. Sustainable produce is grown with fewer and less-toxic pesticides.

4. Sustainable meat is raised with little to no antibiotics or hormones.

5. Sustainably raised animals are more likely to live in healthier habitats — with less crowding, less waste, more roaming and more humane practices.

6. Sustainable foods aren't genetically modified or irradiated.

7. Sustainable foods are grown in a manner that benefits the health of the farmer and workers because they have better working practices and are not exposed to harsh chemicals or harmful gases produced by waste.

8. Sustainable farming supports local economies.

9. Sustainable farming produces less waste due to pasture grazing.

10. Small- and medium-size sustainable farms have less negative impact on local water systems and soil quality.

encourages increased consumption of fruits and vegetables and eating real, wholesome foods made without chemicals or hormones — rather than eating processed food products found in packages.

Question 6: Should I Eat Sugar-Free?

Our motto is "Eat kale and cupcakes!" We believe it is not necessary to eat sugar-free food products when living with diabetes. We have already discussed why you can still eat sugar. "Sugar-free" is not "carbohydrate-free" or "calorie-free." In fact, many sugar-free products replace table (granulated) sugar, otherwise known as sucrose, with sugar alcohols. The Sugar Association defines a sugar alcohol as "a hydrogenated form of carbohydrate." Sugar alcohols are less sweet and less calorically dense than regular table sugar. Sugar alcohols are not as well absorbed as sucrose. In fact, they often cause bloating and have a laxative effect. If a product claims to be sugar-free, it may contain sugar substitutes or nonnutritive sweeteners (NNS), such as aspartame, saccharin, acesulfame potassium and sucralose. These are not supposed to affect your blood sugar, but the body does respond to them in unknown ways.

The American Diabetes Association outlines: "Sucralose affects the glycemic and insulin responses to an oral glucose load in obese people who do not normally consume NNS." While more research is warranted on nonnutritive sweeteners, it's safe to assume they affect our bodies, especially when consumed in large quantities. Always test your blood sugar before a meal or snack and 1 to 2 hours afterward to identify how your body has responded.

Question 7: Is It Better to Follow the Ketogenic Diet?

Once again, the ketogenic diet is becoming quite popular. Previously, it was the standard treatment for individuals with type 1 diabetes before the discovery of insulin in the 1920s. It is best-known for treating epilepsy in both adults and children. The ketogenic diet limits carbohydrates to between 20 and 50 grams, and protein and fat are not restricted. A very low-carbohydrate ketogenic diet (VLCKD) and a low-carbohydrate ketogenic diet (LCKD) put the body into a state of ketosis, identified by measuring ketones in the urine.

Do not mistake nutritional ketosis for the fatal condition of diabetic ketoacidosis (DKA). Nutritional ketosis results from restricting carbohydrate intake. DKA involves elevated blood sugar (levels could be as high as 800 mg/dL, or 44 mmol/L)

■ ■ ■

Sugar alcohols are not as well absorbed as sucrose. In fact, they often cause bloating and have a laxative effect.

■ ■ ■

DID YOU KNOW?

Abnormal Ketone Levels

Abnormal ketone values are defined by Medline Plus as:

- Small is less than 20 mg/dL (1.1 mmol/L)
- Moderate is between 30 and 40 mg/dL (1.7 and 2.2 mmol/L)
- High is greater than 80 mg/dL (4.4 mmol/L)

What Is DKA?

The American Diabetes Association (ADA) defines diabetic ketoacidosis (DKA) as "a serious condition that can lead to diabetic coma (passing out for a long time) or even death. When your cells don't get the glucose they need for energy, your body begins to burn fat for energy, which produces ketones. Ketones are chemicals that the body creates when it breaks down fat to use for energy. The body does this when it doesn't have enough insulin to use glucose, the body's normal source of energy. When ketones build up in the blood, they make it more acidic. They are a warning sign that your diabetes is out of control or that you are getting sick."

ADA's Warning Signs of DKA

DKA usually develops slowly. But when vomiting occurs, this life-threatening condition can develop in a few hours. Early symptoms include the following:

- Thirst or a very dry mouth
- High blood glucose (blood sugar) levels
- High levels of ketones in the urine
- Frequent urination

Then, other symptoms appear:

- Nausea, vomiting or abdominal pain (vomiting can be caused by many illnesses, not just ketoacidosis; if vomiting continues for more than 2 hours, contact your health-care provider)
- Difficulty breathing
- Fruity odor on breath
- A hard time paying attention, or confusion
- Constantly feeling tired
- Dry or flushed skin

with ketone production much greater than nutritional ketoacidosis. DKA results from insulin deficiency, commonly in someone with type 1 diabetes who is experiencing high stress and/or is ill. If your blood sugar is greater than 240 mg/dL (13.3 mmol/L) and you feel abdominal pain, nauseated and mentally foggy, you are likely in a ketotic state. If this is the case, it is recommended that you test your ketone levels.

The University of Colorado Denver's recommendations are to drink extra fluids and call your medical doctor if your ketones measure between 20 and 52 mg/dL (1.1 and 2.9 mmol/L) and to go to the emergency room if they are 54 mg/dL (3 mmol/L) or higher.

"You can't tell the difference between nutritional ketosis and diabetic ketosis on a dipstick," says Dr. Jennifer L. Gaudiani, certified eating disorder specialist and the founder and medical director of the Gaudiani Clinic. "Either there are ketones in the urine, or there aren't. A client with diabetes cannot tell on a dipstick." Since a patient cannot determine whether they are in nutritional ketoacidosis or DKA on the dipstick, Guadiani conducts a "comprehensive metabolic panel to look at the bicarbonate level to see if they've opened up an anion gap." This panel would help the medical doctor determine whether there was an acid-base problem, such as acidosis, which could lead to diabetic ketoacidosis. While she outlines that ketosis is likely not dangerous in someone without diabetes, she would "never recommend a ketogenic diet for someone with diabetes."

> ■ ■ ■
> **While initial weight loss and positive trends in lipids and blood sugar management are observed when following a ketogenic diet, high-quality long-term studies are still needed.**
> ■ ■ ■

While initial weight loss and positive trends in lipids and blood sugar management are observed when following a ketogenic diet, high-quality long-term studies are still needed. This diet can be difficult to sustain because it consists largely of meats, poultry, game, fish, clear soups, gelatin, eggs, butter, olive oil, coffee and tea — and no grains whatsoever. There is additional concern for bone health and kidney function (including kidney stones), but this can possibly be overcome by choosing more alkaline fruits and vegetables.

Finally, while the brain can use ketones made from fat and fatty acids, other organs cannot use these ketones by themselves. Glucose must be made by the liver and kidneys using either protein from the diet or protein found elsewhere in the body. If there is not enough dietary protein, the body will deplete protein from the muscle. You want to prevent this from happening. Muscle is extremely important because it is a metabolically active tissue that helps with insulin sensitivity and metabolic rate.

Question 8: Why Did I Gain Weight When I Started Taking Insulin?

Before you started taking insulin, you may remember that your blood sugar was very high, or perhaps you were diagnosed with type 1 diabetes after an episode of DKA — diabetic ketoacidosis. You may have had a slow increase in blood sugar over a period of time and never knew it. Holly W. LoRusso, registered dietitian and certified diabetes educator at New York–Presbyterian Hospital in New York City, explains: "When your blood sugar is high for an extended period of time and your body is unable to use it properly due to insulin deficiency (type 1 diabetes or type 2 diabetes), you cannot absorb the sugar to create energy. Instead, the sugar is transported to your kidneys and removed through urine."

According to the Joslin Diabetes Center, the world's largest diabetes research center, people with undiagnosed type 1 diabetes and/or unregulated high blood sugar often lose weight due to the sugar and therefore calories lost in the urine. In fact, many times, weight loss is twofold. LoRusso explains that both the loss of calories and the loss of water weight in the form of excessive secretion of urine produce a greater weight loss. When you begin an insulin regimen, you absorb sugar, calories and water. She tells her clients that they "may regain or rehydrate their bodies with the water that was lost." While it appears you have gained weight immediately after starting insulin, it likely means you were not adequately nourished or hydrated prior to insulin treatment.

Additionally, your dietary intake prior to taking insulin may be "falsely" elevated, as it is more difficult to recognize the connection between large portions and weight gain when you are not absorbing the calories or gaining weight at that point. Keep in mind that you may need to make dietary changes, especially in regard to portion sizes, when you start insulin because you will absorb the calories from sugar and store sugar with water as glycogen. As always, it is important to speak with your registered dietitian and/or certified diabetes educator if you have concerns about your diet, insulin and weight management.

Question 9: Can I Drink Coconut Water If I Have Diabetes?

Coconut water is more similar to freshly squeezed orange juice than water because it has both carbohydrates and potassium. It is made from the thin liquid found in the center of an unripe coconut, which is then filtered and pasteurized. It contains about 60 calories and about 15 grams of carbohydrates per 8 ounces (250 mL). While this is about half the calories and carbohydrates of freshly squeezed orange juice, it is most definitely not equivalent to bottled or tap water.

Coconut water contains sodium and is a fabulous source of potassium (as much potassium as 1 banana!). Though coconut water may be sold at gyms and fitness studios, it is not a sports drink. A sports drink has about 75% more sodium for replenishing electrolytes than the average can of coconut water. Athletes need to replace sodium lost in sweat more than they need to replace potassium. Coconut water is a lower-carbohydrate beverage choice for individuals trying to manage their blood sugar. It also provides an easy way to replenish potassium (but not sodium) for people with diabetes who are on potassium-lowering diuretics (of course, check with your medical doctor before drinking coconut water). While it provides potassium and about 15 grams of carbohydrates, it does not contain enough sodium to be considered an ideal sports drink.

Read the nutrition facts on your coconut water. Many brands are adding sugar to the "unflavored" coconut water to help ensure consistent levels of sweetness and to market different flavors to appeal to a greater customer base. While the total carbohydrates typically remains low, be sure to include this drink in your daily carbohydrate count and use blood sugar self-monitoring to see how your body reacts to it.

■ ■ ■

People with undiagnosed type 1 diabetes and/or unregulated high blood sugar often lose weight due to the sugar and therefore calories lost in the urine.

■ ■ ■

Calories and Nutrients in Various Drinks

Drink (per 8 oz/250 mL serving)	Calories	Carbohydrate (g)	Sodium (mg)	Potassium (mg)
Coconut water	45–60	13–15	30–45	470–570
Orange juice, freshly squeezed	112	26	2	500
Water	0	0	5	0
Apple juice, freshly squeezed	120	30	10	0
Sports drink	50	15	110–160	30

Coconut water may be an option for someone trying to manage insulin resistance or someone following a moderate-carbohydrate diet. If you want orange juice but not all of the carbohydrates, this is a great alternative. Do not use coconut water as a replacement for water or as a sports drink. Be moderate and recognize that, like every other food and drink, it should not be consumed in excess.

Question 10: What Produce Should I Buy Organic?

■ ■ ■

Organic farmers, ranchers and food processors follow a defined set of standards to produce organic food.

■ ■ ■

According to the U.S. Department of Agriculture (USDA), organic agriculture produces products using methods that preserve the environment and avoid most synthetic materials, such as pesticides and antibiotics. USDA organic standards describe how farmers may grow crops and raise livestock and which materials they may use.

Organic farmers, ranchers and food processors follow a defined set of standards to produce organic food. The U.S. Congress described general organic principles in the Organic Foods Production Act, and the USDA defines specific organic standards. These standards cover the product from farm to table, including soil and water quality, pest control, livestock practices and rules for food additives.

Organic farms and processors:

- Preserve natural resources and biodiversity
- Support animal health and welfare
- Provide access to the outdoors so that animals can exercise their natural behaviors
- Use only approved materials
- Do not use genetically modified ingredients

- Receive annual onsite inspections
- Separate organic food from nonorganic food

Organic foods are encouraged for children, the elderly and immune-compromised individuals. According to the review article "Contribution of Organically Grown Crops to Human Health" in the *International Journal of Environmental Research and Public Health*, there are higher amounts of pesticide residues and heavy metals in conventionally produced crops as compared to organic crops. There are consequently lower levels of pesticide residues in human urine when eating organic foods. Further, in vitro studies and animal studies showed a clear indication of the benefits of the consumption of organic foods/extracts (such as fertility and increased immunity) when compared to nonorganic foods.

If you can choose to eat organic, go ahead. If cost is a concern, consider organic dairy, meats, fruits and vegetables (and purchase nonorganic breads and grains). Every year, the Environmental Working Group compiles a list, called the Dirty Dozen, of the top 12 foods found to be highest in pesticide residue even after washing and sometimes even after peeling. The 2016 list included strawberries, apples, nectarines, peaches, celery, grapes, cherries, spinach, tomatoes, sweet bell peppers, cherry tomatoes and cucumbers. We believe it's worth spending the extra money on the organic certification when purchasing foods on this list. Check the EWG site (www.EWG.org) annually to find the latest Dirty Dozen. Also take note of the Clean Fifteen, which lists the produce least likely to hold pesticide residues.

Question 11: Why Do I Wake Up with High Blood Glucose Every Morning?

We spoke with Holly LoRusso, registered dietitian and certified diabetes educator in New York City, about why you may have high blood glucose when you wake up in the morning. She told us that high blood sugar in the morning is likely related to what you ate (or didn't eat) the night before. It is important to monitor your blood sugar at night and to be conscious of the foods you are eating before bedtime. Additionally, you are less active during sleeping hours (using less of the sugar in your bloodstream) and you may not have increased insulin sensitivity from contracting muscles. However, it is still important to have a snack at night.

LoRusso outlines: "If you are on insulin or a medication that causes your body to make insulin, your blood sugar may drop overnight, and without having a proper bedtime snack (one with protein and carbohydrate), you can unintentionally cause your body to produce even more sugar overnight for energy. This can result in a high blood sugar in the morning."

Furthermore, high blood glucose in the morning could be caused by the dawn phenomenon. "This is something that happens to everyone with or without diabetes — where between four and five o'clock in the morning, your body produces an excess of hormones. The production of these hormones causes your body to need additional insulin, and for those with diabetes, they may not have the insulin available in the body to use, which causes a higher-than-normal blood sugar in the morning," explains LoRusso.

According to the American Diabetes Association: "The rise in glucose is mostly because your body is making less insulin and more glucagon (a hormone that increases blood glucose) than it needs. The less insulin made by the pancreas, the more glucagon the pancreas makes as a result. This is why high fasting blood glucose levels are common in people with type 2 [diabetes]."

Question 12: Can I Drink Coffee Every Day?

Coffee has been associated with the prevention of diabetes, likely due to coffee's phenolic and antioxidant compounds, which decrease inflammation by reducing oxidative stress. This association is clear in people who do not have diabetes. The bad news is that there is mixed information on coffee consumption in individuals with previously diagnosed diabetes. Here is the scoop. Research gathered from three different studies reported that an increase of 1 cup (250 mL) of coffee a day over 4 years was associated with a 12% decreased risk of type 2 diabetes. Inversely, decreasing coffee consumption by 1 cup (250 mL) a day over 4 years was associated with a 20% increased risk of type 2 diabetes. In these studies, presented in the July 2014 issue of *Diabetologia*, this held true only for caffeinated coffee and not decaffeinated coffee or tea.

In other research, both caffeinated and decaffeinated coffee were associated with decreased risk of type 2 diabetes. Still other studies concluded that caffeine increased blood glucose and decreased insulin sensitivity. Confused? Researchers don't have the final answer yet, but most tend to associate the benefits with caffeine rather than the beverage. Additionally, black coffee (not the fancy coffees with added syrups, flavorings and toppings) decreases the risk of developing diabetes, but if you already have diabetes, it may actually spike blood sugar after consumption. If you have diabetes, be your own detective and test your blood sugar at fasting and after coffee consumption. Let your body be the teacher.

Question 13: How Can I Ever Eat Cake Again?

Diabetes is not about deprivation. Diabetes does not mean that your favorite sweet foods are off-limits. We believe that it is important for you to consume the foods that you enjoy regardless of your diagnoses. Courtney Darsa, registered dietitian in private practice and at the Hospital for Special Surgery in New York City, says: "The biggest difference when you have diabetes versus when you don't is that there needs to be more planning involved."

In our practice, we educate our clients on how to spread out their carbohydrates throughout the day. We also outline that they should consume each macronutrient (carbohydrate, protein, fat) at all meals and at least two of the three macronutrients with snacks — to help maintain a balanced blood sugar. If you want dessert, you can eat it. Pick the time of day you want your cake or cookie. Count how many grams of carbohydrates it contains and moderate it to your meal or snack gram allotment.

Darsa says: "If you are planning to go to a steakhouse for date night, forgo the mashed potatoes and squash in exchange for apple pie as dessert. Eat your protein with nonstarchy vegetables as the entrée (think: steak and roasted Brussels sprouts) and the apple pie for dessert to stay within your carbohydrate count. She reminds clients to "keep portions in mind when planning meals and snacks." Eating too much of one thing can be detrimental and cause deficiencies in other nutrients. Eating too much for your individual needs (large portions and/or too many calories) may result in inflammation and weight gain, leading to metabolic disorders.

With appropriate portion sizes and grams of carbohydrates, you can eat your favorite foods both at home and at your favorite cafés. In most major cities, you can find chain restaurants or franchises that share nutrition information online. In the table below, Darsa shares a sample day for readers following a consistent carbohydrate intake of 45 to

■ ■ ■

With appropriate portion sizes and grams of carbohydrates, you can eat your favorite foods both at home and at your favorite cafés.

■ ■ ■

Sample Day at Pret A Manger

Breakfast	Cranberry Orange Scone + Egg and Spinach Pot
Lunch	Thai Chicken Power Lunch
Snack	Chai Chia Pot
Dinner	Spicy Shrimp and Cilantro Wrap + Melon Medley
Snack	Omega 3 Mix: cranberries, roasted almonds, walnuts, pecans, pistachios, raw green pumpkin seeds (pepitas)

Based on Pret A Manger online menu (www.pret.com); accessed June 28, 2016.

60 grams of carbohydrates per meal and 15 to 30 grams of carbohydrates per snack. Darsa chose menu options from the international food establishment Pret A Manger. With a little planning, you can eat your cake or, in this case, your scone, even when out and about without added anxiety. Always check the nutrition facts on food packaging and on food company websites for updates and changes in carbohydrates and/or ingredients. Remember: this is just a guideline on carbohydrate allotment throughout the day; your overall caloric intake may differ based on your individual needs.

Question 14: What Is the Difference between an Insulin Pump, a Blood Glucose Meter and a Glucosensor?

These are three very helpful instruments for managing blood sugar in individuals with diabetes. While the insulin pump delivers insulin for individuals with absolute insulin deficiency, the others are tools that measure blood sugar. Individuals with type 1 diabetes or type 2 diabetes may benefit from having all three tools at some point, especially if they have diabetes for many years.

Insulin Pump

The insulin pump is an external device used to deliver a basal rate of long-acting insulin and mealtime boluses (doses) with rapid-acting insulin. Using an insulin pump allows for more flexibility with daily activities, greater blood sugar control, and less poking and prodding (fewer finger sticks and daily injections). For instance, you can lower your basal rate when you exercise or increase your rate when stressed or ill. You can program your pump to bolus insulin based on your meal choice as well.

Two Tools for Blood Sugar Reading

The blood glucose meter and the glucosensor (known formally as the continuous glucose monitoring system) are two tools used to read blood sugar. A blood glucose meter gives you one reading at one moment in time. It is essential for blood glucose self-monitoring. You take the reading by obtaining blood and putting it on the strip, which is read by the meter.

More recently, a device to measure blood sugar without interruptions throughout the day and night was created. Medtronic, the maker of the continuous glucose monitor (CGM), describes the tool on their website: "A tiny electrode called a glucose sensor is inserted under the skin to measure glucose levels in tissue fluid. It is connected to a transmitter that sends the information via wireless radio frequency to a monitoring and display device. The device can detect and notify you if your glucose is reaching a high or low limit." The CGM system does not replace finger sticks. You must calibrate the machine every 12 hours by getting a blood sugar reading from a blood glucose meter.

This CGM system acts as a glucosensor/glucose receptor to identify blood sugar highs, lows, trends, rates of falling or increasing blood sugar, and more. Be aware that the CGM measures subcutaneous (under the skin) glucose/sugar, not plasma blood sugar. There is a 10- to 15-minute lag between subcutaneous and plasma blood sugar. The CGM has less accuracy at low glucose levels. Therefore, do not rely solely on this device as an alert for hypoglycemia or low blood sugar.

■ ■ ■

The CGM system does not replace finger sticks. You must calibrate the machine every 12 hours by getting a blood sugar reading from a blood glucose meter.

■ ■ ■

Question 15: Can I Do a Juice Cleanse?

Juicing is one of the latest diet crazes. The Mayo Clinic outlines that juicing "extracts the juice from fresh fruits or vegetables. The resulting liquid contains most of the vitamins, minerals and plant chemicals (phytonutrients) found in the whole fruit. However, whole fruits and vegetables also have healthy fiber, which is lost during most juicing."

Registered dietitian Courtney Darsa says: "When you lose the fiber, you lose the ability to feel as full." This is important for a few reasons and especially relevant when trying to manage blood sugar and weight. First, when doing a juice cleanse, you are likely to spike your blood sugar. Your body will quickly absorb the juice without the help of fiber and/or a more complex macronutrient to slow the rate of digestion and subsequent absorption of the natural sugars. As a consequence, you will likely feel tired and could quickly get hungry. Although your blood sugar surged, your stomach never fully filled.

When your body receives fewer calories on a strict cleanse, your metabolism will slow down in an effort to maximize the limited calories available. This can decrease your metabolism by as much as 30%. Darsa says: "Your body is extremely smart and is trying to adjust to what you are providing it with. Your body is trying to conserve its energy the best it can." Whether you have diabetes or not, you don't want to raise your blood sugar, increase your hunger and slow your metabolism. When your metabolism slows down due to a low caloric intake, you are more likely to binge since your body is literally starving and needs the food it craves.

Since juice is 100% pure carbohydrates and provides no protein or fat, it will raise blood sugar more than a typical meal or snack. For this reason, we recommend that people with diabetes do not participate in a juice cleanse.

DID YOU KNOW?

Realistic Goals

On a cautionary note, as eating-disorder specialists, we commonly see clients who try extreme diets that lead to either evening binging after daytime restricting or even more serious eating disorders. Instead of drastic dietary and lifestyle changes, always identify small and realistic goals that you can adhere to for life.

Question 16: Why Do I Crave Sugar?

Sugar cravings are real. They send the signal to eat, but the signal doesn't always mean you need to eat. The body senses a dip in blood sugar when it is falling dramatically after a higher-carbohydrate meal like pasta (think: 100 to 200 mg/dL, or 5.6 to 11.1 mmol/L). Or perhaps because the blood sugar is falling below the body's lowest norm (below 63 to 70 mg/dL, or 3.5 to 3.9 mmol/L). The body is biologically wired to either seek out food or to make sugar from the body's stores.

This does not mean that all sugar cravings translate to a physical need to eat. If your sugar is spiking or crashing after you eat a bag of gummy candy, check your blood sugar. You could be feeling the change in your blood sugar and may not need more fuel. You can also mistake the signs of hyperglycemia for hypoglycemia and vice versa. Both may result in shaking, sweating and decreased comprehension. Do yourself a favor and take your blood glucose reading.

Cravings for sugar may also feel like an addiction. Knowing this is important especially when understanding that sugar, which is another name for carbohydrates, can and does affect the entire body in various ways in different people. Researchers expect that some people do not produce enough of the reward hormone known as dopamine when they eat, just like some people don't produce enough insulin or leptin (the fullness hormone). They never feel satisfied, and therefore the desire to eat continues. While cravings and overeating for some may be attributed to these deficiencies, others may experience dysfunction in their reward systems, causing the body to become less sensitive to the hormone dopamine. Research on rats suggests one would need to eat more and more to activate the reward feedback with dopamine.

A high sugar and fat intake results in high levels of dopamine. The activation of the brain's reward system leads the body to crave more of the high-sugar, high-fat food to further increase dopamine and activate the brain reward system. However, evidence suggests that, at some point, the brain reward system becomes insensitive to the food, and therefore more sugar and fat need to be consumed to feel pleasure. This is extremely complex because there are other substances — such as the appetite hormone ghrelin and the fullness hormone leptin — that must be considered. To summarize, there exists a type of "addicting" quality to sugar. The best solution at present is to naturally increase dopamine through exercise, to regulate blood sugar with

■ ■ ■

Sugar cravings are real. They send the signal to eat, but the signal doesn't always mean you need to eat.

■ ■ ■

a macronutrient-balanced meal and to regularly practice mindfulness. More information and research, especially in human subjects rather than animals, is warranted.

Lastly, cravings can be caused by changing hormone levels and even the time of day. Did you know that there are very specific times of day the body prepares for food, sleep and even activity? The Women's Health Body Clock diet recommends eating consistently and in sync with the body clock's natural rhythms to reduce cravings. For instance, around three or four o'clock in the afternoon, the body experiences a drop in alertness when your counterregulatory hormone (known as cortisol) is falling. This decrease leads to a feeling of fatigue, which may be misinterpreted as hunger or the need to refuel. You may need to eat, but likely you need instead to do some jumping jacks to get your heart rate up. As always, check your blood sugar and then decide if you need to eat, move or treat with insulin. Keep in mind: this time of day typically coincides with the need for a snack. It is essential for you to be mindful and identify what your individual body needs.

> ■ ■ ■
>
> There exists a type of "addicting" quality to sugar. The best solution at present is to naturally increase dopamine through exercise, to regulate blood sugar with a macronutrient-balanced meal and to regularly practice mindfulness.
>
> ■ ■ ■

Question 17: What Is the Relationship between Low Bone Density and Diabetes?

If you have either type 1 or type 2 diabetes, you have an increased risk for bone loss and therefore fractures and osteoporosis (this is true despite the facts that individuals with type 2 diabetes usually have a higher bone mineral density and typically weigh more than people with type 1 diabetes). One study found that individuals older than 66 years old with diabetes are at a 20% increased risk of having a fracture compared to individuals without diabetes.

It is important to keep in mind that the life expectancy of individuals with diabetes has increased, and therefore so has the likelihood that these individuals will develop osteoporosis.

Symptoms of Osteopenia and Osteoporosis

Osteopenia (weakened bones)	Osteoporosis (bone loss)
• No visible signs • Recent fractures • Bone pain	• Fractures, especially to the hip • Bone pain • Hunched back posture • Loss of height

In individuals with either type 1 or type 2 diabetes, poor glycemic control for extended periods of time results in complications in the smaller blood vessels, which contribute to bone loss and increase the risk of fracture. For example, if an individual with diabetes experiences a complication such as neuropathy or retinopathy, they are more likely to fall and fracture a bone. Furthermore, if an individual with diabetes develops nephropathy (kidney disease), hypercalciuria (excess calcium in the urine) can develop, which can negatively affect vitamin D metabolism and result in vitamin D deficiency.

Need for Both Calcium and Vitamin D

Prevention and early detection are key to maintaining bone density and reversing bone loss. Keep in mind that your body absorbs calcium best when it is taken in doses of 500 mg or less. You must have vitamin D_3 to absorb calcium and form calcitriol, which is a hormone crucial for building new bones and bone formation. Lack of vitamin D_3 can cause the body to take calcium from your bones, preventing new bone growth and leading to osteopenia and osteoporosis.

You can create or take in vitamin D through sun exposure, dietary choices (such as fatty fish), fortified foods and, of course, supplements. See the table below for the recommended daily intakes of both calcium and vitamin D.

The Institute of Medicine, the health arm of the National Academy of Sciences, recommends no more than 4,000 IU of vitamin D per day for adults. However, doctors sometimes prescribe higher doses for people who are deficient in vitamin D.

Recommended Daily Intake of Calcium and Vitamin D for People with Diabetes

	Calcium (mg/day)	Vitamin D (IUs/day)
Women 18–50 years old	1,000	600
Women 50–70 years old	1,200	600
Women 71+ years old	1,200	800
Men 18–70 years old	1,000	600
Men 71+ years old	1,200	800

* Always read your supplement label to ensure that the product meets the United States Pharmacopeia (USP) standards. The upper tolerable level of vitamin D is 4,000 IUs per day for individuals older than 9 years old.

Question 18: What Is Diabetes 1.5?

Have you ever heard of someone having symptoms of both type 1 and type 2 diabetes? Sound weird? After reading the first few chapters of this book, you now know that type 1 diabetes is in part caused by autoimmune factors. Individuals with type 1 diabetes require insulin due to the destruction of the beta cells, the cells in the pancreas that produce insulin. Type 2 diabetes, on the other hand, has nothing to do with antibodies and is caused by a slow decrease in insulin sensitivity and eventually dysfunction, as well as beta cell burnout.

When someone is diagnosed with type 2 diabetes, they will first alter their diet and exercise routine to manage blood sugar. The second step is to try medication, typically an oral hypoglycemic agent (such as metformin), to make the body more sensitive to insulin. Individuals with type 2 diabetes require insulin only when the beta cells have stopped producing insulin after many years of living with diabetes. If you have type 2 diabetes, you will not have autoantibodies that attack your beta cells.

What happens if an individual presents with signs and/ or symptoms of both type 1 and 2 diabetes? It could be what is known as type 1.5 diabetes (formerly known as latent autoimmune diabetes of adults, or LADA). Type 1.5 diabetes shares signs and symptoms of both type 1 and type 2 diabetes, but is completely different. It does not affect children, as its onset is late in adulthood. It often presents as insulin resistance, which often results in a misdiagnosis of type 2 diabetes. Like type 1 diabetes, there is an autoimmune aspect involved in type 1.5 diabetes. Yet destruction of the beta cells by autoantibodies occurs more slowly in type 1.5 than in type 1 diabetes and is therefore typically missed at the time of diagnosis. Most individuals initially respond to oral medications that improve insulin production, but some eventually need treatment with insulin.

Treating type 1.5 diabetes is not very different from treating any other kind of diabetes. It is important to be an advocate for yourself. This means developing a trusting relationship with your diabetes team, educating yourself on the latest diabetes research, practicing self-care and recognizing that you are your best tool in living well with diabetes every day.

■ ■ ■

Destruction of the beta cells by autoantibodies occurs more slowly in type 1.5 than in type 1 diabetes and is therefore typically missed at the time of diagnosis.

■ ■ ■

Question 19: Why Does My Blood Sugar Increase after My Killer Cardio Class?

Having problems keeping your blood sugar down after a cardio class? This is a common problem for some people with diabetes who are initiating an exercise regimen. As mentioned in chapter 2, anaerobic exercise has the potential to raise your blood sugar. Examples of anaerobic exercise are lifting heavy weights, running, cycling and a high-intensity cardio class.

Increased blood sugar with exercise can be frustrating because exercise is recommended to help keep blood sugar down. Thankfully, high blood sugar typically lasts only for a few hours after anaerobic exercise. But why does it happen in the first place? If you don't have enough insulin circulating in your blood before you exercise and your blood sugar is already high (greater than 250 mg/dL, or 13.9 mmol/L), exercise can further increase your blood sugar. This is because anaerobic exercise causes stress hormones — such as adrenaline, norepinephrine, epinephrine, glucagon, growth hormone and cortisol — to be released into your system. These hormones cause glucose to be released into the bloodstream from the liver, thereby raising your blood sugar and leading to a high that is difficult to manage. It's best to delay exercise until your blood sugar decreases to a range previously determined by you and your physician, likely between 100 and 250 mg/dL (5.6 and 13.9 mmol/L).

Everyone's body responds differently to various types and intensities of activity. It's important to understand how your body reacts to physical activity. Measure your blood sugar before, during and after you work out to ensure your safety. Work with your certified diabetes educator to find out what routine is ideal for you and your blood sugar management.

Question 20: Do I Need to Lose Weight?

Depending on your current weight status — more specifically your amount of fat mass — your blood glucose range may improve with weight loss. If you have normal-weight obese syndrome or your weight is classified in the body mass index (BMI) range of "overweight" or "obese," it may be beneficial to lose weight to not only manage your blood glucose, but to also decrease the risk of certain comorbidities (co-occurring disorders or diseases) or at least lessen their symptoms. (See Body Mass Index Numbers, page 11, for more information.)

However, BMI is not always a great indicator for weight status because it doesn't take into account body composition.

■ ■ ■

Yes, losing weight can be difficult. Instead, focus on behaviors and let weight loss be secondary to your healthy lifestyle.

■ ■ ■

Insulin and Weight Gain

Weight gain is common when people start or increase insulin dosages. This doesn't mean you need to lose weight — you may have previously been undernourished. With the help of insulin, sugar can finally be absorbed by your cells and used as an energy source, and this therefore contributes to your total daily calorie intake. See question 8 (page 52) for more clarification on insulin and weight gain.

For example, a collegiate athlete may have a BMI of 26.5, which would put them in the classification of "overweight." Yet this doesn't mean that they are unhealthy or need to lose weight, because lean body mass is greater than fat mass.

A better indicator of whether you need to lose weight is your waist circumference — a more accurate measure of abdominal fat. A waist circumference greater than 35 inches (88 cm) for women and greater than 40 inches (100 cm) for men indicates that you are at risk for metabolic syndrome and heart disease. As discussed in chapter 1, it's possible that inflammation arises secondary to fat mass, not necessarily body weight. Insulin resistance follows, along with leptin resistance. This may lead to abdominal obesity. Keep your body composition in check with lifestyle changes such as diet and exercise.

Most diabetes agencies recommend losing 7% of your current body weight, as this weight loss improves glycemic outcomes and is maintainable for at least 2 years or more as evidenced by the Diabetes Prevention Program. Mindfulness can also improve glycemic outcomes, as discussed in chapter 2. Overall, focus on the four lifestyle factors stressed in *Everyday Diabetes Meals* — nutrition, physical activity, sleep and mindfulness — to lose weight (if needed) and achieve greater health to either prevent or live healthfully with diabetes every day!

Yes, losing weight can be difficult. Instead, focus on behaviors and let weight loss be secondary to your healthy lifestyle. Eat enough, but do not stuff yourself. Eat consistently and don't skip meals. Incorporate balanced meals that include carbohydrates, fats and proteins and prevent blood sugar roller coasters. Move more. For people with diabetes, intense exercise may be even more difficult to achieve and maintain due to comorbidities that may cause weakness and physical pain. Instead, make short-term and realistic exercise goals that you can build on. Consistency is key for long-term success. Don't be discouraged if you are unable to do intense exercises

DID YOU KNOW?

Preventing Diabetes

The Diabetes Prevention Program (DPP), a major multicenter clinical research study, published in 2002, showed that an approximate 7% weight loss through diet and exercise decreases your risk of developing diabetes. The factors that were measured in this program included decreases in overall calories and saturated fat as well 150 minutes a week of exercise. Activities like brisk walking, aerobic dance, skating, swimming and bike riding counted toward the physical activity goal.

like spinning and jogging. Remember: any movement, even brisk walking, is better than none! Sleep 7 to 9 hours each night. Treat sleep disorders such as obstructive sleep apnea with a continuous positive airway pressure (CPAP) machine and practice mindfulness daily.

Question 21: I Was Just Diagnosed with Diabetes. Can I Ever Drink Alcohol Again?

First, you should speak to your medical doctor and certified diabetes educator about whether alcohol is a safe option for you. Alcohol may exacerbate certain comorbidities, like hypertension and diabetic neuropathy. Furthermore, some diabetes-related medications can increase hypoglycemia (low blood sugar) while you are drinking alcohol, so check with your diabetes team before imbibing.

According to the American Diabetes Association, moderate alcohol intake is allowed and people with diabetes should follow the same guidelines on alcohol consumption as people who don't have diabetes. Women can have 1 drink maximum per day and men can have 2 drinks maximum per day. If you do not drink now, it is not recommended to start. Of course, never operate machinery under the influence of alcohol.

Never drink on an empty stomach or if your blood sugar is too low. Always eat something with carbohydrates when you drink. This will help prevent hypoglycemic episodes. Intoxication often mimics the symptoms of hypoglycemia. This is why it's important to avoid becoming intoxicated by staying hydrated, eating a carbohydrate food or a meal with carbohydrates, and not drinking alcohol to excess.

According to Samir Zakhari, PhD, in *Alcohol Research & Health*, the rate at which alcohol is eliminated from the body varies greatly. Several factors affect the rate of alcohol metabolism, including gender, body composition, medications and even sex hormones. During the time it takes for your body to metabolize alcohol, you are at risk for developing hypoglycemia because your liver cannot break down your sugar stores to balance your blood sugar.

> ■ ■ ■
>
> According to the American Diabetes Association, moderate alcohol intake is allowed and people with diabetes should follow the same guidelines on alcohol consumption as people who don't have diabetes.
>
> ■ ■ ■

The American Diabetes Association recommends having a diabetes identification badge so you can get proper care in the case of an emergency, such as hypoglycemia due to drinking alcohol. This could mean wearing an ID bracelet or keeping a card in your wallet. Test your blood sugar before, during and up to 24 hours after you drink alcohol. Always check your blood sugar before you go to bed if you have consumed alcohol, even if you drank several hours before bedtime.

Remember: everyone's body responds differently to alcohol consumption. It is important to test your blood glucose frequently when consuming alcohol to become familiar with your body's response. Speak with your certified diabetes educator and medical doctor to make sure it is safe for you to consume alcohol in accordance with your medication regimen, regardless of whether you take insulin or oral medications for diabetes.

DID YOU KNOW?

Standard Alcoholic Drink Serving Sizes

- **Wine:** 5 oz (150 mL)
- **Spirits:** 1.5 oz (45 mL)
- **Beer:** 12 oz (341 mL)

Sodium Terminology

When you see "reduced sodium" on a label, it means the food's sodium content has been reduced by 25% from its original level. This does not mean it is a low-sodium food. "Low-sodium" foods contain 140 mg of sodium or less, based on a serving of 100 grams. "Very low sodium" identifies foods that contain 35 mg of sodium or less.

If you are preparing a recipe that has more than 600 mg of sodium per serving, choose ingredients that have no added salt or that qualify as reduced sodium, low sodium or very low sodium to help you maintain a daily sodium intake between 1500 and 2300 mg. For instance, low-sodium Worcestershire-style sauce (available in natural foods stores and online) should contain 20 mg sodium per teaspoon (5 mL). If a low-sodium sauce is not available, use a reduced-sodium Worcestershire sauce and factor in the amount of sodium as stated on the label into your daily intake.

About the Nutrient Analyses

The nutrient analysis done on the recipes in this book was derived from Cronometer and Calorie Count, accessed June through December 2016, and through Nutrition Facts labels. Where necessary, data was supplemented using the USDA National Nutrient Database for Standard Reference, Release #28 (2015), revised May 2016 by the USDA Agricultural Research Service: www.nal.usda.gov/fnic/foodcomp/search.

Recipes were evaluated as follows:

- The larger number of servings was used where there is a range.
- Where alternatives are given, the first ingredient and amount listed were used.
- The smaller quantity of an ingredient was used where a range is provided.
- Optional ingredients and ingredients that are not quantified were not included, including optional ingredients outlined in recipe tips.
- Calculations were based on imperial measures and weights.
- When purchasing ground meat and poultry, the terminology on labels differs by country. In the U.S., "lean" contains less than 10% fat (or 90% lean), and "extra-lean" contains less than 5% fat (95% lean). In Canada, "lean" contains 17% fat or less, and "extra-lean" contains 10% fat or less. The nutrient analysis for these recipes has been calculated based on the U.S. fat content, so choose your ground meat accordingly or factor in the different amount of fat to your daily intake.
- Recipes were analyzed prior to cooking.
- Nutrient values were rounded to the nearest whole number.

It is important to note that the cooking method used to prepare the recipe may alter the nutrient content per serving, as may ingredient substitutions and differences among brand-name products.

All percent daily values (%DVs) and nutrition claims that appear in the recipes are based on USDA criteria.

BREAKFAST IS SERVED

Blueberry Boost Parfait

Wellness is easy when you have recipes like this one! Pack this parfait up before leaving for work or keep the ingredients in the office kitchen. Simply combine for a quick, balanced boost of antioxidants, omega-3 and omega-6 fatty acids and fiber. Notice how beautiful the layers look. Take your first bite and be sure to observe all of the textures dancing in your mouth. Love your breakfast and yourself! This is everyday living.

TIPS

If using frozen blueberries, thaw for 15 minutes before using.

If you prefer softer oats, soak them overnight: place in a bowl, add cold water to cover by $\frac{1}{2}$ inch (1 cm), cover and refrigerate. When ready to assemble parfait, drain off excess liquid.

To toast slivered almonds, place a small skillet over medium-low heat. Add almonds and cook, stirring constantly, until fragrant and toasted, about 3 minutes.

If preparing this recipe for two people, simply double all of the ingredients.

$\frac{2}{3}$ cup	vanilla-flavored Greek yogurt	150 mL
1 cup	fresh or thawed frozen blueberries	250 mL
$\frac{1}{4}$ cup	steel-cut oats	60 mL
1 tbsp	slivered almonds, toasted (see tip, at left)	15 mL
2 tsp	hemp hearts	10 mL

1. Spoon half of the yogurt into a parfait glass or other tall, thin glass. Top with blueberries and oats, then spoon in the remaining yogurt. Sprinkle with almonds and hemp hearts.

Health Bite

Frozen fruits and vegetables have been flash-frozen immediately after harvest and have just as much — or even more — nutrition than produce shipped long distances or produce that has been sitting on shelves for long periods. Blueberries contain bursts of cancer-protective plant compounds called antioxidants.

NUTRIENTS PER SERVING			
Calories	461	Fiber	11 g (44% DV)
Fat	15 g	Protein	28 g
Saturated fat	2 g	Calcium	256 mg (26% DV)
Sodium	70 mg (3% DV)	Iron	3 mg (17% DV)
Carbohydrate	56 g	Vitamin D	1 IU (0% DV)

Homemade Granola

Your love for granola will triple when you taste *Everyday Diabetes* granola. Mix with Greek yogurt and stay full until lunch.

TIPS

Let granola cool before storing. Store in an airtight container in the refrigerator for up to 5 days.

If preparing this recipe for one person, cut all of the ingredients in half. Or simply prepare the full recipe and save half for leftovers.

- Preheat oven to 250°F (120°C)
- Rimmed baking sheet, lined with parchment paper

3/4 cup	large-flake (old-fashioned) rolled oats	175 mL
1/4 cup	pecan halves	60 mL
1/4 cup	almonds	60 mL
1 tsp	chia seeds	5 mL
1 tbsp	coconut oil	15 mL
1 1/2 tsp	liquid honey	7 mL

1. In a medium bowl, toss together oats, pecans, almonds and chia seeds.
2. Add coconut oil and honey and mix thoroughly to coat dry ingredients. Spread granola evenly on prepared baking sheet.
3. Bake in preheated oven for 30 minutes. Remove from oven and use a spatula to stir granola. Return baking sheet to oven and bake for another 30 minutes or until brown and toasty. Serve hot or enjoy at room temperature.

Health Bite

Almonds contain many healthful nutrients, such as riboflavin, magnesium, calcium and iron.

NUTRIENTS PER SERVING			
Calories	384	Fiber	7 g (28% DV)
Fat	28 g	Protein	8 g
Saturated fat	8 g	Calcium	64 mg (6% DV)
Sodium	1 mg (0% DV)	Iron	3 mg (17% DV)
Carbohydrate	31 g	Vitamin D	0 IU (0% DV)

Overnight Oats with Peanut Butter

Make ahead and grab this dish to eat when you arrive at the office. This breakfast will make you want to get out of bed and start the day!

TIPS

If you plan to pack this as a portable breakfast, prepare in an airtight container or large-mouth jar.

Choose any unsweetened plant milk to keep the carbohydrates less than or equal to 45 grams of carbohydrate.

If preparing this recipe for two people, simply double all of the ingredients.

1 tsp	unsweetened cocoa powder	5 mL
1 cup	unsweetened almond milk	250 mL
2 tbsp	unsalted smooth peanut butter (at room temperature or warmed)	30 mL
1/2 cup	large-flake (old-fashioned) rolled oats	125 mL
1 tsp	ground cinnamon	5 mL

1. In a medium bowl, combine cocoa powder, almond milk and peanut butter. Add rolled oats and cinnamon. Stir until oats are fully immersed in liquid. Cover the bowl and refrigerate overnight.

2. In the morning, stir and serve cold. (Alternatively, warm in the microwave on High for 30 to 45 seconds or until steaming; stir and serve.)

Health Bite

Peanut butter is packed with fat and protein, complementing the carbs provided by the oats.

NUTRIENTS PER SERVING			
Calories	392	Fiber	8 g (32% DV)
Fat	23 g	Protein	14 g
Saturated fat	4 g	Calcium	244 mg (24% DV)
Sodium	99 mg (4% DV)	Iron	3 mg (17% DV)
Carbohydrate	40 g	Vitamin D	100 IU (25% DV)

Savory Porridge

Your soul will be warmed and your blood sugar balanced with this savory start to your day.

TIPS

Creamy wheat farina is finely milled wheat and is sometimes called cream of wheat. It can be found where hot cereal is stocked in supermarkets.

Feel free to swap types of cheese for different flavors. Try Parmesan or feta for a kick.

If preparing this recipe for two people, simply double all of the ingredients.

Health Bite

Farina is an excellent source of iron, and this recipe represents almost 70% of your daily intake.

FARINA

1 cup	water	250 mL
1/8 tsp	sea salt	0.5 mL
1/4 cup	creamy wheat farina	60 mL
1/4 cup	shredded Cheddar cheese	60 mL

EGG

1 tbsp	apple cider vinegar	15 mL
1	large egg	1
2 tbsp	chopped green onions	30 mL

1. *Farina:* Combine water and salt in a medium pot and bring to a boil over high heat. Reduce heat to low; stir in creamy wheat farina. Increase heat to medium-high and bring to a boil, stirring constantly. Reduce heat to a low simmer as soon as it boils. Cook, stirring constantly, for 2 to 3 minutes or until thick and creamy.

2. Remove from heat and slowly stir in cheese until combined. Transfer farina mixture to a small bowl, cover and set aside.

3. *Egg:* In a medium saucepan, bring 4 inches (10 cm) of water and vinegar to a boil over high heat. Crack egg into a small bowl, being careful not to break the yolk. Use a spoon to create a gentle whirlpool in the boiling water and slowly tip the egg into the water. Reduce heat to a gentle simmer and poach for 3 minutes or until cooked as desired.

4. Using a slotted spoon, drain poached egg and place over farina. Garnish with green onions.

NUTRIENTS PER SERVING			
Calories	363	Fiber	1 g (4% DV)
Fat	15 g	Protein	18 g
Saturated fat	7 g	Calcium	250 mg (25% DV)
Sodium	560 mg (23% DV)	Iron	3 mg (17% DV)
Carbohydrate	37 g	Vitamin D	50 IU (13% DV)

Quinoa Porridge

Protein porridge for breakfast. Diabetes never tasted — or felt — so good. You won't experience a sugar high after eating this naturally lower-carb, higher-protein morning cereal.

TIPS

Use more or less milk to reach your desired consistency.

To toast pine nuts, place a small skillet over medium-low heat. Add pine nuts and cook, stirring constantly, until fragrant and toasted, about 3 minutes.

If preparing this recipe for one person, cut all of the ingredients in half. Or simply prepare the full recipe and save half for leftovers.

1/2 cup	quinoa, rinsed	125 mL
1 cup	water	250 mL
1 cup	2% milk	250 mL
1 tsp	vanilla extract	5 mL
3	dried apricots, chopped	3
2 tbsp	pine nuts, toasted (see tip, at left)	30 mL
1 tbsp	currants or raisins	15 mL
1 tsp	ground cinnamon	5 mL

1. In a medium saucepan, combine quinoa and water over high heat. Bring to a boil, reduce heat and simmer, covered, for 8 to 10 minutes or until all the water has been absorbed and quinoa seeds have popped open and are slightly expanded.

2. Gradually stir in milk and vanilla. Add apricots, pine nuts, currants and cinnamon, stirring to combine. Heat, stirring gently and thoroughly, for about 5 minutes or until the milk is absorbed. Serve hot.

Health Bite

You may call quinoa a super-grain, but this Incan nutritional treasure is actually a seed. It comes from the same plant family as spinach and the sugar beet. Quinoa is sometimes called a psuedocereal because it is a nonlegume (not a bean, nut or pea) that is grown for grain (versus cereal grains, which come from grassy plants). Buckwheat and amaranth are also known as pseudocereals.

NUTRIENTS PER SERVING			
Calories	320	Fiber	6 g (24% DV)
Fat	10 g	Protein	12 g
Saturated fat	3 g	Calcium	194 mg (19% DV)
Sodium	72 mg (3% DV)	Iron	3 mg (17% DV)
Carbohydrate	46 g	Vitamin D	60 IU (15% DV)

Hummus and Smoked Salmon Bagel Breakfast

MAKES 1 SERVING

Everyone loves bagels, but many people think they have to swear them off once diagnosed with diabetes. Not so! Follow this recipe to make your breakfast bagel sandwich a reality.

TIPS

The average New York City–style bagel is about 4 oz (125 g), which is equivalent in carbohydrates to 4 slices of sandwich bread. Try to find a whole-grain bagel slightly smaller than the NY bagel or scoop out an ounce (30 g) of the inner dough to keep your carbohydrate count near 45 grams. Most men and some women can go ahead and have the full-size bagel, if appropriate for your nutrition needs. For example, if you count carbohydrates and take insulin injections, you may be able to take about one additional unit of fast-acting insulin to account for the additional 15 grams of carbohydrate.

If you have high blood pressure, opt for cooked fresh salmon, as it is naturally lower in sodium.

If preparing this recipe for two people, simply double all of the ingredients.

3 oz	whole-grain bagel (see tip, at left)	90 g
2 tbsp	hummus	30 mL
2 oz	smoked salmon	60 g
2	slices tomato	2
2	very thin slices red onion	2

1. Slice bagel in half and toast. Layer hummus, smoked salmon, tomato and onion on each half, dividing evenly. Serve open-face.

Health Bite

This recipe is an ideal blend of carbohydrates, protein and fat, keeping you sustained all morning and your blood sugar balanced.

NUTRIENTS PER SERVING			
Calories	349	Fiber	6 g (24% DV)
Fat	5 g	Protein	21 g
Saturated fat	1 g	Calcium	120 mg (12% DV)
Sodium	831 mg (35% DV)	Iron	5 mg (28% DV)
Carbohydrate	55 g	Vitamin D	26 IU (7% DV)

Italian Baked Eggs with Ciabatta Toast

Who thought Italians ate only family-style? Here, we've individualized the recipe to suit you and one more.

TIPS

Try lacinato kale, also known as Tuscan kale, to make this dish even more authentic.

If preparing this recipe for one person, cut all of the ingredients in half. Or simply prepare the full recipe and save half for leftovers.

Health Bite

Spinach is a good source of folate and iron. The vitamin C from the tomato sauce will help your body absorb the plant-derived iron from spinach.

- Preheat oven to 350°F (180°C)
- Large ovenproof skillet

1 tsp	olive oil	5 mL
1	clove garlic, minced	1
1	medium onion, finely chopped	1
2 cups	lightly packed spinach, roughly chopped	500 mL
1 tsp	dried Italian seasoning	5 mL
1	can (14 oz/398 mL) no-salt-added diced tomatoes, with juice	1
1/2 tsp	freshly ground black pepper	2 mL
2	large eggs	2
1/4 cup	shredded provolone cheese	60 mL
1	medium ciabatta roll (about 4 oz/125 g), split in half	1
1 tbsp	finely chopped fresh basil	15 mL

1. In ovenproof skillet, heat oil over medium-high heat. Add garlic, onion, spinach and Italian seasoning; cook, stirring, for about 3 minutes or until spinach is wilted. Stir in tomatoes and pepper; cover, increase heat to high and cook until bubbling. Reduce heat to medium and simmer for 3 to 5 minutes or until mixture thickens.

2. One at a time, crack eggs into a small bowl, then place on top of tomato mixture in skillet, about 2 inches (5 cm) apart. Sprinkle each egg with cheese, dividing evenly.

3. Bake in preheated oven for 10 to 12 minutes or until eggs are set.

4. Toast ciabatta roll halves until golden brown. Divide eggs and tomato mixture evenly and garnish with basil. Serve with ciabatta halves.

NUTRIENTS PER SERVING			
Calories	366	Fiber	6 g (24% DV)
Fat	13 g	Protein	18 g
Saturated fat	5 g	Calcium	277 mg (28% DV)
Sodium	487 mg (20% DV)	Iron	3 mg (17% DV)
Carbohydrate	46 g	Vitamin D	46 IU (12% DV)

Avocado Toast with a Twist

MAKES 1 SERVING

Dr. Seuss will be green with envy and so will your friends when they see you eating this for breakfast. Avocado is everyone's monounsaturated fat of choice!

TIPS

Try spraying the skillet with olive oil or canola oil nonstick cooking spray rather than frying the eggs in oil, to reduce the quantity of fat. The avocado and eggs already provide fat.

An avocado is ripe and ready to use when it is green below the stem's base. If it is brown, the avocado will be brown inside.

If preparing this recipe for two people, simply double all of the ingredients.

1/2	avocado	1/2
1 tbsp	chopped fresh cilantro	15 mL
1 tbsp	salsa	15 mL
1 tsp	freshly squeezed lemon juice	5 mL
Pinch	sea salt	Pinch
1 tsp	extra virgin olive oil	5 mL
2	large eggs	2
2	slices whole-grain bread, toasted	2

1. Using a spoon, scoop the flesh from the avocado half into a small bowl. Add cilantro, salsa, lemon juice and salt. Using a fork, mash ingredients together until mixture has the consistency of guacamole. Set aside.

2. In a medium skillet, warm oil over medium heat. Crack eggs into the pan and cook, undisturbed, until they reach your preferred consistency for fried eggs.

3. Divide avocado mixture evenly between toast slices. Top each slice with 1 fried egg. Enjoy immediately.

Health Bite

Also known as alligator pear, avocado is high in monounsaturated fat and is a good source of lutein.

NUTRIENTS PER SERVING			
Calories	460	Fiber	10 g (40% DV)
Fat	28 g	Protein	22 g
Saturated fat	6 g	Calcium	132 mg (13% DV)
Sodium	718 mg (30% DV)	Iron	3 mg (17% DV)
Carbohydrate	33 g	Vitamin D	87 IU (22% DV)

Everyday Breakfast Sandwich

You will never go to a fast-food establishment for a breakfast sandwich again! This is your quick-fix fast food made fresh and healthy at home.

TIPS

Don't have Canadian bacon? Use deli ham for a similar taste and texture.

If preparing this recipe for two people, simply double all of the ingredients.

Health Bite

Everyone thinks bananas are the go-to source for potassium, but 2 tbsp (30 mL) avocado has more potassium than the same amount of banana.

1 tsp	olive oil	5 mL
1/4 cup	spinach leaves	60 mL
1	clove garlic, minced	1
1	large egg	1
1	whole wheat English muffin, split in half	1
1	slice Canadian bacon (such as Jones Dairy Farm)	1
1 oz	Cheddar cheese	30 g
1	slice tomato	1
1/4	avocado, sliced	1/4
1 tsp	Sriracha	5 mL

1. In a large skillet, heat oil over medium-high heat. Add spinach and garlic; cook, stirring, for 1 minute. Transfer spinach mixture to a bowl and set aside.

2. Return skillet (no need to wash it) to medium-high heat and crack in egg. Cook for 1 minute, then use a spatula to flip egg over. Cook for 1 more minute or to desired doneness.

3. Meanwhile, toast English muffin halves until golden brown.

4. Layer bacon, egg, cheese, tomato, spinach mixture and avocado on one English muffin half. Top with Sriracha and the other English muffin half. Place on a plate. Microwave sandwich on High for 10 to 15 seconds or until cheese is melted.

NUTRIENTS PER SERVING			
Calories	466	Fiber	7 g (28% DV)
Fat	27 g	Protein	24 g
Saturated fat	8 g	Calcium	420 mg (42% DV)
Sodium	747 mg (31% DV)	Iron	3 mg (17% DV)
Carbohydrate	34 g	Vitamin D	50 IU (13% DV)

"You're the Egg to My Bacon"

Just because you have diabetes doesn't mean you can't eat foods like eggs and bacon. Enjoy this traditional dish! And yes, eggs are okay to eat some of the time. This breakfast provides only 3 grams of carbohydrates per serving, so add a side of toast or whole wheat English muffin to increase carbohydrates, if desired.

TIPS

The cooking time of bacon varies depending on the thickness of slices.

If preparing this recipe for one person, cut all of the ingredients in half. Or simply prepare the full recipe and save half for leftovers.

- Preheat oven to 350°F (180°C)
- Baking sheet, lined with foil

4	slices reduced-sodium turkey bacon	4
4	large eggs	4
1 tbsp	2% milk	15 mL
2 tbsp	shredded Colby Jack cheese	30 mL
1 tsp	olive oil	5 mL
Pinch	freshly ground black pepper	Pinch
2 tsp	chopped green onion	10 mL

1. Arrange bacon slices evenly on prepared baking sheet. Cook bacon in preheated oven for 10 minutes. Flip bacon and cook for another 7 to 10 minutes or until the desired crispiness is reached.

2. Crack eggs into a large bowl. Add milk and whisk thoroughly until air bubbles appear. Add cheese and stir to combine.

3. In a medium skillet, heat oil over medium-low heat. Pour in egg mixture. Use a spoon to constantly stir in a figure-eight motion for about 5 minutes or until eggs are scrambled and set but not dry. Season with pepper.

4. Divide eggs evenly onto warmed plates and flank with bacon. Garnish eggs with green onion.

Health Bite

The USDA's 2015 Dietary Guidelines state that dietary cholesterol does not need to be restricted as previously thought. Research has shown that dietary cholesterol — such as is found in eggs — is only "weakly associated" with cholesterol in your blood. Remember: this doesn't give you a free pass to overconsume foods high in cholesterol. The guidelines also lowered restrictions in overall fat intake.

NUTRIENTS PER SERVING			
Calories	314	Fiber	0 g (0% DV)
Fat	23 g	Protein	23 g
Saturated fat	7 g	Calcium	166 mg (17% DV)
Sodium	744 mg (31% DV)	Iron	2 mg (11% DV)
Carbohydrate	3 g	Vitamin D	107 IU (27% DV)

Fiesta Eggs Benedict

Jalapeños are trending — put the spotlight on your breakfast with this spicy recipe!

TIPS

Always wear kitchen gloves when handling jalapeños and avoid touching your skin and eyes.

A ripe avocado yields slightly when squeezed. To pit the avocado, sink the blade of a chef's knife into the side of the pit, then twist it out.

- Food processor

1 tsp	olive oil	5 mL
1/2 cup	thinly sliced onion	125 mL
1/2 cup	finely chopped bell pepper (any color)	125 mL
2	whole wheat English muffins, split in half	2
1	can (4 1/2 oz/127 mL) mild green chiles, with juice	1
1/2	small jalapeño pepper, seeded and coarsely chopped	1/2
1 tbsp	chopped fresh cilantro	15 mL
1/4 tsp	dried chives	1 mL
1/4 tsp	garlic powder	1 mL
1/4 tsp	onion powder	1 mL
1/4 tsp	dried dillweed	1 mL
1/4 tsp	freshly ground black pepper	1 mL
1 tbsp	plain 2% Greek yogurt	15 mL
1 tbsp	mayonnaise	15 mL
1 tsp	freshly squeezed lemon juice	5 mL
1 tbsp	apple cider vinegar	15 mL
4	large eggs	4
1/4 cup	shredded pepper Jack cheese	60 mL
1/2	avocado, sliced	1/2

1. In a large skillet, heat oil over medium-high heat. Add onion and bell pepper; cook, stirring, for 2 minutes.

2. Push vegetables to one side of skillet. Toast cut sides of two English muffin halves on other side of skillet for about 2 minutes, until evenly browned. Set aside. Repeat with second pair of English muffin halves. Reduce heat to medium-low and cover to keep warm.

NUTRIENTS PER SERVING			
Calories	508	Fiber	8 g (32% DV)
Fat	30 g	Protein	23 g
Saturated fat	9 g	Calcium	540 mg (54% DV)
Sodium	660 mg (28% DV)	Iron	4 mg (22% DV)
Carbohydrate	40 g	Vitamin D	91 IU (23% DV)

TIP

If preparing this recipe for one person, cut all of the ingredients in half. Or simply prepare the full recipe and save half for leftovers.

3. In food processor, combine green chiles, jalapeño, cilantro, chives, garlic powder, onion powder, dill, pepper, yogurt, mayonnaise and lemon juice; process until mixture reaches a smooth consistency.

4. In a large saucepan, bring 4 inches (10 cm) of water and vinegar to a boil over high heat. Crack 1 egg into a small bowl, being careful not to break the yolk. Reduce heat to a gentle simmer. Use a spoon to create a gentle whirlpool in the boiling water and slowly tip the egg into the water. Repeat with each remaining egg. When all the eggs are in the water, poach for 3 minutes or until cooked as desired. Use a slotted spoon to transfer eggs to a plate.

5. Arrange onion and bell pepper evenly on top of English muffin halves. Place a poached egg on top of each English muffin half. Sprinkle with cheese. Top with avocado slices and divide sauce evenly on top of each muffin half.

Health Bite

Jalapeños contain capsaicin, which may help alleviate the pain associated with diabetic neuropathy.

Huevos Rancheros

This recipe comes straight from the South, where Tex-Mex reigns supreme. Invite your gluten-free friend to share this breakfast.

TIPS

Use the remainder of the can of refried beans to make Macro Bowl (page 124) or Spicy Black Bean Burgers with Tangy Veggie Ribbons (page 132).

When using canned foods, choose low-sodium or no-added-salt options.

An avocado is ripe and ready to use when it is green below the stem's base. If it is brown, the avocado will be brown inside.

- Preheat oven to 350°F (180°C)
- Large ovenproof skillet

1 tsp	olive oil	5 mL
1	plum (Roma) tomato, diced	1
1/2 cup	sliced onion	125 mL
1/2 cup	sliced bell pepper (any color)	125 mL
1/2 cup	low-sodium refried beans	125 mL
1 tsp	ground cumin	5 mL
1/4 tsp	chipotle chile powder	1 mL
2	large eggs	2
2	6-inch (15 cm) corn tortillas	2
1 tbsp	chopped fresh cilantro	15 mL
2 tbsp	crumbled queso fresco	30 mL
1/2	avocado, sliced	1/2
1 to 2 tsp	hot pepper sauce	5 to 10 mL

1. In ovenproof skillet, heat oil over medium-high heat. Add tomato, onion and bell pepper; cook, stirring, for about 4 minutes or until onion is translucent.

2. Add refried beans, cumin and chipotle powder. Stir to combine thoroughly with vegetables. Cook, stirring, for about 2 minutes or until ingredients are heated through and thoroughly combined. Remove from heat.

3. Use the back of a spoon to make two small wells in the mixture in the skillet. One at a time, crack an egg into a bowl then drop into a well.

NUTRIENTS PER SERVING			
Calories	310	Fiber	8 g (32% DV)
Fat	17 g	Protein	14 g
Saturated fat	4 g	Calcium	132 mg (13% DV)
Sodium	656 mg (27% DV)	Iron	3 mg (17% DV)
Carbohydrate	29 g	Vitamin D	51 IU (13% DV)

TIP

■ ■ ■ ■ ■ ■ ■ ■ ■ ■ ■ ■ ■ ■ ■ ■

If preparing this recipe for one person, cut all of the ingredients in half.

4. Bake in preheated oven for about 10 minutes or until eggs are set.

5. Wrap tortillas in a damp paper towel and microwave on High for 10 seconds or until warm and pliable.

6. Divide egg, beans and vegetable mixture between tortillas. Top with cilantro, queso fresco and avocado slices. Drizzle with hot sauce to taste.

Health Bite

■ ■

This recipe provides 41% of your daily fiber, helping you to feel full longer.

Shakshuka Eggs

MAKES 2 SERVINGS

Laura first had this absolutely delicious dish at the Art Café in Nyack, New York. It tasted *sooo* good. She went home and recreated this recipe for you. Keep in mind, the recipes in this book are as helpful for preventing diabetes as for managing your blood sugar after a diabetes diagnosis. This is guilt-free eating and living at its best.

TIP

Serve with 1 whole-grain pita for additional calories and to reach the 45 to 60 grams of carbohydrate range per meal.

2 tsp	olive oil	10 mL
1	clove garlic, minced	1
1/2 cup	finely chopped onion	125 mL
1/2 cup	finely chopped red bell pepper	125 mL
1 tsp	hot pepper flakes	5 mL
1	can (28 oz/796 mL) no-salt-added crushed tomatoes	1
1 tsp	paprika	5 mL
1 tsp	ground cumin	5 mL
1/4 tsp	caraway seeds	1 mL
1/4 tsp	freshly ground black pepper	1 mL
3 cups	trimmed spinach leaves, divided	750 mL
2 to 4	large eggs	2 to 4
1/4 cup	crumbled feta cheese	60 mL
	Chopped fresh parsley	

1. In a medium skillet, heat oil over medium heat for 1 to 2 minutes. Add garlic and onion; cook, stirring, for 3 to 4 minutes or until onion is translucent. Add red pepper and cook, stirring, for 3 minutes or until softened.

2. Gradually pour in crushed tomatoes, stirring over medium heat until incorporated. Stir in paprika, cumin, caraway seeds and pepper; reduce heat and simmer, stirring occasionally, for 5 to 8 minutes or until tomatoes are blended into a sauce.

NUTRIENTS PER SERVING			
Calories	309	Fiber	11 g (44% DV)
Fat	18 g	Protein	38 g
Saturated fat	7 g	Calcium	372 mg (37% DV)
Sodium	548 mg (23% DV)	Iron	6 mg (33% DV)
Carbohydrate	26 g	Vitamin D	48 IU (12% DV)

TIP

■ ■ ■ ■ ■ ■ ■ ■ ■ ■ ■ ■ ■ ■ ■ ■

If preparing this recipe for one person, cut all of the ingredients in half.

3. Stir in 1 cup (250 mL) spinach. One at a time, crack eggs into a small bowl, then drop into tomato mixture, spacing evenly. Cover and simmer for 10 to 12 minutes or until egg yolks are almost firm (yolks will remain slightly runny).

4. Divide remaining fresh spinach evenly between two crockery-type bowls or your favorite bowls. Scoop eggs and sauce over spinach, top with feta and garnish with parsley.

Health Bite

■ ■

Tomatoes contain the antioxidant lycopene. This plant compound is more easily absorbed from cooked tomato than from raw. Lycopene may be protective for cardiovascular disease and prostate cancer.

Egg Strata with Spinach, Mushrooms and Chicken Sausage

MAKES 2 SERVINGS

Forget about frittatas; it's all about the strata! Start your morning with this recipe if you have an active day ahead of you.

TIPS

You can prepare this dish up to 24 hours ahead of time. After step 3, cover with plastic wrap and refrigerate. Remove plastic wrap before baking; add 5 minutes to the baking time in step 4.

If you prefer a creamier consistency, increase the milk to ⅔ cup (150 mL) and the Parmesan cheese to ¼ cup (60 mL). Note that the nutritional analysis will change significantly.

If preparing this recipe for one person, cut all of the ingredients in half.

Health Bite

The combination of protein and fat in this recipe will keep you satiated for hours.

- Preheat oven to 350°F (180°C)
- 8-inch (20 cm) glass baking dish, lightly sprayed with canola oil nonstick cooking spray

1 tsp	olive oil	5 mL
6	stalks asparagus (ends snapped off), chopped	6
2	cloves garlic, minced	2
2 cups	trimmed spinach leaves	500 mL
¼ cup	sliced mushrooms	60 mL
4	large eggs	4
¼ cup	2% milk	60 mL
1	link cooked chicken sausage, cut into ¼-inch (0.5 cm) thick slices	1
1 tbsp	grated Parmesan cheese	15 mL
2	slices whole-grain bread, cubed	2

1. In a medium skillet, heat oil over medium-high heat. Add asparagus, garlic, spinach and mushrooms; cook, stirring, for 3 to 5 minutes or until spinach is wilted and asparagus is tender-crisp. Remove from heat.

2. Meanwhile, in a large bowl, whisk together eggs and milk. Stir in vegetables, chicken sausage and cheese until combined.

3. Arrange bread cubes on bottom of baking dish. Pour egg mixture evenly over bread cubes.

4. Bake in preheated oven for 30 minutes or until eggs are set.

NUTRIENTS PER SERVING			
Calories	407	Fiber	7 g (28% DV)
Fat	21 g	Protein	32 g
Saturated fat	6 g	Calcium	442 mg (44% DV)
Sodium	996 mg (42% DV)	Iron	10 mg (56% DV)
Carbohydrate	25 g	Vitamin D	105 IU (26% DV)

Bibimbap Breakfast Bowl

Bibimbap is a favorite Korean dish typically made of leftovers. Feel free to make this dish your own by substituting any on-hand vegetables that have similar carb content. This diabetes-friendly breakfast version is a twist on the typical dinner dish that is fun and, of course, helps to keep you feeling full.

TIPS

To cook soba noodles, add them to a large pot of boiling water; cook, stirring occasionally, for about 8 minutes or according to package directions, until al dente. Drain and rinse noodles with cold water.

If preparing this recipe for two people, simply double all of the ingredients.

Health Bite

Tofu is a good alternative to meat because it contains all the amino acids your body needs to make a complete protein.

3 tsp	peanut oil, divided	15 mL
1 cup	cubed extra-firm tofu	250 mL
3 tsp	seaweed gomasio seasoning (such as Eden Foods), divided	15 mL
2 oz	buckwheat soba noodles, cooked (see tip, at left)	60 g
1/3 cup	shredded or spiraled carrots	75 mL
1/2 cup	shredded or spiraled zucchini (unpeeled)	125 mL
1 tbsp	apple cider vinegar	15 mL
1	large egg	1

1. In a small skillet, heat 2 tsp (10 mL) peanut oil over medium-high heat for 1 minute or until hot. Add tofu and season with 2 tsp (10 mL) gomasio seasoning. Quickly and gently stir-fry tofu for about 2 minutes or until slightly soft and coated with oil and seasoning.

2. Add soba noodles and mix well. Immediately add the remaining peanut oil and gomasio; cook, stirring, for 1 to 2 minutes or until noodles and tofu are completely covered in oil and seasoning. Remove from heat and transfer mixture to a deep serving bowl. Arrange carrots and zucchini along one side of the noodle mixture.

3. In a medium saucepan, bring 4 inches (10 cm) of water and vinegar to a boil over high heat. Crack egg into a small bowl, being careful not to break the yolk. Use a spoon to create a gentle whirlpool in the boiling water and slowly tip the egg into the water. Reduce heat to a gentle simmer and poach for 3 minutes or until cooked as desired.

4. Create a well in the center of the noodle mixture. Using a slotted spoon, drain egg and transfer to the well. Serve immediately.

NUTRIENTS PER SERVING			
Calories	537	Fiber	6 g (24% DV)
Fat	36 g	Protein	37 g
Saturated fat	6 g	Calcium	756 mg (76% DV)
Sodium	405 mg (17% DV)	Iron	7 mg (39% DV)
Carbohydrate	31 g	Vitamin D	44 IU (11% DV)

Buckwheat, Flax and Banana Pancakes

Now you can enjoy fruit and grains for breakfast without going over your carbohydrate range. Cooking for two was never easier or sweeter than with maple syrup!

TIP

If preparing this recipe for one person, cut all of the ingredients in half.

Health Bite

Flax seeds are high in fiber, omega-3 fatty acids and the phytochemical lignan.

* Preheat oven to 200°F (100°C)

	Canola oil nonstick cooking spray	
³⁄₄ cup	buckwheat flour	175 mL
¹⁄₄ cup	ground flax seeds (flaxseed meal)	60 mL
1¹⁄₂ tsp	baking powder	7 mL
1 tsp	ground cinnamon	5 mL
¹⁄₂ tsp	ground allspice	2 mL
2	large eggs, beaten	2
1 cup	unsweetened soy milk	250 mL
1	small banana, thinly sliced	1
4 tsp	pure maple syrup	20 mL

1. Heat a griddle or large skillet over medium heat until hot. Coat with nonstick cooking spray.

2. In a medium bowl, combine buckwheat flour, flax seeds, baking powder, cinnamon and allspice. Stir in eggs and soy milk until mixture is smooth and pourable.

3. For each pancake, use a ¹⁄₂-cup (125 mL) measure to scoop batter onto hot griddle. Add a few banana slices and cook for about 2 minutes or until pancake starts to bubble. Using a spatula, flip pancake and cook for 1 to 2 minutes or until both sides are golden brown; transfer to a plate and keep warm in preheated oven. Repeat with the remaining batter and banana slices, spraying with cooking spray and adjusting the heat as needed between batches.

4. Divide pancakes between plates and drizzle each serving with 2 tsp (10 mL) maple syrup.

NUTRIENTS PER SERVING			
Calories	481	Fiber	17 g (68% DV)
Fat	19 g	Protein	23 g
Saturated fat	2 g	Calcium	472 mg (47% DV)
Sodium	622 mg (26% DV)	Iron	5 mg (28% DV)
Carbohydrate	66 g	Vitamin D	103 IU (26% DV)

Power Pumpkin Pancakes

MAKES 4 PANCAKES (2 PANCAKES PER SERVING)

We bet that you love pancakes! This recipe makes eating easy — it is perfectly portioned, contains all three macronutrients for balanced blood sugar, and tastes awesome (yes, chocolate for breakfast). The power of these pancakes comes from the vitamin A, vitamin Bs and, of course, the protein!

TIPS

We used Bob's Red Mill oat bran pancake mix. If this isn't available in your area, choose a pancake mix that has oat bran or multiple grains as the first ingredients. Look for a fiber content greater than or equal to 3 to 5 grams of fiber per serving.

If preparing this recipe for one person, cut all of the ingredients in half.

- Preheat oven to 200°F (100°C)

	Canola oil nonstick cooking spray	
³⁄₄ cup	oat bran or multigrain pancake mix	175 mL
¹⁄₄ cup	wheat germ	60 mL
1 tsp	ground cinnamon	5 mL
2	large eggs, beaten	2
³⁄₄ cup	unsweetened soy milk	175 mL
¹⁄₄ cup	canned pumpkin purée (not pie filling)	60 mL
¹⁄₄ cup	dark chocolate chips	60 mL

1. Heat a griddle or skillet over medium heat until hot. Coat with nonstick cooking spray.

2. In a medium bowl, combine pancake mix, wheat germ and cinnamon. Stir in eggs, soy milk and pumpkin until mixture is smooth and pourable.

3. For each pancake, use a ¹⁄₂-cup (125 mL) measure to scoop batter onto hot griddle. Drop 1 tbsp (15 mL) chocolate chips onto batter; cook for about 2 minutes or until pancake starts to bubble. Using a spatula, flip pancake and cook for 1 to 2 minutes or until both sides are golden brown; transfer to a plate and keep warm in preheated oven. Repeat with the remaining batter and chocolate chips, spraying with cooking spray and adjusting the heat as needed between batches.

Health Bite

Whether you choose a plant or dairy version of milk, it is ideal for it to contain about 7 grams of protein and 200 mg or more of calcium per serving. Even more important, check the total carbohydrate count for the recipe to ensure that it is less than 45 to 60 grams of carbs. This will make blood sugar management easier.

NUTRIENTS PER SERVING			
Calories	472	Fiber	15 g (60% DV)
Fat	19 g	Protein	25 g
Saturated fat	7 g	Calcium	297 mg (30% DV)
Sodium	212 mg (9% DV)	Iron	7 mg (39% DV)
Carbohydrate	56 g	Vitamin D	89 IU (22% DV)

Rosemary Potato Pancakes with Smoked Salmon

Looking for a savory breakfast option? Look no further. The hint of rosemary, the crunch of cucumber and the color of the salmon make this recipe a feast for your senses.

TIP

Garnish each serving with fresh herbs, such as a sprig of parsley.

- Preheat oven to 400°F (200°C)
- Baking sheet, lined with canola oil nonstick cooking spray

1$\frac{1}{2}$	medium russet potatoes (unpeeled)	1$\frac{1}{2}$
$\frac{1}{4}$ cup	matzo meal	60 mL
$\frac{1}{4}$ tsp	dried rosemary	1 mL
$\frac{1}{4}$ tsp	dried thyme	1 mL
1	large egg, beaten	1
6 tsp	canola oil, divided	30 mL
$\frac{2}{3}$ cup	plain Greek yogurt	150 mL
6 oz	smoked salmon	175 g
$\frac{1}{2}$	large cucumber, thinly sliced	$\frac{1}{2}$
	Freshly ground black pepper	

1. Using the coarse side of a box grater, grate the potatoes into a large bowl.
2. In a small bowl, combine matzo meal, rosemary and thyme; add to grated potatoes and stir to combine. Add egg and stir gently to combine. Be sure to coat grated potato well with the matzo meal mixture and egg.
3. Using a $\frac{1}{2}$-cup (125 mL) measure for each pancake, scoop potato mixture and drop on prepared baking sheet, spacing pancakes at least 1 inch (2.5 cm) apart. Use the back of a spoon to gently flatten each pancake.
4. Bake in preheated oven for 20 minutes or until lightly browned. Reduce oven temperature to 200°F (100°C).

NUTRIENTS PER SERVING			
Calories	506	Fiber	3 g (12% DV)
Fat	21 g	Protein	32 g
Saturated fat	3 g	Calcium	139 mg (14% DV)
Sodium	638 mg (27% DV)	Iron	3 mg (17% DV)
Carbohydrate	49 g	Vitamin D	61 IU (15% DV)

It's difficult to prepare a single serving of this recipe. Instead, prepare the full recipe and store the remaining 3 pancakes in an airtight container in the refrigerator for up to 3 days. Reheat pancakes in a toaster oven or microwave and add toppings just before serving.

5. In a medium skillet, heat 1 tsp (5 mL) oil over medium-high heat. Quickly and gently fry 1 pancake for about 3 minutes, turning once, until golden brown on both sides. Transfer to a plate lined with paper towel and keep warm in oven. Repeat with the remaining oil and pancakes, adjusting the heat as needed between pancakes.

6. Divide pancakes between two plates and top each serving with Greek yogurt, smoked salmon and cucumber slices, dividing evenly. Season to taste with pepper.

Health Bite

Greek yogurt contains twice the protein of regular yogurt and boasts probiotics, which help promote a healthy gut.

Whole Wheat French Toast

All foods fit, even French toast. Whole grains, walnuts, cinnamon and coconut oil make this recipe diabetes-friendly while giving it a unique flavor!

TIPS

Go nuts! Crush your nuts by placing them in a sealable plastic bag and covering the bag with a dish towel. Use a mallet, hammer or rolling pin to pound the bag of nuts. The towel prevents the plastic bag from tearing open.

If preparing this recipe for two people, simply double all of the ingredients.

1	large egg	1
1 tbsp	2% milk	15 mL
$\frac{1}{8}$ tsp	ground cinnamon	0.5 mL
$1\frac{1}{2}$ tsp	coconut oil	7 mL
1	slice whole wheat bread	1
$\frac{1}{2}$	banana, sliced	$\frac{1}{2}$
$\frac{1}{4}$ cup	crushed walnuts	60 mL
1 tsp	pure maple syrup	5 mL

1. In a large bowl, whisk egg. Whisk in milk and cinnamon.

2. In a large skillet, heat coconut oil over medium heat. Dip bread slice in egg mixture until evenly coated and place in hot skillet. Cook for 1 to 2 minutes per side, turning once, until golden brown and slightly crisp.

3. Transfer to a plate and top with banana slices, walnuts and maple syrup.

Health Bite

Walnuts can improve blood cholesterol, are rich in mono- and polyunsaturated fatty acids and support healthy blood vessels.

NUTRIENTS PER SERVING			
Calories	544	Fiber	7 g (28% DV)
Fat	34 g	Protein	19 g
Saturated fat	10 g	Calcium	173 mg (17% DV)
Sodium	321 mg (13% DV)	Iron	3 mg (17% DV)
Carbohydrate	47 g	Vitamin D	51 IU (13% DV)

Toast with Ricotta and Jam

Crunchy meets creamy in this breakfast you will simply love. Nothing can be easier than enjoying toast with ricotta for hits of calcium, vitamin D and protein. A bit of jam adds just enough sweetness.

TIPS

Your slice of pumpernickel should be about 5 by 4 by ⅜ inches (12.5 by 10 by 1 cm).

Replace the raspberry jam with your favorite flavor of jam or fruit preserves, making sure it provides approximately 15 grams of carbohydrate per tablespoon (15 mL).

If preparing this recipe for two people, simply double all of the ingredients.

2 tbsp	ricotta cheese	30 mL
1 tsp	grated lemon zest	5 mL
1	slice pumpernickel bread, toasted	1
1 tbsp	raspberry jam	15 mL
1 tsp	chopped fresh basil	5 mL

1. In a small bowl, use a fork to whip together ricotta and lemon zest until fluffy. Spread ricotta mixture on toast, top with raspberry jam and garnish with basil.

Health Bite

Two tbsp (30 mL) of ricotta cheese provides 64 milligrams of calcium and 4 grams of protein.

NUTRIENTS PER SERVING			
Calories	169	Fiber	3 g (12% DV)
Fat	5 g	Protein	6 g
Saturated fat	3 g	Calcium	128 mg (13% DV)
Sodium	222 mg (9% DV)	Iron	2 mg (11% DV)
Carbohydrate	25 g	Vitamin D	3 IU (1% DV)

Chocobutter Berrywich

Who said breakfast has to be savory? Sweet chocolate and strawberries remind you it's important to eat all foods. Use a chocolate-flavored nut butter such as Peanut Butter & Co's Dark Chocolate Dreams to keep the carbohydrates in check.

TIPS

Go nuts! Crush your nuts by placing them in a sealable plastic bag and covering the bag with a dish towel. Use a mallet, hammer or rolling pin to pound the bag of nuts. The towel prevents the plastic bag from tearing open.

If preparing this recipe for two people, simply double all of the ingredients.

1 tbsp	chocolate-flavored nut butter	15 mL
2	slices whole-grain bread	2
1 tbsp	crushed hazelnuts	15 mL
4	strawberries, thinly sliced	4

1. Spread nut butter evenly over one side of each bread slice. Sprinkle each slice with hazelnuts, dividing evenly. Arrange strawberries over one slice and top with the second slice. Cut in half and serve.

Health Bite

The crushed nuts add texture and protein to balance the carbohydrates and make this a filling breakfast.

NUTRIENTS PER SERVING			
Calories	316	Fiber	7 g (28% DV)
Fat	15 g	Protein	12 g
Saturated fat	2 g	Calcium	116 mg (12% DV)
Sodium	278 mg (12% DV)	Iron	2 mg (11% DV)
Carbohydrate	38 g	Vitamin D	0 IU (0% DV)

Cranberry, Nut and Orange Bread

Make this sweet "tart" breakfast bread for your sweetheart!

TIPS

Top with plain Greek yogurt or cottage cheese for protein, calcium and vitamin D.

Pay attention to your hunger and fullness cues, and be mindful of how long this sweet breakfast keeps you full and how it makes you feel in general.

This bread freezes well: wrap in plastic wrap, then foil, completely enclosing it, and freeze for up to 3 months.

Health Bite

Cranberries contain antioxidants, compounds that fight potentially damaging agents in the body.

- Preheat oven to 350°F (180°C)
- 9- by 5-inch (23 by 12.5 cm) loaf pan, sprayed with canola oil nonstick cooking spray

³⁄₄ cup	almond flour	175 mL
¹⁄₄ cup	coconut flour	60 mL
¹⁄₂ tsp	baking soda	2 mL
3	large eggs	3
2 tbsp	grated orange zest	30 mL
¹⁄₄ cup	freshly squeezed orange juice	60 mL
2 tbsp	liquid honey	30 mL
1 tbsp	melted coconut oil	15 mL
1 cup	fresh or thawed frozen cranberries	250 mL

1. In a medium bowl, combine almond flour, coconut flour and baking soda.

2. In a large bowl, whisk eggs together. Add orange zest, orange juice, honey and coconut oil; whisk to combine.

3. Add flour mixture to egg mixture; stir to combine. Using a spatula, fold in cranberries. Transfer dough to prepared pan, smoothing top.

4. Bake in preheated oven for 45 minutes or until a tester inserted in the center of the loaf comes out clean.

5. Transfer pan to a wire rack and let cool for 20 minutes, then remove from the pan and let cool completely.

NUTRIENTS PER SERVING			
Calories	581	Fiber	12 g (48% DV)
Fat	38 g	Protein	21 g
Saturated fat	12 g	Calcium	154 mg (15% DV)
Sodium	445 mg (19% DV)	Iron	3 mg (17% DV)
Carbohydrate	45 g	Vitamin D	65 IU (16% DV)

Blackberry Coffee Cake Muffins

MAKES 2 MUFFINS (1 MUFFIN PER SERVING)

Diabetes isn't about deprivation. Pour yourself a steamy mug of coffee to savor alongside this coffee cake classic.

TIP

If you don't have a mini chopper, use 2 tbsp (30 mL) roughly or finely chopped almonds in the filling and use a pastry blender or a fork to combine the ingredients thoroughly.

- Preheat oven to 375°F (190°C)
- Muffin pan, 2 cups lined with paper liners
- Mini chopper (see tip, at left)

MUFFINS

2 tbsp	all-purpose flour	30 mL
2 tbsp	whole wheat flour	30 mL
1/2 tsp	baking powder	2 mL
1/2 tsp	baking soda	2 mL
Pinch	salt	Pinch
2 tbsp	granulated sugar	30 mL
1 tbsp	butter, softened	15 mL
1 tbsp	canola oil	15 mL
1	large egg	1
1 tbsp	plain 2% Greek yogurt	15 mL
1/4 tsp	vanilla extract	1 mL
4	blackberries, chopped	4

TOPPING

2 tbsp	sliced almonds	30 mL
1 tbsp	lightly packed brown sugar	15 mL
2 tsp	ground cinnamon	10 mL
Pinch	salt	Pinch
1 tbsp	cold butter	15 mL

1. *Muffins:* In a medium bowl, combine all-purpose flour, whole wheat flour, baking powder, baking soda and salt.

2. In a small bowl, whisk together sugar, butter and oil. Add egg, yogurt and vanilla; whisk to combine.

continued on page 97

NUTRIENTS PER SERVING			
Calories	384	Fiber	4 g (16% DV)
Fat	25 g	Protein	8 g
Saturated fat	9 g	Calcium	148 mg (15% DV)
Sodium	551 mg (23% DV)	Iron	2 mg (11% DV)
Carbohydrate	34 g	Vitamin D	23 IU (6% DV)

Fiesta Eggs Benedict (page 80)

Blueberry Yogurt Scones (page 99)

Tomato Tortellini Soup (page 103)

Bite-Size Turkey Burgers (page 121)

Macro Bowl (page 124)

Chinese Five-Spice Tempeh (page 136)

Citrus Fish Fajitas (page 142)

Angel-Hair Pasta with Shrimp, Sun-Dried
Tomatoes and Peppers (page 160)

Garnish each coffee cake muffin with a small sprig of mint.

It's difficult to prepare a single serving of this recipe. Instead, prepare the full recipe and store the remaining muffin in an airtight container for up to 3 days.

3. Add the egg mixture to the flour mixture and stir just until moistened. Fold in blackberries.

4. *Topping:* In mini chopper, combine almonds, brown sugar, cinnamon, salt and butter. Pulse until crumbly.

5. Scoop batter into two prepared muffin cups, dividing evenly. Sprinkle each evenly with topping.

6. Bake in preheated oven for 10 to 12 minutes or until a tester inserted in the center of a muffin comes out clean.

> ### Health Bite
> ■
>
> The 2% Greek yogurt adds protein and moistness to these muffins.

Kitchen Sink Muffins

**MAKES 4 MUFFINS
(2 MUFFINS PER
SERVING)**

Here is an unexpected
way to use your
leftovers! Fruits,
vegetables and nuts all
in a muffin? Why not!
We promise these will
be your new favorite
muffins.

TIPS

Consider air-drying carrots
and zucchini for a less moist
muffin texture: after grating,
spread vegetables out evenly
on a plate lined with paper
towel for 20 minutes.

If preparing this recipe for
one person, cut all of the
ingredients in half.

Health Bite

Easily convert this recipe
to vegan by replacing
the butter with a vegan
buttery spread (such as
Earth Balance).

- Preheat oven to 350°F (180°C)
- Muffin pan, 4 cups lined with paper liners

1/2 cup	whole wheat flour	125 mL
2 tsp	ground cinnamon	10 mL
1 tsp	ground ginger	5 mL
1 tsp	baking soda	5 mL
1 tsp	grated orange zest	5 mL
1/4 cup	unsweetened applesauce	60 mL
2 tbsp	butter, melted	30 mL
1 tbsp	agave nectar	15 mL
1 tsp	vanilla extract	5 mL
3/4 cup	grated zucchini (unpeeled)	175 mL
1/2 cup	grated carrots	125 mL
1/2 cup	unsweetened dried cranberries	125 mL
1/4 cup	chopped walnuts	60 mL

1. In a large bowl, combine whole wheat flour, cinnamon, ginger and baking soda.

2. In a small bowl, whisk together orange zest, applesauce, butter, agave nectar and vanilla until thoroughly combined.

3. Add the applesauce mixture to the flour mixture and stir just until moistened. Fold in zucchini, carrots, cranberries and walnuts.

4. Scoop batter into prepared muffin cups, dividing evenly.

5. Bake in preheated oven for 20 to 25 minutes or until a tester inserted in the center of a muffin comes out clean.

NUTRIENTS PER SERVING			
Calories	428	Fiber	8 g (32% DV)
Fat	22 g	Protein	8 g
Saturated fat	8 g	Calcium	78 mg (8% DV)
Sodium	657 mg (27% DV)	Iron	2 mg (11% DV)
Carbohydrate	55 g	Vitamin D	9 IU (2% DV)

Blueberry Yogurt Scones

**MAKES 2 SCONES
(1 SCONE PER
SERVING)**

Yes, you can have your scone and eat it, too! Be prepared to take a bite and experience blueberry bliss.

TIPS

Enjoy your scone with Greek yogurt for a source of protein and to balance your blood sugar.

It's difficult to prepare a single serving of this recipe. Instead, prepare the full recipe and store the remaining scone in an airtight container for up to 2 days.

Health Bite

The phytonutrients in blueberries may help to improve insulin sensitivity and therefore decrease the risk of insulin resistance.

- Preheat oven to 400°F (200°C)
- Baking sheet, lined with parchment paper

¼ cup	all-purpose flour	60 mL
¼ cup	whole wheat flour	60 mL
1 tsp	granulated sugar	5 mL
½ tsp	baking powder	2 mL
1 tbsp	cold butter, cut into small pieces	15 mL
1 tsp	grated orange zest	5 mL
1	large egg	1
¼ cup	vanilla-flavored 2% Greek yogurt	60 mL
1 tsp	vanilla extract	5 mL
2 tbsp	blueberries	30 mL
Pinch	salt	Pinch

1. In a large bowl, whisk together all-purpose flour, whole wheat flour, sugar and baking powder. Using a fork, cut in butter until crumbly.

2. In a medium bowl, whisk together orange zest, egg, yogurt and vanilla.

3. Add the egg mixture to the flour mixture, stirring until well combined. Gently fold in blueberries, making sure not to overmix.

4. Divide dough in half and place halves at least 2 inches (5 cm) apart on prepared baking sheet. Sprinkle with salt.

5. Bake in preheated oven for 10 to 12 minutes or until edges are golden brown. Transfer scones to a wire rack to cool. Serve warm or at room temperature.

NUTRIENTS PER SERVING			
Calories	241	Fiber	2 g (8% DV)
Fat	9 g	Protein	10 g
Saturated fat	5 g	Calcium	133 mg (13% DV)
Sodium	244 mg (10% DV)	Iron	2 mg (11% DV)
Carbohydrate	30 g	Vitamin D	26 IU (7% DV)

Coconut Berry Yogurt Smoothie

You may not feel hungry for breakfast every morning, but you still need fuel. This recipe is a favorite among our clients who used to skip their morning meal.

TIPS

. . . .

Too busy to break out the blender in the morning? Try preparing this recipe in advance, then pour the smoothie into an ice pop mold. Freeze overnight for an effortless grab-and-go breakfast!

If preparing this recipe for two people, simply double all of the ingredients.

- **Blender**

²/₃ cup	coconut-flavored 2% Greek yogurt	150 mL
¹/₂ cup	unsweetened almond milk	125 mL
2 tbsp	natural almond butter	30 mL
1 cup	frozen mixed berries	250 mL

1. In blender, combine yogurt, almond milk, almond butter and berries. Blend until smooth.

Health Bite

■ ■

Almond butter contains less saturated fat than peanut butter. Monounsaturated fat has been associated with improved cardiovascular health.

NUTRIENTS PER SERVING			
Calories	431	Fiber	8 g (32% DV)
Fat	23 g	Protein	20 g
Saturated fat	5 g	Calcium	418 mg (42% DV)
Sodium	167 mg (7% DV)	Iron	3 mg (17% DV)
Carbohydrate	40 g	Vitamin D	50 IU (13% DV)

LUNCHES FOR YOU OR TWO

Avocado Cucumber Soup

Who knew avocado could be so versatile? Cool your palate with this inviting chilled soup.

TIPS

A ripe avocado yields slightly when squeezed. To pit the avocado, sink the blade of a chef's knife into the side of the pit, then twist it out.

If preparing this recipe for one person, cut all of the ingredients in half.

- Blender

1	avocado, halved	1
1	clove garlic	1
$1/2$	cucumber, peeled and quartered	$1/2$
2 tsp	chopped green onion	10 mL
1 cup	ready-to-use low-sodium vegetable broth	250 mL
$1/2$ cup	plain Greek yogurt	125 mL
2 tbsp	freshly squeezed lime juice	30 mL
1 tbsp	olive oil	15 mL

1. In blender, combine avocado, garlic, cucumber, green onion, broth, yogurt, lime juice and oil. Purée until smooth. Feel free to add additional broth to achieve a thinner consistency.

2. Transfer soup to a large bowl, cover tightly with plastic wrap and refrigerate for 30 minutes. Divide into two even portions. Serve cold soup immediately to prevent browning (also known as oxidation).

Health Bite

Fruits — such as lime — that are high in vitamin C and other antioxidants can help your immune system fight germs like those that cause cold and flu.

NUTRIENTS PER SERVING			
Calories	269	Fiber	5 g (20% DV)
Fat	23 g	Protein	4 g
Saturated fat	6 g	Calcium	110 mg (11% DV)
Sodium	116 mg (5% DV)	Iron	1 mg (6% DV)
Carbohydrate	15 g	Vitamin D	4 IU (1% DV)

Tomato Tortellini Soup

Dazzle your friend with this impressive soup for two! Sautéing the spices and vegetables before blending them develops this soup's flavor and will make it seem like you cooked for hours.

TIPS

Store this soup in an airtight container in the refrigerator for up to 4 days or in the freezer for up to 2 months.

If preparing this recipe for one person, cut all of the ingredients in half. Or simply prepare the full recipe and save half for leftovers.

- Blender

2 tbsp	unsalted butter	30 mL
1/2	onion, roughly chopped	1/2
1/2 tsp	onion powder	2 mL
1/2 tsp	garlic powder	2 mL
1/2 tsp	dried basil	2 mL
1/2 tsp	hot pepper flakes	2 mL
1/2 tsp	ground allspice	2 mL
1 cup	ready-to-use low-sodium vegetable broth	250 mL
1	can (28 oz/796 mL) crushed tomatoes	1
1 cup	cheese tortellini, cooked	250 mL

1. In a large saucepan, melt butter over medium heat. Add onion, onion powder, garlic powder, basil, hot pepper flakes, allspice, broth and tomatoes. Bring to a boil, then reduce heat to a simmer. Cook, uncovered, stirring occasionally, for about 30 minutes or until onions are translucent and ingredients are well blended.

2. Working in batches, transfer soup to blender and purée until your desired consistency is reached. Return soup to the saucepan and add cooked tortellini. Stir to combine and heat through. Serve warm.

Health Bite

Tomatoes contain the antioxidant lycopene. This plant compound is more easily absorbed from cooked tomato than from raw. Lycopene may be protective for cardiovascular disease and prostate cancer.

NUTRIENTS PER SERVING			
Calories	322	Fiber	5 g (20% DV)
Fat	17 g	Protein	10 g
Saturated fat	10 g	Calcium	213 mg (21% DV)
Sodium	665 mg (28% DV)	Iron	5 mg (28% DV)
Carbohydrate	37 g	Vitamin D	22 IU (6% DV)

Turkey Noodle Soup

Warm up a rainy day with this twist on a classic soup. Even leftover turkey can be used for this recipe.

TIPS

Soups are great for freezing. Make this recipe when you have leftover turkey. Let soup cool completely before transferring to a glass container to freeze. Thaw in the refrigerator the night before you have this soup for lunch. To reheat, transfer soup to a medium pot set over medium-high heat and heat, stirring occasionally, until soup reaches a rolling boil.

If preparing this recipe for one person, cut all of the ingredients in half. Or simply prepare the full recipe and save half for leftovers. Store leftover soup in an airtight container in the refrigerator for up to 3 days.

Health Bite

The protein from the turkey balances the carbohydrates provided by the egg noodles.

8 oz	boneless skinless turkey breast	250 g
Pinch	salt	Pinch
1 tsp	freshly ground black pepper	5 mL
1 tsp	olive oil	5 mL
2	cloves garlic, minced	2
2	stalks celery, chopped	2
1	carrot, sliced	1
½ cup	chopped onion	125 mL
4 cups	ready-to-use low-sodium vegetable broth	1 L
4 oz	medium-width egg noodles	125 g
1	bay leaf	1
1 tsp	dried thyme	5 mL
½ tsp	dried oregano	2 mL
1	sprig fresh parsley, chopped	1

1. Season turkey with salt and pepper. Heat oil in a medium pot over medium-high heat. Add turkey and cook for about 5 minutes per side or until turkey is no longer pink inside. Transfer to a cutting board and let rest for 10 minutes.

2. Add garlic, celery, carrot and onion to the pot and cook for 2 minutes, stirring occasionally. Add broth, noodles, bay leaf, thyme and oregano; stir to combine. Cover, bring to a boil over medium-high heat and cook for 5 to 7 minutes or until noodles are al dente.

3. Meanwhile, use two forks to shred turkey; add to soup. Discard bay leaf. Divide soup between bowls and top with parsley.

NUTRIENTS PER SERVING			
Calories	364	Fiber	4 g (16% DV)
Fat	6 g	Protein	35 g
Saturated fat	1 g	Calcium	70 mg (7% DV)
Sodium	502 mg (21%)	Iron	3 mg (17% DV)
Carbohydrate	42 g	Vitamin D	0 IU (0% DV)

Arugula, Pear, Trout and Blue Cheese Salad

No need to dine out when you can dig in to this beloved pear, trout and blue cheese salad at home. Your taste buds will be impressed.

TIPS

If you'd like a smaller salad, use 2 cups (500 mL) arugula.

Pears ripen from the inside out. To tell when a pear is ready to eat, lightly press your thumb into the top of the pear, near the stem. If the pear is firm, it's not ripe yet. If the pear gives in to the light pressure, it is ideal for eating.

Try this salad with grilled chicken in place of the trout.

If preparing this recipe for two people, simply double all of the ingredients.

	Canola oil nonstick cooking spray	
6 oz	skin-on trout fillet	175 g
1 tbsp	olive oil	15 mL
1 tsp	raspberry-flavored or plain balsamic vinegar	5 mL
1 tsp	freshly squeezed lemon juice	5 mL
1/4 tsp	poppy seeds	1 mL
3 cups	arugula	750 mL
1 oz	blue cheese, crumbled	30 g
1	pear (peeled, if desired), sliced	1
2 tbsp	walnuts	30 mL

1. Lightly spray a small skillet with cooking spray. Place over medium heat and add trout, skin side down. Cover and cook for about 5 minutes or until trout is opaque and flakes easily when tested with a fork. Transfer to a cool dish to prevent overcooking; set aside.

2. In a small ramekin or bowl, whisk together oil, vinegar, lemon juice and poppy seeds.

3. Place arugula in a serving bowl and arrange blue cheese, pear and walnuts over top. Whisk vinaigrette again and quickly pour over salad.

4. Slide a spatula between the trout and its skin and arrange trout over salad. Discard skin.

Health Bite

Not just delicious, pears are also good sources of vitamin C, calcium, potassium and fiber.

NUTRIENTS PER SERVING			
Calories	630	Fiber	8 g (32% DV)
Fat	37 g	Protein	45 g
Saturated fat	9 g	Calcium	400 mg (40% DV)
Sodium	400 mg (17% DV)	Iron	3 mg (17% DV)
Carbohydrate	33 g	Vitamin D	457 IU (114% DV)

Kale Salad with Pine Nuts, Endive and Champagne Vinaigrette

This bright salad will make you crave kale. Live the message of moderation "Eat kale and cupcakes." Enjoy one of the *Everyday Diabetes* cupcakes (pages 218–219) as a snack on the same day you enjoy this salad.

TIPS

Massaging the kale with olive oil and lemon juice helps break down the cellular walls of the kale. Not only does this make the kale less fibrous, it can also decrease its bitterness.

If preparing this recipe for one person, cut all of the ingredients in half. Or simply prepare the full recipe up to the end of step 3 and store in separate airtight containers in the refrigerator. When ready to enjoy leftovers, up to 2 days later, toss salad with vinaigrette.

Health Bite

The pine nuts not only add a crunch to this lunch, they are also chock full of antioxidants and healthy fat.

SALAD

5	large kale leaves, stemmed	5
	Juice of 1/2 lemon	
1 tsp	olive oil	5 mL
1	medium endive	1
1/4 cup	pine nuts, toasted (see tip, page 74)	60 mL
1/4 cup	grated Parmesan cheese	60 mL

CHAMPAGNE VINAIGRETTE

2 tbsp	freshly squeezed lemon juice	30 mL
2 tbsp	champagne vinegar or white wine vinegar	30 mL
2 tbsp	olive oil	30 mL
1 tsp	Dijon mustard	5 mL
1 tbsp	chopped shallots	15 mL
1/2 tsp	freshly ground black pepper	2 mL

1. *Salad:* In a large bowl, combine kale, lemon juice and oil. Use your fingertips to massage the kale, as if you were kneading bread, for 2 to 4 minutes or until tender. Thinly slice kale leaves and return to bowl with the oil mixture.

2. Slice the endive lengthwise into two sections, then slice each section horizontally into smaller pieces. Add to the kale and stir to combine.

3. *Champagne Vinaigrette:* In a small bowl, whisk together lemon juice, vinegar, oil, mustard, shallots and pepper.

4. Top kale and endives with pine nuts and cheese. Toss with vinaigrette.

NUTRIENTS PER SERVING			
Calories	374	Fiber	10 g (40% DV)
Fat	32 g	Protein	10 g
Saturated fat	5 g	Calcium	274 mg (27% DV)
Sodium	350 mg (15% DV)	Iron	4 mg (22% DV)
Carbohydrate	18 g	Vitamin D	3 IU (1% DV)

Pesto Pasta Salad with Vegetables

Become a pesto pro with this easy-to-follow recipe! Walnuts are a great alternative to pine nuts, which can be quite costly for homemade pesto.

TIPS

If you want to prepare this pasta ahead of time, toss with 1/2 tsp (2 mL) olive oil to avoid sticky pasta.

You can also use this pesto sauce in Pesto Grilled Cheese (page 117) or as a base on homemade pizza (marinara sauce usually has a higher sugar content).

If preparing this recipe for one person, cut all of the ingredients in half.

Health Bite

The fiber from the whole wheat pasta along with the omega-3 fatty acids from the walnuts can help to prevent a spike in blood sugar.

- Small food processor

4 oz	whole wheat farfalle pasta	125 g
10	spears asparagus (ends snapped off), chopped	10
1/2 cup	diced zucchini (unpeeled)	125 mL
2	cloves garlic	2
1/2 cup	loosely packed fresh basil leaves, divided	125 mL
1/2 cup	walnuts	125 mL
1/4 cup	grated Parmesan cheese	60 mL
Pinch	salt	Pinch
1/3 cup	olive oil	75 mL
1/4 cup	dry-packed sun-dried tomatoes, chopped	60 mL
1/2 tsp	hot pepper flakes (or to taste)	2 mL

1. In a large pot of boiling salted water, cook pasta according to package directions. Two minutes before the pasta is ready, add asparagus and zucchini to the pot and blanch until tender-crisp. Drain pasta and vegetables, cool with cold running water and transfer to a bowl.

2. Meanwhile, in food processor, combine garlic, half the basil, walnuts, cheese and salt. Process until roughly combined, scraping down the sides as needed. With the motor running, slowly pour in oil through the feed tube until incorporated. Add the remaining basil and continue processing to your preferred texture, scraping down the sides as needed.

3. Add sun-dried tomatoes and pesto to the bowl and stir until evenly coated. Season with hot pepper flakes and serve immediately.

NUTRIENTS PER SERVING			
Calories	716	Fiber	10 g (40% DV)
Fat	49 g	Protein	18 g
Saturated fat	8 g	Calcium	178 mg (18% DV)
Sodium	440 mg (18% DV)	Iron	5 mg (28% DV)
Carbohydrate	57 g	Vitamin D	3 IU (1% DV)

Pasta Salad with Grilled Chicken

One of the biggest accomplishments you'll achieve in following the recipes in this book is learning how to eat pasta. This recipe is an ideal example of pairing pasta with protein and fat to create a complex dish that is digested slowly — and therefore the sugars are also slowly released into your bloodstream. Welcome to the world of easy eating.

TIPS

Substitute shrimp, salmon or steak for the chicken.

If preparing this recipe for one person, cut all of the ingredients in half. Or simply prepare the full recipe and save half for leftovers. Store leftovers in an airtight container in the refrigerator for up to 3 days.

Health Bite

Vitamin E–rich black olives can neutralize damaging free radicals in the body's fat tissues.

	Canola oil nonstick cooking spray	
1	boneless skinless chicken breast (6 oz/175 g)	1
1 tbsp	steak seasoning	15 mL
4 oz	rotini pasta	125 g
1 tbsp	olive oil	15 mL
1 tbsp	balsamic vinegar	15 mL
1 tsp	dried oregano	5 mL
1/2	red onion, chopped	1/2
1/2	tomato, chopped	1/2
1/2 cup	black olives, pitted	125 mL
1/2 cup	broccoli florets	125 mL

1. Spray a medium skillet with cooking spray. Season both sides of chicken breast with steak seasoning. Add chicken to skillet and cook over medium-high heat for 6 to 8 minutes per side or until no longer pink inside. Remove from heat, let rest for about 5 minutes and cut into thin strips.

2. Meanwhile, in a medium pot of boiling salted water, cook pasta according to package directions. Drain and rinse with cold water.

3. In a small bowl, whisk together olive oil, vinegar and oregano.

4. In a large bowl, combine onion, tomato, olives, broccoli and cooled pasta. Pour in dressing and toss to combine. Divide into two portions and serve with sliced chicken on top.

NUTRIENTS PER SERVING			
Calories	381	Fiber	5 g (20% DV)
Fat	16 g	Protein	32 g
Saturated fat	3 g	Calcium	102 mg (10% DV)
Sodium	403 mg (17% DV)	Iron	4 mg (22% DV)
Carbohydrate	28 g	Vitamin D	4 IU (1% DV)

Grilled Salmon over Chopped Greek Salad

Homemade Greek salad is so much better than a diner's version. No need for lettuce when you have farm-fresh cucumbers and tomatoes. This salad is topped with salmon for extra flavor and, of course, a dose of the favored omega-3 fatty acids. Serve with warmed whole wheat pita.

TIP
■ ■ ■ ■ ■ ■ ■ ■ ■ ■ ■ ■ ■ ■ ■ ■

If preparing this recipe for two people, simply double all of the ingredients.

Health Bite
■ ■ ■ ■ ■ ■ ■ ■ ■ ■ ■ ■ ■ ■

There have been mixed research results on omega-3 fatty acid supplementation versus dietary intake — and omega-3s and their relationship to disease. But one large-scale study spanning almost 20 years and involving 2,000 men found that serum long-chain omega-3 concentration (a biomarker for fish consumption) was associated with lower risk of type 2 diabetes in middle-aged and older men.

- Preheat oven to 350°F (180°C)
- Baking sheet, lined with foil

4 oz	piece skin-on salmon fillet	125 g
1 tbsp	olive oil	15 mL
2 tsp	balsamic vinegar	10 mL
1 tsp	dried oregano	5 mL
Pinch	salt	Pinch
2	plum (Roma) tomatoes, quartered	2
1	cucumber, cut into eighths	1
1/4 cup	black olives, pitted	60 mL
1/4 cup	chopped fresh parsley	60 mL
1 oz	feta cheese	30 g
1	6-inch (15 cm) whole wheat pita, warmed	1

1. Place salmon, skin side down, on prepared baking sheet. Bake in preheated oven for about 15 minutes or until salmon is opaque and flakes easily when tested with a fork.

2. Meanwhile, in a small bowl, whisk together olive oil, vinegar, oregano and salt.

3. In a medium bowl, combine tomatoes, cucumber, olives and parsley. Pour in vinaigrette and stir to combine. Crumble feta over salad and let stand while the salmon bakes.

4. Arrange salmon over salad and serve with warmed pita.

NUTRIENTS PER SERVING			
Calories	329	Fiber	5 g (20% DV)
Fat	17 g	Protein	21 g
Saturated fat	4 g	Calcium	139 mg (14% DV)
Sodium	471 mg (20% DV)	Iron	3 mg (17% DV)
Carbohydrate	25 g	Vitamin D	200 IU (50% DV)

Chickpea Salad with Savory Greek Yogurt Dressing

Chickpeas are great for hummus, roasting and adding to salads for texture. In this recipe, they act as a substitute for chicken in a "flexitarian" vegetarian lunch. Chickpeas are a great source of soluble fiber and are approved as part of the Mediterranean diet.

TIPS

If a 15-oz (425 mL) can of chickpeas is not available, you can use a 14-oz (398 mL) can, or measure $1\frac{2}{3}$ cups (400 mL) drained rinsed chickpeas from a larger can.

You can substitute green olives for the kalamatas.

You can substitute goat cheese for the feta.

CHICKPEA SALAD

1	can (15 oz/425 mL) no-salt added chickpeas, drained and rinsed (see tip, at left)	1
5	medium dry-packed sun-dried tomatoes, finely chopped	5
2	stalks celery, diced	2
$\frac{1}{3}$ cup	finely chopped onion	75 mL
$\frac{1}{4}$ cup	diced cucumber	60 mL
2 tbsp	chopped pitted kalamata olives	30 mL
Pinch	salt	Pinch
$\frac{1}{4}$ cup	crumbled feta cheese	60 mL

YOGURT DRESSING

$\frac{1}{4}$ cup	plain 2% Greek yogurt	60 mL
2 tbsp	freshly squeezed lemon juice	30 mL
2 tbsp	olive oil	30 mL
1 tbsp	white wine vinegar	15 mL
1 tsp	dried oregano	5 mL
$\frac{1}{2}$ tsp	freshly ground black pepper	2 mL
$\frac{1}{2}$ tsp	dried rosemary	2 mL

1. *Chickpea Salad:* In a medium bowl, using a potato masher, gently mash chickpeas, leaving some intact for texture. Add sun-dried tomatoes, celery, onion, cucumber, olives and salt. Stir until thoroughly combined.

NUTRIENTS PER SERVING			
Calories	575	Fiber	16 g (64% DV)
Fat	29 g	Protein	23 g
Saturated fat	6 g	Calcium	263 mg (26% DV)
Sodium	586 mg (24% DV)	Iron	3 mg (17% DV)
Carbohydrate	61 g	Vitamin D	3 IU (1% DV)

Store this dish in an airtight container in the refrigerator for up to 5 days.

If preparing this recipe for one person, cut all of the ingredients in half. Or simply prepare the full recipe and save half for leftovers.

2. *Yogurt Dressing:* In a small bowl, whisk together yogurt, lemon juice, oil, vinegar, oregano, pepper and rosemary until thoroughly combined. Pour dressing over chickpea mixture and stir until evenly coated.

3. Refrigerate for at least 1 hour or for up to 2 days. Top salad with cheese before serving.

Health Bite

Choose chickpeas and chickpea flour over wheat and white flour. In a study measuring blood sugar response, those who ate a single chickpea meal had a lower blood-sugar range than those who ate a single flour-based meal.

CABB Salad (Chicken, Apple, Brussels Sprouts and Bacon)

Long gone are the Cobb salads at the local diner. The new salad favorite is the CABB salad. Brussels sprouts have become one of the most popular vegetables and are even more delicious when partnered with bacon. The best part is that this salad travels well. Pack it up for lunch at the office and it will still be crispy and crunchy.

TIPS

Use a mandoline or a knife to shred Brussels sprouts.

If preparing this recipe for two people, simply double all of the ingredients.

	Canola oil nonstick cooking spray	
4 oz	boneless skinless chicken cutlet	125 g
2	slices bacon ($\frac{1}{2}$ oz/15 g)	2
1 tbsp	olive oil	15 mL
1 tbsp	apple cider vinegar	15 mL
2 tsp	Dijon mustard	10 mL
2 cups	shredded Brussels sprouts	500 mL
$\frac{1}{2}$	apple (unpeeled), diced	$\frac{1}{2}$

1. Coat a grill pan or medium skillet with cooking spray and heat over medium heat until hot but not smoking. Add chicken and cook, turning once, for about 3 minutes per side or until no longer pink inside. Transfer to a plate lined with paper towel.

2. Add bacon to the grill pan and cook, turning once, for 2 minutes per side or until crispy. Transfer to the plate lined with paper towel to absorb excess fat.

3. In a small bowl, whisk together olive oil, vinegar and mustard.

4. Chop chicken and crumble bacon; transfer to a serving bowl. Add Brussels sprouts, apple and vinaigrette; toss to combine.

Health Bite

The Brussels sprouts in this recipe will meet your daily requirement for vitamins C and K while also delivering plenty of manganese, B vitamins, folate, potassium and fiber.

NUTRIENTS PER SERVING			
Calories	460	Fiber	9 g (36% DV)
Fat	22 g	Protein	37 g
Saturated fat	4 g	Calcium	81 mg (8% DV)
Sodium	504 mg (21% DV)	Iron	4 mg (22% DV)
Carbohydrate	31 g	Vitamin D	6 IU (2% DV)

Chicken Waldorf Salad

This traditional salad is modified to meet your carbohydrate needs. Crunchy celery, savory chicken and sweet apple — what more could you ask for?

TIPS

To lower the saturated fat in this recipe, opt for canola oil mayonnaise.

Store this salad in an airtight container in the refrigerator for up to 5 days.

If preparing this recipe for two people, simply double all of the ingredients.

1	cooked chicken breast (4 oz/125 g)	1
1	stalk celery, finely chopped	1
1/2	apple (such as Gala, Red Delicious or Granny Smith; unpeeled), chopped	1/2
1/4 cup	red seedless grapes, halved	60 mL
2 tbsp	chopped walnuts	30 mL
1/4 cup	plain Greek yogurt	60 mL
2 tbsp	mayonnaise	30 mL
2 tsp	freshly squeezed lemon juice	10 mL
2 cups	shredded romaine lettuce	500 mL

1. In a medium bowl, combine chicken, celery, apple, grapes and walnuts.
2. In a small bowl, combine yogurt, mayonnaise and lemon juice. Add to chicken mixture and gently toss to combine.
3. Arrange romaine lettuce on a serving plate and top with Waldorf salad.

Health Bite

Although celery contains a high percentage of water, it also provides a good amount of dietary fiber.

NUTRIENTS PER SERVING			
Calories	503	Fiber	6 g (24% DV)
Fat	25 g	Protein	41 g
Saturated fat	6 g	Calcium	167 mg (17% DV)
Sodium	282 mg (12% DV)	Iron	3 mg (17% DV)
Carbohydrate	29 g	Vitamin D	10 IU (3% DV)

Curry and Harissa Chicken Salad

Excite your taste buds with this quick lunch that kicks it up with curry and harissa powders. This filling salad includes chicken and yogurt, which provide protein, as well as walnuts, which provide fats for staying power.

TIPS

Harissa is a traditional hot sauce or paste used in North African cuisine. You can find it in the international foods section at the grocery store.

Store this salad in an airtight container in the refrigerator for up to 5 days.

If preparing this recipe for one person, cut all of the ingredients in half. Or simply prepare the full recipe and save half for leftovers.

1 tsp	olive oil	5 mL
6 oz	boneless skinless chicken breasts, cubed	175 g
1/2 tsp	freshly ground black pepper	2 mL
Pinch	salt	Pinch
1	stalk celery, chopped	1
1/2 cup	chopped apple (unpeeled)	125 mL
1/4 cup	walnuts, coarsely chopped	60 mL
2 tbsp	dried cranberries	30 mL
1 tbsp	curry powder	15 mL
1/2 tsp	harissa powder	2 mL
1/4 cup	plain 2% Greek yogurt	60 mL
1 tbsp	mayonnaise	15 mL

1. In a medium skillet, heat oil over medium-high heat. Add chicken and season with pepper and salt. Cook, stirring, for about 8 minutes or until chicken is no longer pink inside. Transfer to a plate lined with paper towel and let cool.

2. Meanwhile, in a medium bowl, combine celery, apple, walnuts, cranberries, curry powder, harissa powder, yogurt and mayonnaise. Add cooled chicken to bowl; stir to combine. Cover and refrigerate for 1 hour before serving.

Health Bite

Walnuts are rich in mono- and polyunsaturated fatty acids, which can help to keep blood vessels healthy.

NUTRIENTS PER SERVING			
Calories	338	Fiber	5 g (19% DV)
Fat	19 g	Protein	26 g
Saturated fat	2.5 g	Calcium	83 mg (8% DV)
Sodium	214 mg (9% DV)	Iron	2 mg (11% DV)
Carbohydrate	19 g	Vitamin D	1 IU (0% DV)

Italian Hero Sandwich

This sandwich is inspired by Laura's father's favorite hero at the local Italian deli. Low-sodium turkey is used to balance the higher-fat and higher-sodium deli meats in the sandwich.

TIPS

Serve raw bell peppers on the side or top with roasted red peppers for a filling lunch.

If preparing this recipe for two people, simply double all of the ingredients.

To minimize sodium intake, avoid the salt shaker and choose low-sodium deli meats when available.

1	whole wheat roll (about 2½ inches/6 cm in diameter)	1
3	slices low-sodium turkey breast	3
1	slice soppressata salami	1
1	slice Genoa salami	1
1	slice provolone	1
2 tsp	red wine vinegar	10 mL
1 tsp	olive oil	5 mL

1. Cut roll in half. Layer turkey, soppressata salami, Genoa salami and provolone on one half of roll.

2. In a small bowl, combine vinegar and oil. Pour mixture onto other half of roll, place over meats and cheese, and cut hero into two.

Health Bite

About one-third of the population is salt-sensitive.

NUTRIENTS PER SERVING			
Calories	392	Fiber	3 g (10% DV)
Fat	19 g	Protein	35 g
Saturated fat	7 g	Calcium	275 mg (28% DV)
Sodium	1120 mg (47% DV)	Iron	2 mg (11% DV)
Carbohydrate	20 g	Vitamin D	6 IU (2% DV)

No Skimpy Shrimp Salad Sandwich

All foods fit when you have diabetes. Here is a great recipe exemplifying how to eat a brioche filled with creamy shrimp salad.

TIPS

For even better flavor, prepare the celery mixture 1 day ahead of serving. Store in an airtight container in the refrigerator overnight. Combine with the shrimp right before you eat lunch.

If preparing this recipe for one person, cut all of the ingredients in half. Or simply prepare the full recipe up to the end of step 2 and store in an airtight container in the refrigerator. When ready to enjoy leftovers, up to 2 days later, continue with step 3.

10 oz	medium shrimp, peeled and deveined	300 g
3 tbsp	chopped celery	45 mL
2 tbsp	finely chopped green onion	30 mL
1/2 cup	plain 2% Greek yogurt	125 mL
2 tbsp	freshly squeezed lemon juice	30 mL
1 tsp	dried tarragon	5 mL
1 tsp	dried dillweed	5 mL
2	brioche buns (each 1$\frac{1}{3}$ oz/39 g)	2
	Sea salt	

1. Bring a medium pot of water to a boil over high heat. Reduce heat to a simmer and add shrimp. Cook for 2 to 3 minutes or until pink, firm and opaque. Quickly drain shrimp into a colander and rinse under cold running water. Chop cooled shrimp and set aside.

2. In a medium bowl, combine celery, green onion, yogurt, lemon juice, tarragon and dill; mix well. Add shrimp to the bowl and mix thoroughly.

3. Slice open each brioche and divide shrimp salad evenly between sandwiches. Season to taste with sea salt. If desired, fill each brioche with less shrimp salad and serve any extra on the side.

Health Bite

The antioxidant astaxanthin, which provides the pinkish color to shrimp, is associated with a reduction in inflammation, a known trigger of disease and aging.

NUTRIENTS PER SERVING			
Calories	341	Fiber	1 g (4% DV)
Fat	7 g	Protein	44 g
Saturated fat	3 g	Calcium	203 mg (20% DV)
Sodium	349 mg (15% DV)	Iron	3 mg (17% DV)
Carbohydrate	25 g	Vitamin D	11 IU (3% DV)

Pesto Grilled Cheese

This ain't your mama's grilled cheese! This is what you will call a party in your mouth. Your taste buds will dance with the earthy spiced pesto combined with the ooey-gooey cheese.

TIPS

Provolone is naturally lower in saturated fat than other cheeses. Want a different flavor? Swap with another lower-saturated-fat cheese, such as Swiss cheese.

If preparing this recipe for two people, simply double all of the ingredients.

1 tbsp	pesto (store-bought or see step 2 of Pesto Pasta Salad with Vegetables, page 107)	15 mL
2	slices (each 1½ oz/45 g) sourdough bread	2
2 oz	reduced-sodium provolone cheese slices	60 g
	Canola oil nonstick cooking spray	

1. Spread pesto evenly over bread slices. Top one slice of bread with both slices of cheese and cover with the remaining bread slice.

2. Spray a small skillet with nonstick cooking spray and heat over medium heat. Toast sandwich, turning once, for 2 to 3 minutes per side or until cheese is melted and bread is golden brown. Cut in half and serve.

Health Bite

Add a raw non-starchy vegetable — such as cauliflower or broccoli — for a crunchy side dish and added fiber.

NUTRIENTS PER SERVING			
Calories	532	Fiber	3 g (12% DV)
Fat	27 g	Protein	22 g
Saturated fat	11 g	Calcium	538 mg (54% DV)
Sodium	653 mg (27% DV)	Iron	4 mg (22% DV)
Carbohydrate	45 g	Vitamin D	1 IU (0% DV)

Mozzarella, Basil and Tomato Panini

Bread is something we all love, yet many people deprive themselves of it because they think carbs don't mix with diabetes. There's good news. This recipe is all about bread. Go to the bakery and get a fresh ciabatta roll, if you can. The trip to the bakery will make this sandwich memorable.

TIPS

James Beard said: "Good bread is the most fundamentally satisfying of all foods; and good bread with fresh butter, the greatest of feasts."

If you have a panini maker, go ahead and use it! Cheese-filled sandwiches are perfect for grilled paninis.

If preparing this recipe for two people, simply double all of the ingredients.

- Preheat oven to 400°F (200°C)
- Baking sheet, lined with foil

1	medium ciabatta roll (about 4 oz/125 g)	1
1 tsp	olive oil	5 mL
1 tsp	garlic powder	5 mL
1 tsp	balsamic vinegar	5 mL
3 oz	reduced-sodium mozzarella cheese, sliced	90 g
1	plum (Roma) tomato, sliced	1
6	basil leaves	6

1. Cut roll in half and brush oil over cut sides. Sprinkle garlic powder over oil.

2. Drizzle vinegar over bottom half of roll and top with two-thirds of the mozzarella, tomato slices and basil. Add the remaining mozzarella and cover with top half of roll.

3. Place sandwich on prepared baking sheet and bake in preheated oven for 5 to 6 minutes or until cheese is melted and roll is golden brown. Slice in half and serve.

Health Bite

Fresh basil leaves contain magnesium, iron, potassium, vitamins A, K and C — and even calcium.

NUTRIENTS PER SERVING			
Calories	457	Fiber	3 g (12% DV)
Fat	21 g	Protein	30 g
Saturated fat	10 g	Calcium	680 mg (68% DV)
Sodium	332 mg (14% DV)	Iron	2 mg (11% DV)
Carbohydrate	36 g	Vitamin D	11 IU (3% DV)

Deviled Egg Wrap

MAKES 1 SERVING

Deviled eggs are en vogue. Learn how to make them part of your consistent carbohydrate intake. It's easy: mash your deviled eggs and wrap them in a tortilla. Lunch is served.

TIPS

To hard-cook eggs, place eggs in a medium pot of cold water. Bring to a boil over high heat. Watch closely! When you begin to see tiny bubbles (light boil), cover the pot and remove from heat. Let eggs stand for 15 minutes. To stop the cooking, plunge eggs into a bowl filled with ice and water for 10 minutes or until chilled.

If preparing this recipe for two people, simply double all of the ingredients.

2	hard-cooked large egg whites (see tip, at left)	2
1	hard-cooked whole large egg	1
1 tbsp	plain 2% Greek yogurt	15 mL
2 tsp	spicy mustard (such as Dijon)	10 mL
1 tsp	paprika	5 mL
1	8-inch (20 cm) whole wheat tortilla	1
1	reduced-sodium dill pickle	1

1. In a small bowl, using a potato masher or fork, mash egg whites and whole egg.
2. In another small bowl, combine yogurt, mustard and paprika. Scrape dressing into mashed eggs and mix well.
3. Place tortilla on a work surface and spoon egg salad in a line down the middle of the tortilla, stopping approximately one-third of the way from the bottom. Fold the bottom edge of the tortilla in and roll tortilla up. Serve with dill pickle.

> ## Health Bite
>
> Eggs are a valuable source of protein! The yolk contains the fat, and the whites provide the protein. If you have diabetes, be mindful of overall egg consumption.

NUTRIENTS PER SERVING			
Calories	292	Fiber	5 g (20% DV)
Fat	11 g	Protein	19 g
Saturated fat	4 g	Calcium	180 mg (18% DV)
Sodium	656 mg (27% DV)	Iron	3 mg (17% DV)
Carbohydrate	29 g	Vitamin D	44 IU (11% DV)

Classic Tuna Wrap

You will love this easy go-to lunch option. Keep cans of tuna and mandarin oranges in your pantry and celery and tortillas in your refrigerator at all times. That way, when you're too busy to get to the grocery store, you can easily create a balanced lunch.

TIPS

To lower the saturated fat in this recipe, opt for canola oil mayonnaise.

Use a snack-size single serving (4 oz/125 mL) of mandarin oranges to prevent food waste.

If preparing this recipe for two people, simply double all of the ingredients.

1	can (5 to 6 oz/142 to 170 g) water-packed low-sodium chunk light tuna, drained	1
1 tbsp	mayonnaise	15 mL
1/2 cup	drained juice-packed mandarin orange segments, halved	125 mL
2 tbsp	diced celery	30 mL
1	8-inch (20 cm) whole wheat tortilla	1

1. In a medium bowl, combine tuna and mayonnaise, breaking up tuna with a fork. Stir in mandarin oranges and celery until fully incorporated.

2. Place tortilla on a work surface and spoon tuna salad in a line down the middle of the tortilla. Roll and secure with a toothpick.

Health Bite

Chunk light tuna is three times lower in mercury than albacore (white) tuna. For more information, visit the Environmental Defense Fund website (www.edf.org).

NUTRIENTS PER SERVING			
Calories	385	Fiber	6 g (24% DV)
Fat	9 g	Protein	39 g
Saturated fat	1 g	Calcium	111 mg (11% DV)
Sodium	684 mg (29% DV)	Iron	3 mg (17% DV)
Carbohydrate	39 g	Vitamin D	96 IU (24% DV)

Bite-Size Turkey Burgers

MAKES 4 BURGERS (2 BURGERS PER SERVING)

Even though these burgers are on the smaller side, they pack a big, bold flavor.

TIPS

You can substitute ground chicken or beef for the ground turkey.

If preparing this recipe for one person, cut all of the ingredients in half. Or simply prepare the full recipe and save half for leftovers. Store cooled cooked patties and tahini sauce in separate airtight containers in the refrigerator for up to 2 days. Reheat patties in the microwave on High for 1 to 2 minutes or until warmed. Assemble burgers just before serving.

2 tbsp	finely chopped fresh parsley	30 mL
1/4 tsp	onion powder	1 mL
1/4 tsp	garlic powder	1 mL
8 oz	lean ground turkey	250 g
	Canola oil nonstick cooking spray	
1 tbsp	tahini	15 mL
1 tsp	freshly squeezed lemon juice	5 mL
4	slices tomato	4
4	mini pitas (each about 3 to 4 inches/ 7.5 to 10 cm)	4

1. In a large bowl, combine parsley, onion powder and garlic powder. Add ground turkey and mix until combined. Divide turkey mixture into 4 equal portions, shaping each into a $1\frac{1}{2}$-inch (4 cm) patty.

2. Spray a large skillet with cooking spray and place over medium heat. Arrange patties in pan and cook, turning once, for 4 minutes per side or until an instant-read thermometer inserted in the thickest part of a patty registers 165°F (74°C).

3. Meanwhile, in a small bowl, combine tahini and lemon juice. Divide sauce and tomatoes among pitas and fill each with a patty.

Health Bite

Mini pitas keep the carbohydrates in check, while ground turkey provides protein and fat to balance this lunch.

NUTRIENTS PER SERVING			
Calories	438	Fiber	5 g (20% DV)
Fat	19 g	Protein	40 g
Saturated fat	4 g	Calcium	138 mg (14% DV)
Sodium	345 mg (14% DV)	Iron	4 mg (22% DV)
Carbohydrate	31 g	Vitamin D	9 IU (2% DV)

No-Cook Zucchini Marinara with Roasted Chickpeas

Fresh, fast cooking is best for everyday health. When you're hungry and need a quick fix, choose this no-cook, low-carb "pasta" dish. Serve with ricotta cheese or canned tuna to keep you full longer.

TIPS

Add ¼ cup (60 mL) ricotta cheese or a 5- to 6-oz (142 to 170 g) can of water-packed chunk light tuna, drained, to each serving for extra protein and staying power.

This sauce can be stored in an airtight container in the refrigerator for up to 1 week or in the freezer up to 3 months.

- Preheat oven to 400°F (200°C)
- Baking sheet, lined with foil and brushed with olive oil
- Blender or food processor

¾ cup	rinsed drained canned chickpeas	175 mL
1 tbsp	olive oil	15 mL
1½ cups	chopped vine-ripened tomatoes	375 mL
¼ cup	chopped red bell pepper	60 mL
¼ cup	chopped orange bell pepper	60 mL
¼ cup	chopped strawberries	60 mL
¼ cup	fresh basil leaves, torn	60 mL
2 tsp	chopped garlic	10 mL
2 tsp	granulated sugar	10 mL
½ tsp	dried parsley	2 mL
¼ tsp	sea salt	1 mL
2	small zucchinis (or 1 large zucchini, about 6 oz/175 g)	2

1. Spread chickpeas out on prepared baking sheet. Brush chickpeas with oil. Bake in preheated oven for 20 to 30 minutes or until chickpeas are slightly crisp and golden brown.

2. Meanwhile, in blender or food processor, combine tomatoes, red pepper, orange pepper, strawberries, basil, garlic, sugar, parsley and sea salt; process until smooth.

NUTRIENTS PER SERVING			
Calories	307	Fiber	8 g (32% DV)
Fat	18 g	Protein	8 g
Saturated fat	3 g	Calcium	79 mg (8% DV)
Sodium	463 mg (19% DV)	Iron	2 mg (11% DV)
Carbohydrate	32 g	Vitamin D	0 IU (0% DV)

TIPS

We suggest using 1 cup (250 mL) sauce per serving, but there will be extra sauce. The nutritional information provided was calculated using the entire amount of sauce.

This recipe doesn't work well if halved to a single serving. Instead, find a friend or family member to share it with.

3. Use a peeler or spiralizer to create ribbons from the zucchini and divide evenly between two bowls. Top each bowl with half of the chickpeas and the desired amount of sauce (see tip, at left). Serve at room temperature or chilled.

Health Bite

Adding $\frac{1}{4}$ cup (60 mL) whole-milk ricotta cheese provides 107 calories, 8 g fat, 5 g saturated fat, 52 mg sodium, 2 g carbohydrate, 7 g protein, 127 mg calcium, 0.2 mg iron and 6 IU vitamin D. Adding 5 oz (142 g) tuna provides 122 calories, 1 g fat, 350 mg sodium, 0 g carbohydrates, 28 g protein, 24 mg calcium and 67 IU vitamin D.

Macro Bowl

Here is a meat-free meal that is 100% adequate in protein and even provides calcium! The sweet potato serves as a carbohydrate, while the beans serve as both carbohydrate and protein. Kale is also a carbohydrate, but due to its high level of fiber and the amount you will be eating in this recipe, it affects your blood sugar minimally. Tofu serves as a protein source while adding extra value by providing calcium for bone support. Keep in mind: fat is necessary in your diet. Olive oil and hemp are the fat in the bowl!

TIP

Massaging the kale with olive oil helps break down the cellular walls of the kale. Not only does this make the kale less fibrous, it can also decrease its bitterness.

1	small sweet potato (unpeeled)	1
3 tsp	olive oil, divided	15 mL
1½ cups	shredded trimmed kale	375 mL
1 cup	firm cubed tofu	250 mL
½ cup	rinsed drained no-salt-added canned black beans	125 mL
1½ tsp	hemp hearts	7 mL
1 tsp	low-sodium vegan Worcestershire sauce (such as Robbie's Worcestershire Pure & Mild Sauce)	5 mL
1 tsp	pure maple syrup	5 mL
	Salt (optional)	
¼ cup	chopped mango	60 mL

1. Use a fork to poke sweet potato five times. Microwave on High for 5 minutes or until hot, steamy and flesh is soft. Transfer to a medium bowl and drizzle with 1 tsp (5 mL) oil. Use fork to mash potato and break up skin into small pieces.

2. In a small bowl, combine shredded kale and 1 tsp (5 mL) oil. Use your fingertips to massage the kale, as if you were kneading bread, for 2 to 4 minutes or until tender (see tip, at left). Arrange kale over sweet potato.

NUTRIENTS PER SERVING			
Calories	623	Fiber	16 g (64% DV)
Fat	32 g	Protein	35 g
Saturated fat	5 g	Calcium	672 mg (67% DV)
Sodium	253 mg (11% DV)	Iron	8 mg (44% DV)
Carbohydrate	55 g	Vitamin D	1 IU (0% DV)

TIPS
■ ■ ■ ■ ■ ■ ■ ■ ■ ■ ■ ■ ■ ■

Look for low-sodium Worcestershire-style sauce in natural foods stores and online. It should contain 20 mg sodium per teaspoon (5 mL). If a low-sodium sauce is not available, use a reduced-sodium Worcestershire sauce and factor in the amount of sodium as stated on the label into your daily intake.

If preparing this recipe for two people, simply double all of the ingredients.

3. In another medium bowl, combine tofu, beans, hemp hearts, Worcestershire sauce, maple syrup and the remaining oil. Arrange tofu mixture over kale and, if desired, season to taste with salt. Top with chopped mango.

Health Bite
■ ■

It's a good idea to aim for one meat-free meal a week. Think about Meatless Mondays! Doing so will help you achieve a flexitarian dietary approach, defined as someone who eats mostly plant-based foods, but occasionally eats meat, poultry and fish, which is consistent with a Mediterranean diet. Eating less red meat and more fruits, vegetables, legumes, whole grains and healthy fats has been shown to reduce your risk of heart disease and other chronic conditions.

Italian Tuna-Stuffed Peppers

MAKES 2 SERVINGS

Stuffed peppers are definitely delicious, but they're time-consuming to make for just one or two people. Here is a quick, easy version of stuffed peppers that's ideal for everyday prep.

TIPS

Any remaining tuna can be added to No-Cook Zucchini Marinara with Roasted Chickpeas (page 122) for a source of protein and omega-3 fatty acids.

If preparing this recipe for one person, cut all of the ingredients in half. Or simply prepare the full recipe and save half for leftovers. Store leftover stuffed pepper in an airtight container in the refrigerator for up to 3 days; garnish with avocado just before serving.

2	red bell peppers	2
1 tbsp	olive oil	15 mL
2 tsp	balsamic vinegar	10 mL
1 tsp	dried oregano	5 mL
	Salt (optional)	
1	stalk celery, diced	1
1	carrot, diced	1
1½	cans (each 5 to 6 oz/142 to 170 g) water-packed chunk light tuna, drained (about 8 oz/250 g drained tuna)	1½
½ cup	cooked quinoa	125 mL
¼ cup	chopped orange bell pepper	60 mL
2 tbsp	finely chopped red onion	30 mL
½	avocado, sliced	½

1. Slice off tops of red peppers and remove the ribs and seeds, creating a hole to fill each pepper. Pat dry with a paper towel. Set aside.

2. In a small bowl, whisk together oil, vinegar, oregano and salt to taste (if using).

3. In another small bowl, combine celery, carrot, tuna, cooked quinoa, orange pepper and onion; pour in vinaigrette and stir to coat. Fill each red pepper with tuna mixture, dividing evenly. Arrange avocado slices and any remaining filling alongside red peppers.

Health Bite

This recipe is high in omega-3 fatty acids and naturally low in carbohydrates.

NUTRIENTS PER SERVING			
Calories	408	Fiber	9 g (36% DV)
Fat	13 g	Protein	31 g
Saturated fat	2 g	Calcium	76 mg (8% DV)
Sodium	428 mg (18% DV)	Iron	5 mg (28% DV)
Carbohydrate	45 g	Vitamin D	53 IU (13% DV)

Tuscan Sausage and Polenta

Nothing is better than eating Italian food in Italy — except making it in your own kitchen and, of course, not worrying about whether it will affect your blood sugar. This meal is perfect for the fall and winter seasons. Pair it with a full-bodied red wine, if your heart desires.

TIPS

Garnish with a few leaves of fresh basil, if desired.

If preparing this recipe for one person, cut all of the ingredients in half. Or simply prepare the full recipe up to the end of step 3, let cool, and store polenta and sauce in separate airtight containers in the refrigerator. When ready to enjoy leftovers, up to 2 days later, reheat sauce and polenta in the microwave on High for 1 to 2 minutes, or until heated through, and continue with step 4.

1¾ cups	ready-to-use low-sodium chicken or vegetable broth	425 mL
¾ cup	stone-ground cornmeal	175 mL
1 tbsp	grated Parmesan cheese	15 mL
2 cups	no-sugar-added marinara sauce	500 mL
5 oz	chicken sausage (about 5 links), sliced	150 g
2 tsp	dried oregano	10 mL

1. In a medium saucepan, bring broth to a boil over high heat. Slowly add cornmeal, stirring to combine. Reduce heat to medium and cook, stirring constantly. When cornmeal starts to thicken, after about 5 minutes, stir in cheese.

2. Cook, stirring often, for about 30 minutes or until thick and all the liquid is absorbed. Remove from heat and transfer to two pasta bowls, dividing evenly.

3. Meanwhile, in a small saucepan, combine marinara sauce, sausage slices and oregano. Bring to a boil over high heat, then reduce heat to medium. Cook for about 20 minutes or until sausage is cooked through.

4. Spoon sauce and sausage slices over polenta, dividing evenly.

Health Bite

Stone-ground cornmeal still contains the bran and hull, which makes it a good source of fiber and nutrients.

NUTRIENTS PER SERVING			
Calories	380	Fiber	8 g (32% DV)
Fat	12 g	Protein	20 g
Saturated fat	3 g	Calcium	89 mg (9% DV)
Sodium	670 mg (28% DV)	Iron	5 mg (28% DV)
Carbohydrate	52 g	Vitamin D	3 IU (1% DV)

Beef Tacos

MAKES 2 SERVINGS

Here's a finger-food favorite filled with beef, cheese and tomato. The best part is that you and your guest can prepare this meal together.

TIPS

You can substitute queso blanco for the Mexican cheese blend.

If preparing this recipe for one person, cut all of the ingredients in half. Or simply prepare the full recipe up to the end of step 1, let cool, and store in an airtight container in the refrigerator. When ready to enjoy leftovers, up to 2 days later, reheat the ground beef mixture in the microwave on High for 1 to 2 minutes or until heated through and continue with step 2.

1 tsp	canola oil	5 mL
8 oz	lean ground beef	250 g
1/2 tsp	chili powder	2 mL
1/4 tsp	garlic powder	1 mL
1/4 tsp	ground cumin	1 mL
2 tbsp	finely chopped red onion	30 mL
4	6-inch (15 cm) corn tortillas	4
1/4 cup	shredded Mexican cheese blend	60 mL
1	small tomato, diced	1
1/4 cup	chopped romaine lettuce	60 mL
2 tbsp	sour cream	30 mL
2 tbsp	chopped fresh cilantro	30 mL

1. In a medium skillet, heat oil over medium-high heat. Add beef, chili powder, garlic powder and cumin. Cook, breaking up beef with the back of a spoon, for 2 minutes. Add onion and cook, stirring often, for about 10 minutes or until beef is well browned and no longer pink. Drain fat from skillet.

2. Divide ground beef mixture among tortillas. Top evenly with cheese, tomato and lettuce. Dollop with sour cream and garnish with cilantro.

Health Bite

Cilantro contains a high level of beta-carotene, which has antioxidant abilities and can decrease the risk of numerous conditions.

NUTRIENTS PER SERVING			
Calories	456	Fiber	4 g (12% DV)
Fat	25 g	Protein	35 g
Saturated fat	10 g	Calcium	139 mg (14% DV)
Sodium	134 mg (6% DV)	Iron	4 mg (22% DV)
Carbohydrate	24 g	Vitamin D	6 IU (2% DV)

DINNER, PARTY OF TWO

Mexican Quinoa and Veggie–Stuffed Peppers

Perfect for a Meatless Monday meal, this dinner recipe is not only filling, it's nutrient-rich. The quinoa is a healthy carbohydrate choice and pairs well with the protein in the black beans. This dish will be sure to impress any dinner partner!

TIPS

Make the quinoa and veggie mixture up to 2 days in advance (steps 2 and 3). Store in an airtight container in the refrigerator. When ready to bake, complete step 1, warm quinoa and veggie mixture in the microwave on High for 1 minute, then follow steps 4 and 5.

Use the remaining black beans for Spicy Black Bean Burgers with Tangy Veggie Ribbons (page 132).

- Preheat oven to 350°F (180°F)
- 8-inch (20 cm) square glass baking dish

4	small bell peppers (any color)	4
2/3 cup	water	150 mL
1/3 cup	quinoa, rinsed	75 mL
1 tsp	olive oil	5 mL
1/4 cup	finely chopped onion	60 mL
1/2	can (10 oz/284 mL) diced tomatoes with green chiles, drained	1/2
1 tbsp	taco seasoning (half a 1-oz/28 g packet)	15 mL
1/3 cup	rinsed drained canned no-salt-added black beans	75 mL
1/4 cup	shredded Mexican cheese blend	60 mL
1/4 cup	sour cream	60 mL

1. Cut the tops off the bell peppers and carefully remove the pith and seeds. Discard tops. Set peppers aside.
2. Bring 2/3 cup (150 mL) water to a bowl and add quinoa. Cook according to package instructions (or until quinoa soaks up water and is fluffy when tossed with a fork, 10 to 12 minutes). Transfer to a large bowl.
3. In a medium skillet, heat oil over medium-high heat. Add onion, tomatoes with green chiles and taco seasoning; stir to thoroughly combine. Cook, stirring, for 3 minutes. Add black beans, reduce heat to medium, stir to combine and cook for 5 to 7 minutes or until heated through. Transfer to the large bowl and stir to combine with quinoa.

NUTRIENTS PER SERVING			
Calories	385	Fiber	9 g (36% DV)
Fat	12 g	Protein	16 g
Saturated fat	6 g	Calcium	165 mg (17% DV)
Sodium	863 mg (36% DV)	Iron	13 mg (72% DV)
Carbohydrate	55 g	Vitamin D	7 IU (2% DV)

TIP

If preparing this recipe for one person, cut all of the ingredients in half. Or simply prepare the full recipe and save half for leftovers. Store leftovers in an airtight container in the refrigerator for up to 2 days. Reheat in the microwave on High for 1 to 2 minutes or until heated through.

4. Distribute filling evenly among bell peppers and arrange peppers in baking dish, propping them up against each other so they stay upright. Top each stuffed pepper with cheese. Cover baking dish with foil.

5. Bake in preheated oven for about 30 minutes or until cheese is melted and peppers are tender. To serve, top each filled pepper with sour cream.

Health Bite

This recipe provides about one-third of the daily recommended fiber intake, which helps to lower cholesterol levels and keeps you feeling full for longer.

Spicy Black Bean Burgers with Tangy Veggie Ribbons

MAKES 2 SERVINGS

Say goodbye to frozen processed burgers and hello to these everyday black bean burgers in a whole wheat pita pocket and topped with avocado. Yes, these black bean burgers hold together!

TIPS

Wash your hands and remove any jewelry before combining patty ingredients.

Add up to 4 tsp (20 mL) additional hot sauce for extra-spicy burgers.

Swap in apple cider vinegar for the white vinegar to help you absorb the non-heme iron found in the black beans (see health bite, page 133).

- Preheat oven to 400°F (200°C)
- Baking sheet, lined with foil and brushed with canola oil

¹/₂ cup	rinsed drained canned no-salt-added black beans	125 mL
¹/₄ cup	large-flake (old-fashioned) rolled oats	60 mL
2 tbsp	finely chopped red onion	30 mL
1 tsp	garlic powder	5 mL
1 tsp	onion powder	5 mL
2 tsp	hot pepper sauce	10 mL
1 tsp	canola oil	5 mL
1	carrot	1
3	stalks celery	3
¹/₂ cup	white vinegar	125 mL
2	6¹/₂-inch (16 cm) whole wheat pita pockets	2
¹/₄ cup	mashed avocado	60 mL

1. In a small bowl, use a fork or potato masher to mash the beans. Add oats, onion, garlic powder, onion powder and hot pepper sauce; use your hands to combine mixture and divide into 2 round patties, about ³/₄ inch (2 cm) thick. Brush with oil.

2. Place patties on prepared baking sheet and bake in preheated oven for 10 minutes or until firm and slightly crispy.

NUTRIENTS PER SERVING			
Calories	374	Fiber	12 g (48% DV)
Fat	8 g	Protein	16 g
Saturated fat	1 g	Calcium	130 mg (13% DV)
Sodium	225 mg (9% DV)	Iron	5 mg (28% DV)
Carbohydrate	62 g	Vitamin D	0 IU (0% DV)

You can substitute an equal amount of your favorite guacamole for the avocado.

If preparing this recipe for one person, cut all of the ingredients in half. Or simply prepare the full recipe up to the end of step 2, let leftover burger cool and store in an airtight container in the refrigerator for up to 2 days. Reheat in the microwave on High for 1 to 2 minutes, or until heated through, and continue with step 3.

3. Meanwhile, use a peeler or spiralizer to create ribbons from the carrot and celery. Arrange ribbons in a medium bowl and pour in vinegar.

4. Arrange each burger in a pita pocket and top with avocado. Drain vegetable ribbons and serve on the side.

Health Bite

■ ■

There are two different forms of iron found in our foods. Non-heme iron is from plant sources and is best absorbed with heme iron from animal products, vitamin C and/or acids (such as citric acid, found in apple cider vinegar).

Orange-Glazed Tofu with Sautéed Vegetables

Whether or not you're vegetarian, this tangy Asian recipe will become a go-to weeknight dish. The glaze packs a pop of flavor with fresh ginger and orange zest.

TIPS

We've used a reduced-sodium soy sauce with 550 mg sodium per tablespoon (15 mL) for the nutrient analysis for this recipe. If you wish to reduce the sodium further, look for a "Lite" product with even lower sodium (about 50% less than regular). If the soy sauce you have has more sodium listed on the label, reduce the amount you add to the recipe, or factor in the increase in sodium to your meal.

Add 1 to 2 tbsp (15 to 30 mL) reduced-sodium teriyaki sauce just before serving to add more flavor to this dish, but be aware that this will increase the sodium considerably.

GLAZE

1 tbsp	cornstarch	15 mL
2 tbsp	water	30 mL
1 tsp	grated gingerroot	5 mL
1 tsp	grated orange zest	5 mL
2 tbsp	freshly squeezed orange juice	30 mL
1 tbsp	reduced-sodium soy sauce	15 mL
2 tsp	unseasoned rice vinegar	10 mL

TOFU AND VEGETABLES

1 tbsp	canola oil	15 mL
2	cloves garlic, minced	2
1 cup	roughly chopped broccoli florets	250 mL
14 oz	firm tofu, drained, cubed	400 g
1	small orange bell pepper, finely chopped	1
1	small red bell pepper, finely chopped	1
1/2	large onion, finely chopped	1/2
1 cup	cooked brown rice (warm)	250 mL

1. *Glaze:* In a small bowl, whisk cornstarch into water until combined. Add ginger, orange zest, orange juice, soy sauce and vinegar; whisk until fully combined.

NUTRIENTS PER SERVING			
Calories	409	Fiber	7 g (28% DV)
Fat	16 g	Protein	24 g
Saturated fat	2 g	Calcium	366 mg (37% DV)
Sodium	393 mg (16% DV)	Iron	6 mg (33% DV)
Carbohydrate	43 g	Vitamin D	0 IU (0% DV)

TIPS

If desired, substitute 1½ cups (375 mL) cooked quinoa for the brown rice to keep the carbohydrate count the same.

If preparing this recipe for one person, cut all of the ingredients in half. Or simply prepare the full recipe up to the end of step 2, let cool, and store leftovers in an airtight container in the refrigerator for up to 2 days. Reheat tofu mixture and rice in the microwave on High for 1 to 2 minutes, or until heated through, and continue with step 3.

2. *Tofu and Vegetables:* In a large skillet, heat oil over medium-high heat. Add garlic and cook, stirring, for 1 minute. Add broccoli, cover and cook, stirring occasionally, until broccoli is tender-crisp, about 4 minutes. Add tofu, orange pepper, red pepper and onion. Increase heat to high and cook, stirring, for 2 minutes or until onion is translucent and peppers are tender. Pour glaze over the mixture and cook, stirring, for about 2 minutes or until heated through.

3. Divide rice between two bowls and top with tofu mixture, dividing evenly.

Health Bite

One serving provides 27% of the recommended daily value for fiber, aiding in blood sugar management and even helping you to feel satiated!

Chinese Five-Spice Tempeh

Prepare yourself for all meat lovers to embrace their inner vegetarian. The bountiful servings of vegetables are sure to fill the extra-hungry dinner guest. Feel free to serve with a grain, even an instant rice or couscous.

TIPS

Peanut oil has a higher smoke point, so it can be heated on high heat. If using another oil, reduce the heat to medium-high in step 1. If you don't have peanut oil, which offers an authentic flavor in this recipe, substitute canola oil.

We've used a reduced-sodium tamari with 700 mg sodium per tablespoon (15 mL) for the nutrient analysis for this recipe. If you wish to reduce the sodium further, look for a "Lite" product with even lower sodium (about 50% less than regular). If the tamari you have has more sodium listed on the label, reduce the amount you add to the recipe, or factor in the increase in sodium to your meal.

- Large skillet or wok

1 tbsp	peanut oil	15 mL
1/2	large Vidalia onion, diced	1/2
1 tbsp	minced garlic	15 mL
1 1/2 tsp	grated gingerroot	7 mL
1 tsp	Chinese five-spice powder	5 mL
10 oz	tempeh, cubed	300 g
1/4 cup	ketchup	60 mL
2 tbsp	reduced-sodium tamari	30 mL
1 tbsp	unseasoned rice vinegar	15 mL
1 to 2 tbsp	Sriracha	15 to 30 mL
1	large red bell pepper, julienned	1
3 cups	broccoli florets	750 mL
1 cup	shredded red cabbage	250 mL
2 tbsp	chopped fresh cilantro	30 mL

1. In a large skillet or wok, heat peanut oil over high heat. Add onion, garlic, ginger and five-spice powder; cook, stirring, for 1 minute. Add tempeh and stir to coat in oil. Fry tempeh, turning often, for 3 to 5 minutes or until evenly browned.

2. Meanwhile, in a small saucepan, combine ketchup, tamari, vinegar and Sriracha to taste; bring to a simmer and cook for 2 minutes, stirring occasionally.

NUTRIENTS PER SERVING			
Calories	494	Fiber	11 g (44% DV)
Fat	23 g	Protein	33 g
Saturated fat	4 g	Calcium	259 mg (26% DV)
Sodium	870 mg (36% DV)	Iron	5 mg (28% DV)
Carbohydrate	44 g	Vitamin D	0 IU (0% DV)

Garnish each dish with 5 chopped cashews for added texture.

If preparing this recipe for one person, cut all of the ingredients in half. Or simply prepare the full recipe up to the end of step 4, let cool, and store leftovers in an airtight container in the refrigerator for up to 2 days. Reheat in the microwave on High for 1 to 2 minutes, or until heated through, and continue with step 5.

3. Add red pepper, broccoli and cabbage to tempeh mixture in the skillet; stir to combine. Cook, stirring, until tender-crisp, about 8 minutes.

4. Pour sauce over tempeh and vegetable mixture. Toss until thoroughly coated.

5. Transfer tempeh and vegetables to two bowls, dividing evenly, and garnish with cilantro.

Health Bite

The antioxidant anthocyanin is present in red cabbage and may help slow cancer growth and stop the formation of new tumors.

Garlicky Tofu and Green Beans

Choose this recipe when you need a break from your weekly meat-heavy dinners. It is delicious, inexpensive to prepare and cooks up quickly.

TIPS

For a more filling meal, serve with ¾ cup (175 mL) cooked wild rice per serving.

If preparing this recipe for one person, cut all of the ingredients in half. Or simply prepare the full recipe and save half for leftovers. Store leftovers in an airtight container in the refrigerator for up to 2 days. Reheat in the microwave on Medium (50%) power for 1 to 2 minutes or until heated through.

2 tbsp	extra virgin olive oil	30 mL
3	cloves garlic, minced	3
4 oz	green beans, trimmed	125 g
10 oz	extra-firm tofu, cubed	300 g

1. In a medium skillet, heat oil over medium heat for about 1 minute. Add garlic and cook, stirring, for 1 minute. Add beans and cook, stirring, for about 5 minutes or until tender-crisp.

2. Add tofu and cook, stirring occasionally, for about 3 minutes or until heated through.

Health Bite

Tofu is an excellent source of iron, calcium and protein.

NUTRIENTS PER SERVING			
Calories	487	Fiber	7 g (28% DV)
Fat	40 g	Protein	26 g
Saturated fat	7 g	Calcium	630 mg (63% DV)
Sodium	42 mg (2% DV)	Iron	3 mg (17% DV)
Carbohydrate	16 g	Vitamin D	0 IU (0% DV)

Personal Crustless Quiche

This quiche is crustless, so you can eat it with a carbohydrate of your choice — or even dessert! — all the while keeping within your carbohydrate range.

TIPS

If you use a 6-inch (15 cm) shallow baking dish, decrease the baking time in step 3 to 15 minutes.

Serve with your favorite vegetable or soup. This is a great dish to eat when you plan to have fruit or a higher-carbohydrate dessert immediately after your entrée.

If preparing this recipe for two people, simply double all of the ingredients, using two separate baking dishes.

- Preheat oven to 350°F (180°C)
- 4- to 6-inch (10 to 15 cm) shallow baking dish or ramekin

1 tsp	olive oil	5 mL
1/2 cup	chopped trimmed spinach	125 mL
1	clove garlic, minced	1
1/4 cup	shredded Cheddar cheese	60 mL
2	large eggs	2
1/4 cup	milk	60 mL

1. In a small skillet, heat oil over medium heat. Add spinach and garlic; cook, stirring, for 3 minutes or until spinach is wilted. Transfer spinach mixture to the baking dish and top with cheese.

2. In a small bowl, whisk together eggs and milk; pour over the cheese and spinach mixture.

3. Bake in preheated oven for about 20 minutes (see tip, at left) or until firm and pulling away from the edges of the ramekin and a tester inserted into the center comes out clean.

Health Bite

Garlic is recognized by the National Cancer Institute as having potential anticancer properties. Be sure to eat garlic in its natural state, not as a supplement.

NUTRIENTS PER SERVING			
Calories	345	Fiber	1 g (4% DV)
Fat	26 g	Protein	22 g
Saturated fat	10 g	Calcium	342 mg (34% DV)
Sodium	637 mg (27% DV)	Iron	2 mg (11% DV)
Carbohydrate	6 g	Vitamin D	123 IU (31% DV)

Margherita Flatbread

MAKES 2 SERVINGS

If there ever was a perfect meal, it might just be pizza. It has carbohydrates, proteins and fats. Of course, this flatbread has loads of vitamin A from spinach, too. You will never think of pizza the same way after eating this!

TIP

Most frozen pizza dough comes in a package of 16 oz (464 g). If you don't have a kitchen scale to weigh out a portion, divide the dough in half, then cut off one-quarter of one half and you'll be left with your 6-oz (175 g) portion. Place extra dough in an oiled resealable plastic bag or covered bowl and refrigerate for up to 2 days. The extra dough can be used to make Prosciutto Flatbread (page 256) or baked as a plain crust and frozen for later.

- Preheat oven to 400°F (200°C)
- Baking sheet, sprayed with canola oil nonstick cooking spray

6 oz	thawed frozen whole-grain pizza dough (see tip, at left)	175 g
	All-purpose flour (optional)	
1 tbsp	olive oil	15 mL
1/4 tsp	dried oregano	1 mL
Pinch	sea salt	Pinch
1/2 cup	no-salt-added unsweetened tomato sauce, divided	125 mL
3/4 cup	lightly packed trimmed baby spinach	175 mL
1/4 cup	partly skimmed ricotta cheese	60 mL
2	slices mozzarella cheese (2 oz/60 g total)	2
1 tbsp	grated Parmesan cheese	15 mL

1. On a work surface, roll out pizza dough into a long, thin rectangular shape, about 12 by 5 inches (30 by 12.5 cm), dusting with flour, if necessary, to prevent sticking. Place on prepared baking sheet. Brush oil over the dough and sprinkle with oregano and salt.

2. Bake in preheated oven for about 15 minutes or until golden brown and crispy (don't turn oven off).

3. Transfer flatbread to a large cutting board and let cool for 5 minutes. Top the flatbread with half the tomato sauce, followed by spinach and ricotta.

NUTRIENTS PER SERVING			
Calories	413	Fiber	7 g (28% DV)
Fat	21 g	Protein	17 g
Saturated fat	8 g	Calcium	299 mg (30% DV)
Sodium	644 mg (27% DV)	Iron	3 mg (17% DV)
Carbohydrate	41 g	Vitamin D	9 IU (2% DV)

TIPS

■ ■ ■ ■ ■ ■ ■ ■ ■ ■ ■ ■ ■ ■ ■ ■ ■

This pizza recipe is a favorite among kids. Ask them to help you assemble it!

If you do not have sliced mozzarella, you can use 1/2 cup (125 mL) shredded mozzarella cheese.

If preparing this recipe for one person, cut all of the ingredients in half. This flatbread doesn't work well as leftovers.

4. Use a pizza cutter or serrated knife to cut flatbread in half. Return to baking sheet. Top each half with 1 slice of mozzarella, the remaining tomato sauce and a sprinkle of Parmesan.

5. Bake for 5 minutes to warm the toppings and melt the cheese. Serve immediately.

Health Bite

■ ■

The vitamin C from the tomato aids in absorbing the iron from the spinach.

Citrus Fish Fajitas

MAKES 2 SERVINGS

Serve this recipe when you're yearning for summer. The citrus flavors are balanced by the creamy, savory salad of avocado and beans. Eating never tasted so good!

TIPS

You can experiment with different red chile peppers, such as cherry, Anaheim or serrano.

A ripe avocado yields slightly when squeezed. To pit the avocado, sink the blade of a chef's knife into the side of the pit, then twist it out.

- Mini colander or sieve

10 oz	skinless white fish fillet (such as cod, scrod or tilapia)	300 g
1 tbsp	freshly squeezed lime juice	15 mL
1/4 cup	finely chopped red onion	60 mL
2 tsp	olive oil	10 mL
2	8-inch (20 cm) sprouted-grain tortillas	2

FRUIT TOPPING

1/2 cup	diced mango	125 mL
1/4 cup	finely chopped red onion	60 mL
2 tbsp	chopped fresh cilantro	30 mL
1 tbsp	minced hot red chile pepper	15 mL
2 tbsp	freshly squeezed or unsweetened orange juice	30 mL
1 tsp	olive oil	5 mL

SALAD

1	small avocado, sliced	1
1/4 cup	rinsed drained canned black beans	60 mL
1/2 cup	halved cherry tomatoes	125 mL
2 tsp	freshly squeezed lime juice	10 mL
	Salt and freshly ground black pepper	

1. In a sealable plastic bag, marinate white fish in lime juice and red onion for up to 30 minutes at room temperature, flipping bag halfway through and making sure marinade covers the whole fish.

2. *Fruit Topping:* In a small bowl, combine mango, onion, cilantro, chile pepper, orange juice and oil. Let stand while you prepare the salad and cook the fish.

NUTRIENTS PER SERVING			
Calories	607	Fiber	18 g (72% DV)
Fat	23 g	Protein	44 g
Saturated fat	3 g	Calcium	156 mg (16% DV)
Sodium	347 mg (15% DV)	Iron	5 mg (28% DV)
Carbohydrate	62 g	Vitamin D	65 IU (16% DV)

If preparing this recipe for one person, cut all of the ingredients in half. Or simply prepare the full recipe and save half for leftovers, refrigerating each component separately in an airtight container and reheating fish in the microwave on Medium (50%) power for 1 to 2 minutes before assembling fajita.

3. *Salad:* In a small bowl, gently stir together avocado, black beans, tomatoes and lime juice. Season to taste with salt and pepper. Set aside.

4. In a medium skillet, heat 2 tsp (10 mL) oil over low heat for about 2 minutes or until hot. Add fish and marinade, increase heat to medium and cook, turning fish once, for about 3 minutes per side or until fish is opaque and flakes easily when tested with a fork. Remove from heat and flake fish into chunks in the skillet.

5. Position a mini colander over the skillet and pour the fruit topping into the colander, letting the juices drip over the fish for added flavor. Set aside the fruit topping solids.

6. Arrange tortillas on a work surface and top with fish mixture, dividing evenly. Top with fruit topping and roll up tortilla, securing with a toothpick. Serve with black bean salad on the side.

Health Bite

Fruits — such as lime — that are high in vitamin C and other antioxidants can help your immune system fight germs like those that cause cold and flu.

Herb-Roasted Salmon with Garlic Mashed Potatoes

Lemon is one of Lisa's favorite fruits to cook with, and this recipe certainly highlights its versatility. The lemon dill marinade pairs perfectly with the salmon, which is high in omega-3 fatty acids and protein to balance out the carbohydrates from the potatoes. Serve with a side of asparagus to add a pop of green to this meal.

TIP

Substitute trout, tilapia or branzino for the salmon, reducing the baking time as necessary depending on the thickness of the fish.

- Preheat oven to 325°F (160°C)
- Ovenproof skillet

LEMON DILL MARINADE

3 tbsp	chopped fresh dill	45 mL
1 tsp	freshly ground black pepper	5 mL
Pinch	salt	Pinch
2 tbsp	freshly squeezed lemon juice	30 mL
2 tsp	olive oil	10 mL
2 tsp	Dijon mustard	10 mL
2	pieces (each 4 oz/125 g) skin-on salmon fillet	2
2	medium potatoes (unpeeled)	2
2 tbsp	sour cream	30 mL
1 tbsp	butter	15 mL
2	cloves garlic, minced	2
1 tsp	dried Italian seasoning	5 mL
1 tsp	olive oil	5 mL

1. *Lemon Dill Marinade:* Whisk together dill, pepper, salt, lemon juice, oil and mustard.

2. Place salmon in a sealable plastic bag and pour marinade over top. Seal bag and let marinate in the refrigerator for at least 1 hour or for up to 12 hours.

NUTRIENTS PER SERVING			
Calories	526	Fiber	5 g (20% DV)
Fat	25 g	Protein	34 g
Saturated fat	7 g	Calcium	100 mg (10% DV)
Sodium	294 mg (12% DV)	Iron	4 mg (22% DV)
Carbohydrate	40 g	Vitamin D	397 IU (99% DV)

If desired, garnish with fresh dill.

If preparing this recipe for one person, cut all of the ingredients in half. Or simply prepare the full recipe and save half for leftovers. Store salmon and potatoes in separate airtight containers in the refrigerator for up to 2 days. Reheat in the microwave on Medium (50%) power for 1 to 2 minutes or until heated through.

3. In a small pot of boiling water, cook potatoes for 30 minutes or until easily pierced with a fork. Drain. When cool enough to handle, cube potatoes and return to the pot. Add sour cream, butter, garlic and Italian seasoning. Use a potato masher or fork to mash potatoes until they reach a smooth consistency.

4. Meanwhile, in ovenproof skillet, heat oil over medium-high heat. Increase heat to high and transfer salmon to the skillet flesh-side down (reserving marinade). Sear for 1 minute.

5. Pour reserved marinade over salmon, flip salmon over and transfer skillet to preheated oven. Bake for 10 to 12 minutes or until fish is opaque and flakes easily when tested with a fork. Serve with potatoes.

Health Bite

For a sustainable choice, opt for wild-caught salmon instead of farm-raised. Farmed salmon may contain more contaminants and fewer omega-3 fatty acids.

Salmon with Peaches

Warm your soul with this sweet peach recipe. Serve with Brussels sprouts or your favorite vegetable side. Of course, feel free to add carbs to meet your grams per meal allotment.

TIPS

Leftover peaches? Use them in Cinnamon Chia Peach Pudding (page 224).

If preparing this recipe for two people, simply double all of the ingredients.

- **Preheat oven to 375°F (190°C)**
- **Baking sheet, lined with foil and sprayed with canola oil nonstick cooking spray**

1/2 cup	diced drained canned juice-packed peaches	125 mL
1/4 tsp	brown sugar	1 mL
1/4 tsp	ground ginger	1 mL
1/4 tsp	ground cinnamon	1 mL
1/4 tsp	vanilla extract	1 mL
1 tbsp	chopped fresh cilantro	15 mL
1	piece (4 oz/125 g) skin-on salmon fillet	1

1. In a medium bowl, combine peaches, brown sugar, ginger, cinnamon and vanilla; stir to mix thoroughly. Add cilantro, stirring until well combined.

2. Place salmon, skin side down, on prepared baking sheet. Spread peach mixture evenly across salmon.

3. Bake in preheated oven for 15 minutes or until salmon is opaque and flakes easily when tested with a fork and the peach mixture is ooey-gooey.

Health Bite

Salmon is a good source of omega-3 fatty acids, which can help prevent blood clots from forming and can protect against the development of irregular heartbeats.

NUTRIENTS PER SERVING			
Calories	341	Fiber	2 g (8% DV)
Fat	12 g	Protein	37 g
Saturated fat	2 g	Calcium	42 mg (4% DV)
Sodium	94 mg (4% DV)	Iron	2 mg (11% DV)
Carbohydrate	20 g	Vitamin D	493 IU (123% DV)

Weeknight Salmon Patties

When Lisa was growing up, her mom made this dinner on busy weeknights because it's simple, yet scrumptious. Serve over a bed of leafy greens or, if you and your dinner partner are looking to meet your meal's carbohydrate range, serve on 100% whole wheat hamburger buns for an additional 25 grams of carbohydrates each.

TIPS

Fifteen saltine crackers contain approximately the same number of carbohydrates (30 grams) as ½ cup (125 mL) dry whole wheat bread crumbs. So if you don't have saltine crackers, use bread crumbs!

If preparing this recipe for one person, cut all of the ingredients in half. Or simply prepare the full recipe and save half for leftovers. Store leftover patties in an airtight container in the refrigerator for up to 2 days. Reheat in the microwave on High for 1 to 2 minutes or until heated through.

- Medium skillet, sprayed with canola oil nonstick cooking spray

15	saltine crackers, crumbled	15
1	can (5 oz/142 g) water-packed boneless salmon, drained	1
1	clove garlic, minced	1
½ cup	finely chopped onion	125 mL
1	large egg	1
1 tbsp	low-sodium Worcestershire sauce (such as Robbie's Worcestershire Pure & Mild Sauce)	15 mL
1 tsp	garlic powder	5 mL
½ tsp	freshly ground black pepper	2 mL

1. In a medium bowl, use your hands to mix together saltine crackers, salmon, garlic, onion, egg, Worcestershire sauce, garlic powder and pepper. Shape into 4 equally sized patties, about ¾ inch (2 cm) thick.

2. In prepared skillet, cook salmon patties over medium-high heat, turning once, for about 4 minutes per side or until beginning to brown.

Health Bite

Incredibly high in vitamin D, at about 400 IUs per serving, this recipe is packed with nutrition.

NUTRIENTS PER SERVING			
Calories	265	Fiber	2 g (8% DV)
Fat	8 g	Protein	23 g
Saturated fat	2 g	Calcium	243 mg (24% DV)
Sodium	328 mg (14% DV)	Iron	3 mg (17% DV)
Carbohydrate	25 g	Vitamin D	433 IU (108% DV)

Swordfish Steaks with Lemon and Mustard Vinaigrette

You don't have to go to a fancy seafood restaurant to enjoy a top-notch swordfish steak. The flavor of the fish is elevated by the tangy vinaigrette. Serve with roasted asparagus.

TIP

Garnish each portion with a tarragon leaf and a slice of lemon.

- Preheat oven to 375°F (190°C)
- Ovenproof skillet

2	pieces (each 5 oz/150 g) swordfish steak (about 1 inch/2.5 cm thick)	2
1/2 tsp	freshly ground black pepper	2 mL
Pinch	salt	Pinch
1/2	lemon	1/2
1 tbsp	butter	15 mL
1	clove garlic, minced	1

LEMON AND MUSTARD VINAIGRETTE

2 tbsp	freshly squeezed lemon juice	30 mL
1 tbsp	Dijon mustard	15 mL
1 tsp	olive oil	5 mL
1 tsp	dried tarragon	5 mL

1. Place swordfish on a plate. Season both sides of swordfish with pepper and salt. Drizzle lemon juice over both sides.

2. In ovenproof skillet, melt butter over medium-high heat. Add garlic and cook, stirring, for 1 minute. Arrange swordfish in skillet and sear, turning once, for 1 to 2 minutes per side or until lightly browned.

3. Transfer skillet to preheated oven and bake for about 10 minutes or until fish is opaque and flakes easily when tested with a fork.

NUTRIENTS PER SERVING			
Calories	335	Fiber	1 g (4% DV)
Fat	20 g	Protein	34 g
Saturated fat	7 g	Calcium	26 mg (3% DV)
Sodium	474 mg (20% DV)	Iron	1 mg (6% DV)
Carbohydrate	4 g	Vitamin D	948 IU (237% DV)

TIP

If preparing this recipe for one person, cut all of the ingredients in half. Or simply prepare the full recipe and save half for leftovers. Store leftovers in an airtight container in the refrigerator for up to 2 days. Reheat in the microwave on Medium (50%) power for 1 to 2 minutes or until heated through.

4. *Lemon and Mustard Vinaigrette:* Meanwhile, in a small saucepan, whisk together lemon juice, mustard, oil and tarragon; bring to a simmer over low heat. Simmer, whisking, for 3 minutes or until slightly thickened.

5. Transfer swordfish to a serving dish and pour heated vinaigrette on top.

Health Bite

According to the U.S. Food and Drug Administration, almost all fish contain traces of mercury. In general, the mercury found in fish and shellfish will not cause harm to the general public. However, women who are planning on becoming pregnant or who are pregnant, nursing mothers and young children should be cautious with their mercury intake. It is recommended that these groups of people avoid shark, swordfish, king mackerel and tilefish, since these fish contain high concentrations of mercury.

Tuna Casserole

MAKES 2 SERVINGS

Craving comfort? This tuna casserole brings you back to fond memories of Grandma's kitchen! This recipe is diabetes-friendly and has been tailored to meet your nutrition needs. The whole wheat noodles, carrots and celery not only add fiber, they add crunch for even more mouth satisfaction.

TIPS

Serve with a side of steamed or roasted broccoli.

If preparing this recipe for one person, cut all of the ingredients in half. Or simply prepare the full recipe and save half for leftovers. Store leftovers in an airtight container in the refrigerator for up to 2 days. Reheat in the microwave on High for 1 to 2 minutes or until heated through.

- Preheat oven to 375°F (190°C)
- 9-inch (23 cm) square glass baking dish

6 oz	whole wheat elbow macaroni	175 g
2 tsp	olive oil	10 mL
1 cup	finely chopped onion	250 mL
1/2 cup	diced celery	125 mL
1/4 cup	diced carrots	60 mL
2	cans (each 5 to 6 oz/142 to 170 g) water-packed, no-salt-added chunk light tuna, drained (about 5 oz/150 g drained)	2
1/2	can (10 oz/284 mL) condensed cream of mushroom soup	1/2
1 tbsp	dry bread crumbs	15 mL

1. In a pot of boiling water, cook macaroni according to package directions until al dente. Drain and set aside.

2. In a medium saucepan, heat oil over medium heat. Add onion, celery and carrots; cook, stirring occasionally, for about 10 minutes or until onion is translucent and carrots are tender. Transfer to baking dish and add tuna, soup and cooked noodles; stir gently until combined.

3. Bake in preheated oven for about 20 minutes or until mushroom sauce is bubbling. Remove casserole from the oven and preheat the broiler. Sprinkle casserole with bread crumbs and broil for 5 minutes or until golden brown.

Health Bite

Tuna is a good low-saturated-fat source of protein.

NUTRIENTS PER SERVING			
Calories	377	Fiber	5 g (20% DV)
Fat	8 g	Protein	38 g
Saturated fat	1 g	Calcium	108 mg (11% DV)
Sodium	329 mg (14% DV)	Iron	3 mg (17% DV)
Carbohydrate	32 g	Vitamin D	206 IU (52% DV)

Peel-and-Eat Old Bay Shrimp

Cover your kitchen table with newspaper and tie a bib around your neck. Think gingham or red-and-white for the classic picnic theme. This four-ingredient recipe will be a feast for your senses, especially touch. You are never too young or old to eat finger foods, especially peel-and-eat shrimp! This recipe was inspired by the Cross Street Market, located at Federal Hill in Baltimore, Maryland. It goes great with a cold beer and french fries.

TIPS

Use reduced-sodium Old Bay seasoning if you have high blood pressure or want to limit your sodium intake.

If you are a big fan of Old Bay seasoning, increase to 3 tbsp (45 mL).

If preparing this recipe for one person, cut all of the ingredients in half. Or simply prepare the full recipe and save half for leftovers. Store leftovers in an airtight container in the refrigerator for up to 2 days. Reheat in the microwave on Medium (50%) power for 1 to 2 minutes or until heated through.

- Preheat barbecue grill to medium
- Three 12-inch (30 cm) wooden skewers, soaked for 30 minutes

10 oz	deveined shell-on medium shrimp	300 g
¼ cup	olive oil	60 mL
1 tbsp	freshly squeezed lemon juice	15 mL
2 tbsp	Old Bay seasoning (see tips, at left)	30 mL

1. In a large bowl, toss shrimp with oil and lemon juice. Season with Old Bay seasoning; toss to coat thoroughly.

2. Push shrimp onto skewers (through the meat near the head of the shrimp) and arrange on preheated grill; grill, turning once, for about 4 minutes per side or until pink, firm and opaque. Slide shrimp off skewers and serve.

Health Bite

The antioxidant astaxanthin, which provides the pinkish color to shrimp, is associated with a reduction in inflammation, a known trigger of disease and aging.

NUTRIENTS PER SERVING			
Calories	624	Fiber	0 g (0% DV)
Fat	54 g	Protein	34 g
Saturated fat	8 g	Calcium	102 mg (10% DV)
Sodium	319 mg (13% DV)	Iron	1 mg (6% DV)
Carbohydrate	2 g	Vitamin D	0 IU (0% DV)

Grilled Shrimp and Kale Caesar

Eat this salad when you need to feel satiated. The kale Caesar will let your belly know it has been fed by providing bulk from the kale and a decent amount of fat from the olive oil and anchovy paste.

TIPS

Add ¾ cup (175 mL) cooked quinoa or your favorite grain to the salad.

If preparing this recipe for one person, cut all of the ingredients in half. This salad doesn't work well as leftovers.

Health Bite

Vitamin K helps with blood clotting. Many people who take blood-thinning medication avoid all vegetables containing vitamin K, such as kale and broccoli, because they fear the vitamin will counter their medication. However, if you talk with your medical doctor, you can determine an amount of vitamin K–containing foods to eat every single day (but never skipping a day).

KALE CAESAR

5 oz	kale, stemmed (about 3¼ cups/800 mL)	150 g
¼ cup	extra virgin olive oil	60 mL
1 tbsp	Dijon mustard	15 mL
1½ tsp	apple cider vinegar	7 mL
1 tsp	anchovy paste	5 mL
½ tsp	Worcestershire sauce	2 mL
1	clove garlic, minced	1
¼ tsp	freshly cracked black pepper	1 mL
Pinch	sea salt	Pinch

SHRIMP

1 tsp	olive oil	5 mL
1	clove garlic, minced	1
8 oz	medium shrimp, peeled and deveined	250 g
¼ cup	ready-to-use low-sodium chicken or vegetable broth	60 mL

1. *Kale Caesar:* Chop kale into bite-size pieces and transfer to a medium bowl.

2. In a small bowl, stir together oil, mustard, vinegar, anchovy paste, Worcestershire sauce and garlic. Season with pepper and salt. Pour dressing over kale, toss and let marinate while you prepare the shrimp.

3. *Shrimp:* In a small skillet, heat oil over medium heat. Add garlic and cook, stirring, for 1 minute. Add shrimp and pour broth over shrimp. Reduce heat to medium-low and cook, stirring often, for about 5 minutes or until shrimp are pink, firm and opaque.

4. Top the kale Caesar with shrimp and serve.

NUTRIENTS PER SERVING			
Calories	467	Fiber	7 g (28% DV)
Fat	30 g	Protein	35 g
Saturated fat	4 g	Calcium	328 mg (33% DV)
Sodium	693 mg (29% DV)	Iron	2 mg (11% DV)
Carbohydrate	21 g	Vitamin D	2 IU (0% DV)

Rosemary and Garlic Shrimp Bruschetta

You no longer have to avoid bruschetta! This recipe is portioned to meet your needs. Entertain your savory side with this shrimp recipe. Serve with a salad for a pop of color and to make a complete meal.

TIPS

Easily substitute crumbled feta cheese for the mozzarella in this recipe.

Garnish each baguette slice with 1 tsp (5 mL) chopped fresh basil and a drizzle of balsamic vinaigrette before serving.

If preparing this recipe for one person, cut all of the ingredients in half.

Health Bite

While shrimp is known for being a source of cholesterol, all fish and animal products contain cholesterol. What matters is the saturated fat! Be mindful of saturated fats, which the body turns into cholesterol.

- Preheat oven to 375°F (190°C)

4	slices (each about 1 inch/2.5 cm thick) French baguette	4
2 tsp	olive oil, divided	10 mL
10	extra-large shrimp, peeled and deveined	10
1 tsp	freshly ground black pepper	5 mL
1 tsp	garlic powder	5 mL
1 tsp	dried rosemary	5 mL
½ cup	diced plum (Roma) tomatoes	125 mL
2 tbsp	shredded mozzarella cheese	30 mL

1. Brush one side of baguette slices with half the oil and arrange on a baking sheet.

2. In a medium bowl, season shrimp with pepper, garlic powder and rosemary; stir to coat.

3. In a medium skillet, heat the remaining oil over medium-high heat. Add shrimp and cook, stirring, for about 5 minutes or until pink, firm and opaque. Transfer to a bowl and let cool for about 10 minutes or until cool enough to handle.

4. Dice shrimp and transfer to a clean bowl. Add tomatoes and stir to combine.

5. Distribute shrimp mixture on top of baguette slices, dividing equally. Top with cheese. Bake in preheated oven for about 5 minutes or until edges of bread are golden brown and cheese is melted.

NUTRIENTS PER SERVING			
Calories	284	Fiber	3 g (12% DV)
Fat	7 g	Protein	15 g
Saturated fat	2 g	Calcium	80 mg (8% DV)
Sodium	505 mg (21% DV)	Iron	3 mg (17% DV)
Carbohydrate	42 g	Vitamin D	2 IU (0% DV)

Stir-Fried Peppered Shrimp with Cockles

This recipe is worth every minute of preparation. If you don't have a traditional molcajete (typically used for making guacamole), you can easily use your mortar and pestle. Cockles are small saltwater clams that add such fun and flavor to this recipe. Go ahead, flex your muscles and work for your meal.

TIPS

The U.S. Food and Drug Administration recommends that people do a "tap test" to determine if clams are safe to cook. If a live clam closes upon tapping, it is safe to cook. If it remains open, do not use it. After cooking, eat only cockles that have opened.

While peanut oil adds great flavor, feel free to swap in canola oil in this recipe.

- Mortar and pestle (or molcajete)
- Large skillet or wok with lid

2 tbsp	whole black peppercorns	30 mL
3 tbsp	all-purpose flour	45 mL
Pinch	sea salt	Pinch
8 oz	medium shrimp, peeled and deveined	250 g
3 tsp	peanut oil, divided	15 mL
2 cups	shredded green cabbage	500 mL
2 cups	snow peas, stemmed	500 mL
1	hot red chile pepper, seeded and chopped	1
4 oz	cockles (little clams), rinsed	125 g
1 tbsp	freshly squeezed lime juice	15 mL
1 tbsp	reduced-sodium tamari	15 mL

1. In large skillet, lightly toast peppercorns over medium heat, about 2 minutes. Transfer to mortar and pestle. Add flour and salt; grind until the mixture is powderlike. Transfer to a bowl.

2. Dredge shrimp in the flour mixture, turning to coat evenly, and transfer to a plate. Discard any excess flour mixture.

3. In the same skillet (no need to wash it), heat 2 tsp (10 mL) oil over medium-high heat. Add shrimp and cook, turning once, for about 3 minutes per side or until pink, firm and opaque. Transfer shrimp to a plate lined with paper towel.

NUTRIENTS PER SERVING			
Calories	319	Fiber	4 g (16% DV)
Fat	8 g	Protein	40 g
Saturated fat	1 g	Calcium	160 mg (16% DV)
Sodium	599 mg (25% DV)	Iron	12 mg (67% DV)
Carbohydrate	24 g	Vitamin D	1 IU (0% DV)

TIPS

We've used a reduced-sodium tamari with 700 mg sodium per tablespoon (15 mL) for the nutrient analysis for this recipe. If you wish to reduce the sodium further, look for a "Lite" product with even lower sodium (about 50% less than regular). If the tamari you have has more sodium listed on the label, reduce the amount you add to the recipe, or factor in the increase in sodium to your meal.

If preparing this recipe for one person, cut all of the ingredients in half. This recipe doesn't work well as leftovers.

4. In the same skillet (no need to wash it), heat the remaining oil (only if pan seems dry) over high heat. Add cabbage and snow peas; stir-fry for about 3 minutes or until softened slightly but still bright in color. Add red chile, cockles, lime juice and tamari. Cook, covered, until cockles open, about 5 minutes.

5. Add shrimp to skillet, stir and immediately remove from heat. Divide and serve immediately.

Health Bite

Fiber found in cabbage helps to prevent constipation and maintain a health digestive system.

Pasta and Shrimp with Spicy Tomato Spinach and Cream Sauce

Learning how to incorporate pasta into living every day with diabetes is essential. This dish is inspired by favorite dishes, such as penne à la vodka and fettuccine Alfredo. It's moderated by whole wheat pasta and balanced by the protein in the shrimp.

TIP

To make this recipe gluten-free, swap the whole wheat pasta for brown rice pasta or quinoa pasta.

4 oz	whole wheat pasta (such as spaghetti)	125 g
3 tsp	olive oil, divided	15 mL
1	clove garlic, minced	1
8 oz	medium shrimp, peeled and deveined	250 g
1½ tsp	hot pepper flakes	7 mL
¼ cup	diced dry-packed sun-dried tomatoes	60 mL
1½ cups	diced fresh tomatoes	375 mL
1 cup	packed trimmed spinach leaves	250 mL
¼ cup	heavy or whipping (35%) cream	60 mL
2 tbsp	grated Parmesan cheese	30 mL

1. In a medium pot of boiling water, cook pasta according to package directions or until al dente. Drain and set aside.

2. In a medium skillet, heat 2 tsp (10 mL) oil over medium heat. Add garlic and cook, stirring, for 1 minute. Add shrimp, increase heat to high and cook, turning once, for 3 to 4 minutes per side or until shrimp are pink, firm and opaque. Remove from heat and set aside.

3. In a medium saucepan, heat hot pepper flakes over medium heat and toast for 30 seconds. Add the remaining oil and sun-dried tomatoes; cook, stirring occasionally, for 30 seconds. Add fresh tomatoes and bring to a simmer; simmer for 2 minutes.

NUTRIENTS PER SERVING			
Calories	419	Fiber	5 g (20% DV)
Fat	21 g	Protein	35 g
Saturated fat	9 g	Calcium	191 mg (19% DV)
Sodium	454 mg (19% DV)	Iron	3 mg (17% DV)
Carbohydrate	27 g	Vitamin D	21 IU (5% DV)

If preparing this recipe for one person, cut all of the ingredients in half. Or simply prepare the full recipe and save half for leftovers. Store leftovers in an airtight container in the refrigerator for up to 2 days. Reheat in the microwave on Medium (50%) power for 1 to 2 minutes or until heated through; moisten with a little water, if necessary.

4. Add spinach and cream; cook, stirring occasionally, for 2 minutes. Add shrimp mixture and cooked pasta. Toss together and cook, stirring gently, for 1 minute or until heated through. Divide mixture between bowls, top with cheese and serve.

Health Bite

The antioxidant astaxanthin, which provides the pinkish color to shrimp, is associated with a reduction in inflammation, a known trigger of disease and aging.

Baked Seafood Scampi with Shrimp and Clams

Escape to Cape Cod without leaving your kitchen! Garlicky clams, buttery shrimp and tender-crisp asparagus — yum, yum, yum! Serve with an arugula side salad.

TIP

Wash clams thoroughly by scrubbing their shells. Do not use any clams that have an odor. In a large pot, submerge clams in 8 cups (2 L) lukewarm water mixed with 1 tsp (5 mL) salt and let soak in the refrigerator for 20 minutes before cooking. (Make sure clams are completely submerged; add more water if necessary.) Drain water and repeat this process two times, for a total of 1 hour. Do not use any clams that float.

- Preheat oven to 350°F (180°C)
- Large ovenproof skillet with lid

4 oz	whole-grain angel-hair pasta	125 g
2 tbsp	unsalted butter, divided	30 mL
2	cloves garlic, minced	2
1/2	medium onion, sliced	1/2
3/4 cup	dry white wine (such as pinot grigio)	175 mL
1/4 cup	freshly squeezed lemon juice	60 mL
1 lb	clams (about 10; littlenecks or steamers recommended), soaked and chilled (see tip, at left)	500 g
10	extra-large shrimp, peeled and deveined	10
1 tsp	freshly ground black pepper	5 mL
12	spears asparagus (ends snapped off), chopped	12
2 tbsp	coarsely chopped pine nuts	30 mL
1/4 cup	grated Parmesan cheese	60 mL
1 tsp	chopped fresh flat-leaf (Italian) parsley	5 mL

1. In a large pot of boiling water, cook pasta according to package directions. Drain and set aside.

2. In ovenproof skillet, melt 1 tbsp (15 mL) butter over medium-high heat. Add garlic, onion, wine and lemon juice; stir to combine. Bring to a boil, stirring, and cook for about 2 minutes or until onion is translucent and liquid is simmering. Add clams and the remaining butter, cover and cook for 10 to 12 minutes or until clams open. Discard any clams that do not open.

NUTRIENTS PER SERVING			
Calories	570	Fiber	9 g (36% DV)
Fat	22 g	Protein	28 g
Saturated fat	10 g	Calcium	219 mg (22% DV)
Sodium	832 mg (35% DV)	Iron	9 mg (50% DV)
Carbohydrate	49 g	Vitamin D	4 IU (1% DV)

TIP

If preparing this recipe for one person, cut all of the ingredients in half. Or simply prepare the full recipe and save half for leftovers. Store leftovers in an airtight container in the refrigerator for up to 2 days. Reheat in the microwave on Medium-High (70%) power for 1 to 2 minutes or until heated through.

3. While clams are cooking, season shrimp with pepper. Add shrimp and asparagus to skillet. Cover and cook for about 3 minutes or until shrimp are pink, firm and opaque and asparagus is tender-crisp.

4. Add pasta to mixture in skillet. Sprinkle with pine nuts and Parmesan; toss to combine. Transfer skillet to preheated oven and bake, uncovered, for 3 to 5 minutes or until cheese is melted and sauce is bubbling. Divide into two portions and garnish with parsley.

Health Bite

The whole-grain angel-hair pasta in this dish adds fiber to lower the total carbohydrates absorbed by the body.

Angel-Hair Pasta with Shrimp, Sun-Dried Tomatoes and Peppers

MAKES 2 SERVINGS

Want a taste of the Mediterranean in under 30 minutes? Try this savory dish to take your taste buds on a trip. Serve with a side of sautéed spinach or broccoli.

TIPS

You can substitute Romano or manchego cheese for the fontina.

Garnish with fresh basil or parsley.

If preparing this recipe for one person, cut all of the ingredients in half. Or simply prepare the full recipe and save half for leftovers. Store leftovers in an airtight container in the refrigerator for up to 2 days. Reheat in the microwave on Medium (50%) power for 1 to 2 minutes or until heated through.

Health Bite

Red bell peppers are commonly recognized for having higher amounts of antioxidants, but green peppers are also a significant source of phytochemicals as well.

12	medium shrimp, peeled and deveined	12
1 tsp	freshly ground black pepper	5 mL
1 tsp	dried Italian seasoning	5 mL
4 oz	angel-hair pasta	125 g
2 tsp	olive oil	10 mL
1	clove garlic, minced	1
1	medium green bell pepper, finely chopped	1
1/2 cup	dry-packed sun-dried tomatoes, finely chopped	125 mL
1/4 cup	chopped onion	60 mL
1/2 cup	shredded fontina cheese	125 mL
1 tsp	hot pepper flakes	5 mL

1. In a medium bowl, season shrimp with pepper and Italian seasoning, tossing to coat. Set aside.

2. In a pot of boiling water, cook pasta according to package directions. Drain and set aside.

3. In a large skillet, heat oil over medium-high heat. Add garlic, green pepper, sun-dried tomatoes and onion. Cook, stirring occasionally, for about 2 minutes or until green pepper is tender-crisp and onion is slightly softened.

4. Add seasoned shrimp to skillet and cook, stirring occasionally, for 5 minutes or until shrimp are pink, firm and opaque. Remove from heat.

5. Add pasta to skillet. Top with cheese and sprinkle with hot pepper flakes. Toss and serve immediately.

NUTRIENTS PER SERVING			
Calories	454	Fiber	6 g (24% DV)
Fat	15 g	Protein	28 g
Saturated fat	6 g	Calcium	167 mg (17% DV)
Sodium	425 mg (18% DV)	Iron	4 mg (22% DV)
Carbohydrate	55 g	Vitamin D	6 IU (2% DV)

Shrimp Pad Thai

MAKES 2 SERVINGS

Here's a favorite Vietnamese dish made delicious by the full-flavored fish sauce. Using just the right amount of fish sauce is key to making this dish irresistible.

TIPS

We've used a reduced-sodium soy sauce with 550 mg sodium per tablespoon (15 mL) for the nutrient analysis for this recipe. If you wish to reduce the sodium further, look for a "Lite" product with even lower sodium (about 50% less than regular). If the soy sauce you have has more sodium listed on the label, reduce the amount you add to the recipe, or factor in the increase in sodium to your meal.

To make this a vegetarian meal, swap the shrimp for 1 package (14 oz/400 g) extra-firm tofu, cubed, and 2 eggs, scrambled.

If preparing this recipe for one person, cut all of the ingredients in half. Or simply prepare the full recipe up to the end of step 3 and save half for leftovers. Store leftovers in an airtight container in the refrigerator for up to 2 days. Reheat in the microwave on Medium (50%) power for 1 to 2 minutes, or until heated through, and continue with step 4.

4 oz	long, thin brown rice noodles	125 g
2 tbsp	smooth natural peanut butter	30 mL
1 tbsp	reduced-sodium soy sauce	15 mL
2 tsp	Sriracha	10 mL
1 tsp	fish sauce	5 mL
1 tsp	unseasoned rice vinegar	5 mL
2 tsp	peanut oil	10 mL
10	medium shrimp, peeled and deveined	10
1	clove garlic, minced	1
1	green onion, chopped	1
1/2 cup	bean sprouts	125 mL
10	unsalted roasted peanuts, chopped	10
1	lime, halved	1
1 tbsp	chopped fresh cilantro	15 mL

1. In a large pot of boiling water, cook noodles according to package directions. Drain and set aside.

2. In a small bowl, whisk together peanut butter, soy sauce, Sriracha, fish sauce and vinegar.

3. In a medium skillet, heat oil over medium-high heat. Add shrimp and cook, turning once, for 2 to 3 minutes per side or until shrimp are pink, firm and opaque. Add garlic, green onion, noodles and peanut butter sauce; mix thoroughly.

4. Divide mixture between two bowls. Top evenly with bean sprouts and peanuts; squeeze a half lime over each bowl. Garnish with cilantro.

Health Bite

Shrimp are higher in cholesterol than most types of meat and poultry, but they're also lower in saturated fat.

NUTRIENTS PER SERVING			
Calories	434	Fiber	6 g (24% DV)
Fat	18 g	Protein	19 g
Saturated fat	3.4 g	Calcium	67 mg (7% DV)
Sodium	674 mg (28% DV)	Iron	2 mg (11% DV)
Carbohydrate	56 g	Vitamin D	0 IU (0% DV)

Fried Cauliflower Rice with Shrimp

There's no question that shrimp fried rice is a staple at most Chinese restaurants. This modified takeout favorite will exceed your flavor expectations. You'll be reaching for a cutting board rather than a menu!

TIPS

We've used a reduced-sodium soy sauce with 550 mg sodium per tablespoon (15 mL) for the nutrient analysis for this recipe. If you wish to reduce the sodium further, look for a "Lite" product with even lower sodium (about 50% less than regular). If the soy sauce you have has more sodium listed on the label, reduce the amount you add to the recipe, or factor in the increase in sodium to your meal.

If you like a little kick of heat, try adding 1 tsp (5 mL) Sriracha per serving — either in step 3 with the vegetables or on top of the dish before eating.

- Food processor

1	medium head of cauliflower, roughly chopped (about 2½ cups/625 mL)	1
1 tbsp	olive oil, divided	15 mL
2	cloves garlic, minced	2
12	extra-large shrimp, peeled and deveined	12
2	green onions, chopped	2
1 cup	snow peas, stemmed	250 mL
1 cup	sliced mushrooms	250 mL
½ cup	chopped carrots	125 mL
½ cup	finely chopped onion	125 mL
2	large eggs	2
1 tbsp	reduced-sodium soy sauce	15 mL

1. In food processor, pulse cauliflower until the consistency is similar to rice.

2. In a large skillet, heat half the oil over medium-high heat. Add garlic and cook, stirring, for 1 minute. Add shrimp and cook, stirring occasionally, for 3 to 5 minutes or until pink, firm and opaque. Transfer shrimp to a plate and set aside.

NUTRIENTS PER SERVING			
Calories	239	Fiber	7 g (28% DV)
Fat	11 g	Protein	17 g
Saturated fat	2 g	Calcium	117 mg (12% DV)
Sodium	487 mg (20% DV)	Iron	3 mg (17% DV)
Carbohydrate	21 g	Vitamin D	50 IU (13% DV)

TIP

If preparing this recipe for one person, cut all of the ingredients in half. Or simply prepare the full recipe and save half for leftovers. Store leftovers in an airtight container in the refrigerator for up to 2 days. Reheat in the microwave on Medium (50%) power for 1 to 2 minutes or until heated through.

3. Add chopped cauliflower to skillet and use a spatula to evenly flatten cauliflower; cook, stirring occasionally, for 4 to 5 minutes or until it starts to brown. Add the remaining oil to skillet; stir to combine. Add green onions, snow peas, mushrooms, carrots and onion. Reduce heat to medium and cook, stirring often, for about 5 minutes or until vegetables are tender-crisp.

4. Make two wells in the middle of the vegetable mixture and crack in eggs. Scramble eggs into mixture, cooking just until eggs are set. Add shrimp and soy sauce to skillet and stir to thoroughly combine.

Health Bite

Using cauliflower instead of white rice avoids an unwanted spike in blood sugar without losing the crunch and flavor of fried rice.

Barbecue Chicken with Corn Muffins

MAKES 2 SERVINGS

There's nothing like chicken drowning in tangy barbecue sauce with freshly baked corn muffins. If desired, pat some butter on the steaming-hot muffins as soon as they come out of the oven.

TIPS

Serve with a bowl of steamed greens, such as collard greens or Swiss chard.

If you eat foods with gluten, you can use an equal amount of all-purpose flour in place of the quinoa flour.

If preparing this recipe for one person, cut all of the ingredients in half. Or simply prepare the full recipe and save half for leftovers. Store chicken leftovers in an airtight container in the refrigerator for up to 2 days (corn muffins can be stored in an airtight container at room temperature). Reheat chicken in the microwave on High for 1 to 2 minutes or until heated through.

Health Bite

Stone-ground cornmeal still contains the bran and hull, which makes it a good source of fiber and nutrients.

- Preheat oven to 425°F (220°C)
- Muffin pan, 4 cups lined with paper liners

2	boneless skinless chicken breasts (each 5 oz/150 g)	2
3 tbsp	barbecue sauce	45 mL
1/2 cup	stone-ground cornmeal	125 mL
1/4 cup	quinoa flour	60 mL
1 tbsp	granulated sugar	15 mL
1/4 tsp	baking powder	1 mL
1/4 tsp	ground cinnamon	1 mL
1 tbsp	drained canned corn	15 mL
1	large egg	1
1/2 cup	milk	125 mL
1 1/2 tsp	canola oil	7 mL
1/4 tsp	vanilla extract	1 mL

1. Arrange chicken breasts on a baking sheet and brush with barbecue sauce. Bake in preheated oven for about 30 minutes or until chicken is no longer pink inside.

2. Meanwhile, in a medium bowl, combine cornmeal, flour, sugar, baking powder and cinnamon.

3. In a small bowl, whisk together corn, egg, milk, oil and vanilla. Add corn mixture to flour mixture and stir just until moistened.

4. Divide batter equally among prepared muffin cups. Bake alongside chicken in preheated oven for about 20 minutes or until golden brown and a tester inserted in the center of a corn muffin comes out clean. Let cool in pan on a wire rack for about 3 minutes before serving.

NUTRIENTS PER SERVING			
Calories	588	Fiber	3 g (12% DV)
Fat	15 g	Protein	53 g
Saturated fat	4 g	Calcium	157 mg (16% DV)
Sodium	519 mg (22% DV)	Iron	4 mg (22% DV)
Carbohydrate	57 g	Vitamin D	59 IU (15% DV)

Baked Chicken with Dates, Capers and Olives

MAKES 2 SERVINGS

This simple yet satisfying dish is perfect for a relaxing Sunday night dinner. Prepare on Saturday to allow enough time for the rich flavors to develop. Enjoy with ½ cup (125 mL) couscous or ⅓ cup (75 mL) cooked pasta to stay within your carbohydrate range for this dinner. Alternatively, this is a great recipe to serve right before you indulge in a dessert.

TIP

If preparing this recipe for one person, cut all of the ingredients in half. Or simply prepare the full recipe and save half for leftovers. Store leftovers in an airtight container in the refrigerator for up to 2 days. Reheat in the microwave on High for 1 to 2 minutes or until heated through.

4	skinless chicken thighs (each about 3 to 4 oz/90 to 125 g)	4
½ tsp	freshly ground black pepper	2 mL
4	pitted dates, diced	4
3	cloves garlic, minced	3
2 tbsp	chopped pitted green olives	30 mL
1 tbsp	caper juice	15 mL
2 tbsp	drained capers	30 mL
1 tbsp	olive oil	15 mL
1 tbsp	red wine vinegar	15 mL
½ tsp	dried oregano	2 mL
¼ cup	dry white wine	60 mL

1. In a large glass bowl, season chicken thighs with pepper. Add dates, garlic, olives, caper juice, capers, oil, vinegar and oregano; stir to combine. Cover and refrigerate for up to 24 hours.

2. Preheat oven to 400°F (200°F).

3. Transfer chicken mixture to a large baking dish, spreading evenly. Pour white wine over top.

4. Bake for 35 to 40 minutes, basting with pan juices occasionally, until juices run clear when chicken is pierced and internal temperature of chicken reaches 165°F (74°C).

Health Bite

According to the National Institutes of Health, garlic is used to treat several conditions associated with the blood system and heart, such as high cholesterol, atherosclerosis, heart attack and hypertension.

NUTRIENTS PER SERVING			
Calories	426	Fiber	3 g (12% DV)
Fat	26 g	Protein	34 g
Saturated fat	6 g	Calcium	43 mg (4% DV)
Sodium	365 mg (15% DV)	Iron	3 mg (17% DV)
Carbohydrate	14 g	Vitamin D	11 IU (3% DV)

Mama's Chicken Parmesan

Somehow Laura's German mother taught her how to make the best Italian food. The secrets? Wheat germ, no-added-sugar tomato sauce and, of course, a big, heaping portion of love.

TIPS

If preferred, use canola oil instead of olive oil.

Plate each serving with 1 oz (30 g) whole wheat noodles, cooked, and/or steamed greens.

If preparing this recipe for one person, cut all of the ingredients in half. Or simply prepare the full recipe and save half for leftovers. Store leftovers in an airtight container in the refrigerator for up to 2 days. Reheat in the microwave on High for 1 to 2 minutes or until heated through.

Health Bite

Wheat germ is free of sodium but is packed with folate, vitamin E, potassium, zinc, iron and magnesium. In just 2 tbsp (30 mL), there are 50 calories and 4 grams of protein!

- Preheat oven to 375°F (190°C)
- 9-inch (23 cm) square glass baking dish

1	large egg	1
³⁄₄ cup	2% milk	175 mL
¹⁄₂ cup	dry bread crumbs	125 mL
2 tbsp	wheat germ	30 mL
1 tbsp	dried oregano	15 mL
8 oz	chicken breast cutlets, thinly sliced	250 g
2 tbsp	olive oil	30 mL
1 cup	no-sugar-added tomato sauce	250 mL
2 oz	mozzarella cheese, thinly sliced	60 g

1. In a wide, shallow container, whisk together egg and milk.

2. In another wide, shallow container, stir together bread crumbs, wheat germ and oregano.

3. Working with one chicken slice at a time, dip chicken into egg mixture, letting excess liquid drain off, then dredge through bread crumb mixture, coating thinly and evenly. As they are coated, transfer to a plate. Discard any excess egg and bread crumb mixtures.

4. In a large skillet, heat oil over medium heat. Arrange chicken slices in the skillet and cook, turning once, for 2 or 3 minutes per side or until golden brown. Transfer to a plate lined with paper towel.

5. Spoon ¹⁄₄ cup (60 mL) tomato sauce into baking dish and spread to coat. Arrange chicken slices on top. Spoon ¹⁄₂ cup (125 mL) tomato sauce over chicken and top with cheese. Add remaining tomato sauce over cheese.

6. Bake in preheated oven for 15 minutes or until cheese is melted and sauce is bubbling.

NUTRIENTS PER SERVING			
Calories	586	Fiber	5 g (20% DV)
Fat	29 g	Protein	45 g
Saturated fat	8 g	Calcium	378 mg (38% DV)
Sodium	532 mg (22% DV)	Iron	4 mg (22% DV)
Carbohydrate	38 g	Vitamin D	71 IU (18% DV)

Chicken Burrito Bowl

Prepare your own Mexican quick fix with this Chipotle-inspired bowl. Carbs are moderated by filling the bowl with beans, extra veggies and chicken. No need for rice, since the beans count as carbs.

TIPS

Use the remaining black beans in Spicy Black Bean Burgers (page 132).

If you love tomatoes, increase the quantity to ½ cup (125 mL), but note that the carbohydrates will also increase.

If preparing this recipe for one person, cut all of the ingredients in half. Or simply prepare the full recipe up to the end of step 2 and store leftover chicken and vegetable-bean mixture in separate airtight containers in the refrigerator for up to 2 days. Reheat in the microwave on High for 1 to 2 minutes, or until heated through, and continue with step 3.

Health Bite

The iron, calcium, magnesium, manganese, copper and zinc in black beans help to keep bones strong and healthy.

6 oz	boneless skinless chicken breast (about 1 medium)	175 g
¼ tsp	chili powder	1 mL
¼ tsp	chipotle chile powder	1 mL
2 tsp	olive oil, divided	10 mL
½ cup	chopped onion	125 mL
½ cup	chopped green bell pepper	125 mL
½ cup	rinsed drained canned black beans	125 mL
1 cup	chopped romaine lettuce	250 mL
2 tbsp	diced tomato	30 mL
2 tbsp	shredded Mexican blend cheese	30 mL
2 tbsp	sour cream	30 mL
½	avocado, sliced	½
2 tbsp	chopped fresh cilantro	30 mL

1. Season chicken with chili powder and chipotle powder. In a medium skillet, heat 1 tsp (5 mL) oil over medium-high heat. Add chicken and cook, turning once, for 4 minutes per side or until no longer pink inside. Transfer chicken to a cutting board and let rest for 10 minutes, then cut into cubes.

2. In the same skillet (no need to wash it), heat the remaining oil over medium heat. Add onion and green pepper; cook, stirring, for about 8 minutes or until tender-crisp. Reduce heat to medium-low, add black beans and cook, stirring, until heated through.

3. Divide romaine lettuce and tomatoes between two bowls. Top with vegetable and bean mixture, then chicken. Sprinkle with cheese, dollop with sour cream, top with avocado and garnish with cilantro.

NUTRIENTS PER SERVING			
Calories	410	Fiber	9 g (36% DV)
Fat	21 g	Protein	34 g
Saturated fat	6 g	Calcium	143 mg (14% DV)
Sodium	286 mg (12% DV)	Iron	3 mg (17% DV)
Carbohydrate	22 g	Vitamin D	8 IU (2% DV)

Chicken Marsala

Who says you have to travel to Sicily to enjoy a traditional chicken marsala? You can complement this traditional Italian dish beautifully with a side of "zoodles" (zucchini noodles; see tip, below. If you want to increase your grams of carbohydrate for this meal, add $1/2$ cup (125 mL) mashed potatoes (or smashed potatoes, page 182).

TIP

To make zoodles, cut ends off 2 medium zucchinis and use a spiralizer to create "noodles." In a medium saucepan, heat 1 tsp (5 mL) olive oil over medium-high heat. Add zucchini and cook, stirring occasionally, for about 5 minutes or until tender. One cup (250 mL) zoodles contains about 5 grams carbohydrates.

- Preheat oven to 350°F (180°C)
- Medium ovenproof skillet

CHICKEN

2	boneless skinless chicken breasts (each 4 oz/125 g), pounded to $1/2$ inch (1 cm) thick	2
$1/2$ tsp	freshly ground black pepper	2 mL
1 tbsp	all-purpose flour	15 mL
1 tbsp	butter	15 mL

MARSALA SAUCE

1 tbsp	butter	15 mL
1 cup	sliced mushrooms	250 mL
3	cloves garlic, minced	3
$1/4$ cup	all-purpose flour	60 mL
1 cup	ready-to-use low-sodium beef broth	250 mL
3 tbsp	marsala wine	45 mL
$1/2$ tsp	freshly ground black pepper	2 mL

1. *Chicken:* Season chicken breasts with pepper. Sprinkle flour on both sides of each chicken breast. In skillet, melt butter over medium-high heat. Cook chicken, turning once, for 2 to 3 minutes per side or until beginning to brown. Transfer to a plate.

2. *Marsala Sauce:* In the same skillet (no need to wash it), melt butter over medium heat. Add mushrooms and cook, stirring, for 3 minutes or until tender. Transfer mushrooms to the plate with the chicken.

NUTRIENTS PER SERVING			
Calories	350	Fiber	1 g (4% DV)
Fat	16 g	Protein	30 g
Saturated fat	9 g	Calcium	18 mg (2% DV)
Sodium	390 mg (16% DV)	Iron	3 mg (17% DV)
Carbohydrate	20 g	Vitamin D	11 IU (3% DV)

TIP

■ ■ ■ ■ ■ ■ ■ ■ ■ ■ ■ ■ ■ ■ ■ ■

If preparing this recipe for one person, cut all of the ingredients in half. Or simply prepare the full recipe and save half for leftovers. Store leftovers in an airtight container in the refrigerator for up to 2 days. Reheat in the microwave on High for 1 to 2 minutes or until heated through.

3. Add garlic to the skillet and cook, stirring, for 30 seconds or until fragrant. Slowly whisk in flour until fully combined. Gradually pour in broth and marsala while whisking, and season with pepper.

4. Quickly bring mixture to a boil over medium-high heat, stirring often, then reduce heat to low. Add mushrooms and chicken to skillet; stir to combine.

5. Transfer skillet to preheated oven and bake for 25 to 30 minutes or until chicken is no longer pink inside.

Health Bite

■ ■

Besides animal products, mushrooms are the only food source of vitamin D. No other plants provide vitamin D!

Chicken Tetrazzini

It has been said that this is one of the earliest dishes brought from Italy in the early 1900s when immigrants began new lives in the United States. Named for Luisa Tetrazzini, the operatic soprano known as the Florentine Nightingale, this dish is sure to make you and your guest sing its praise.

TIPS

The standard mushroom is the white mushroom, sometimes called button mushrooms. For a bit bolder flavor, try brown (cremini) mushrooms or get creative and try shiitake or chanterelle mushrooms.

Use a damp paper towel to scrub dirt from mushrooms (do not clean with water, as mushrooms will absorb excess water). Use a spoon to remove the gills.

- Preheat oven to 350°F (180°C)
- Medium skillet, sprayed with canola oil nonstick cooking spray
- Small or medium glass baking dish, sprayed with canola oil nonstick cooking spray

4 oz	whole wheat spaghetti	125 g
6 oz	boneless skinless chicken breast (about 1 medium)	175 g
Pinch	salt	Pinch
Pinch	freshly ground black pepper	Pinch
2 tsp	olive oil	10 mL
1 cup	frozen cut or chopped fresh green beans	250 mL
$1/2$ cup	sliced mushrooms	125 mL
$1/2$ cup	chopped onion	125 mL
$1/4$ cup	whole wheat flour	60 mL
1 tsp	dried Italian seasoning	5 mL
$1^1/2$ cups	2% milk	375 mL
2 tbsp	grated Parmesan cheese	30 mL

1. In a large pot of boiling water, cook spaghetti according to package directions or until al dente, 9 to 11 minutes. Drain and return to pot.

2. Meanwhile, season chicken with salt and pepper. Heat prepared skillet over medium-high heat. Add chicken and cook, turning once, for 4 minutes per side or until no longer pink inside. Transfer to a cutting board and let rest for 5 minutes; use two forks to shred chicken.

3. Return skillet (no need to wash it) to medium-high heat. Add oil, beans, mushrooms and onion; cook, stirring, for 3 minutes or until tender-crisp.

NUTRIENTS PER SERVING			
Calories	473	Fiber	6 g (24% DV)
Fat	13 g	Protein	41 g
Saturated fat	4 g	Calcium	352 mg (35% DV)
Sodium	341 mg (14% DV)	Iron	4 mg (22% DV)
Carbohydrate	48 g	Vitamin D	97 IU (24% DV)

TIP

If preparing this recipe for one person, cut all of the ingredients in half. Or simply prepare the full recipe and save half for leftovers. Store leftovers in an airtight container in the refrigerator for up to 2 days. Reheat in the microwave on High for 1 to 2 minutes or until heated through.

4. Transfer bean mixture to prepared baking dish and stir in spaghetti and chicken.

5. In a measuring cup or a small bowl, whisk flour and Italian seasoning into milk. Pour over ingredients in baking dish and mix well.

6. Bake in preheated oven for 50 minutes or until bubbling. Top with cheese and bake for 2 minutes or until cheese is melted.

Health Bite

Different mushrooms provide different health benefits. Exotic mushrooms, like shiitake, maiki and oyster, are thought to have anticancer properties.

Tortellini and Chicken Pasta Salad

MAKES 2 SERVINGS

Pair this dinner with a side of steamed broccoli or spinach for an easy weeknight dinner.

TIPS

If you have about 8 oz (250 g) leftover cooked chicken, skip step 1 to make this recipe even more simple!

If preparing this recipe for one person, cut all of the ingredients in half. Or simply prepare the full recipe and save half for leftovers. Store leftovers in an airtight container in the refrigerator for up to 2 days. Reheat in the microwave on High for 1 to 2 minutes or until heated through.

Health Bite

Using whole wheat tortellini provides insoluble fiber, which is important for glycemic goals.

2	boneless skinless chicken breasts (each 4 oz/125 g)	2
1/2 tsp	freshly ground black pepper	2 mL
Pinch	salt	Pinch
1 tsp	olive oil	5 mL
4 oz	cheese-filled whole wheat tortellini	125 g
3/4 cup	drained roasted red bell peppers, chopped	175 mL
2 tbsp	chopped green onions	30 mL
2 tbsp	chopped black olives	30 mL

VINAIGRETTE

3 tbsp	olive oil	45 mL
2 tbsp	red wine vinegar	30 mL
2 tsp	dried oregano	10 mL
1 tsp	garlic powder	5 mL

1. Season chicken breasts with pepper and salt. In a skillet, heat oil over medium-high heat. Add chicken and cook, turning once, for 3 to 4 minutes per side or until no longer pink inside. Transfer to a cutting board and let cool. Cut into bite-size pieces.

2. Meanwhile, in a large pot of boiling water, cook tortellini according to package directions. Drain and let cool for 10 minutes.

3. *Vinaigrette:* In a small bowl, whisk together oil, vinegar, oregano and garlic powder until emulsified.

4. In a large bowl, combine tortellini, chicken, roasted peppers, green onions and olives. Add vinaigrette and toss gently to coat. Serve warm.

NUTRIENTS PER SERVING			
Calories	568	Fiber	4 g (16% DV)
Fat	34 g	Protein	34 g
Saturated fat	7 g	Calcium	92 mg (9% DV)
Sodium	642 mg (27% DV)	Iron	3 mg (17% DV)
Carbohydrate	33 g	Vitamin D	0 IU (0% DV)

Hoisin Chicken

Are you in the mood for some Chinese takeout? Fear no more for your blood sugar. Now you can make your own Chinese food without the added cornstarch and MSG.

TIPS

You can substitute 2 tsp (10 mL) freeze-dried garlic or 1 tbsp (15 mL) prepared minced garlic in oil for the garlic cloves.

If preparing this recipe for one person, cut all of the ingredients in half. Or simply prepare the full recipe and save half for leftovers. Store the chicken and greens in separate airtight containers in the refrigerator for up to 2 days. Reheat in the microwave on Medium (50%) power for 1 to 2 minutes or until heated through.

HOISIN CHICKEN

1 tbsp	granulated sugar or liquid honey	15 mL
1/3 cup	hoisin sauce	75 mL
3 tbsp	reduced-sodium tamari (see tip, page 136)	45 mL
10 oz	chicken breast cutlets	300 g
3	green onions, chopped	3
1/4 cup	sesame seeds	60 mL

GARLICKY GREENS

2 tsp	olive oil	10 mL
2	cloves garlic, minced	2
5 cups	lightly packed trimmed spinach leaves (5 oz/150 g)	1.25 L

1. *Hoisin Chicken:* In a small bowl, combine sugar, hoisin sauce and tamari. Scrape into a large skillet and cook sauce over medium heat, stirring, for 1 minute. Add chicken cutlets and cook, turning once, for about 5 minutes per side or until no longer pink inside. Transfer to a cutting board. Wash and dry the skillet.

2. *Garlicky Greens:* In skillet, heat oil and garlic over medium heat for 1 minute. Add spinach and cook, stirring, for about 3 minutes or until spinach is wilted.

3. Divide garlicky greens between two plates. Slice each cutlet crosswise a few times and arrange over greens, spooning any remaining sauce over top. Garnish with green onions and sesame seeds.

Health Bite

If you are having difficulty with high blood sugar, omit the sugar and tamari, and serve the hoisin as a dipping sauce on the side instead. Decrease the hoisin sauce to 5 tsp (25 mL), omitting it from step 1, and cook the chicken cutlets in 1/2 cup (125 mL) ready-to-use low-sodium chicken broth.

NUTRIENTS PER SERVING			
Calories	385	Fiber	4 g (16% DV)
Fat	12 g	Protein	41 g
Saturated fat	2 g	Calcium	49 mg (5% DV)
Sodium	1837 mg (77% DV)	Iron	3 mg (17% DV)
Carbohydrate	32 g	Vitamin D	0 IU (0% DV)

Chinese Chicken Salad

This dish is perfect for a summer lunch when you're craving crisp Asian flavors. The red cabbage, wonton strips and almond provide a crunchy texture. Enjoy with a side of miso soup.

TIPS

We've used a reduced-sodium soy sauce with 550 mg sodium per tablespoon (15 mL) for the nutrient analysis for this recipe. If you wish to reduce the sodium further, look for a "Lite" product with even lower sodium (about 50% less than regular). If the soy sauce you have has more sodium listed on the label, reduce the amount you add to the recipe, or factor in the increase in sodium to your meal.

It's a good idea to rinse canned mandarin oranges to remove any excess sugary syrup.

If you have extra mandarin oranges, blend them into a smoothie or use to top yogurt.

Wonton strips can be found in the salad-topper section near the croutons at well-stocked grocery stores. Alternatively, substitute croutons or baked tortilla chips.

2 tsp	cornstarch	10 mL
2 tbsp	reduced-sodium soy sauce	30 mL
2 tbsp	water	30 mL
2 tsp	olive oil, divided	10 mL
2	boneless skinless chicken breasts (each 4 oz/125 g), cut into 1-inch (2.5 cm) cubes	2
1/2 tsp	freshly ground black pepper	2 mL
Pinch	salt	Pinch
2	cloves garlic, minced	2
2	stalks celery, chopped	2
1 cup	shredded carrots	250 mL
1 cup	shredded red cabbage	250 mL
1/2 cup	chopped onion	125 mL
1	medium head romaine lettuce, shredded	1
1 cup	thawed frozen shelled edamame	250 mL
1/2 cup	rinsed drained canned mandarin oranges	125 mL
1 oz	wonton strips (about 1/4 cup/60 mL) (see tip, at left)	30 g
1/4 cup	slivered almonds	60 mL

1. In a small bowl, combine cornstarch, soy sauce and water. Set aside.

2. In a large skillet, heat 1 tsp (5 mL) oil over medium-high heat. Add chicken, pepper and salt; cook, stirring, for about 5 minutes or until chicken is no longer pink inside. Transfer to a large bowl.

NUTRIENTS PER SERVING			
Calories	550	Fiber	7 g (28% DV)
Fat	20 g	Protein	43 g
Saturated fat	3 g	Calcium	191 mg (19% DV)
Sodium	1078 mg (45% DV)	Iron	4 mg (22% DV)
Carbohydrate	50 g	Vitamin D	0 IU (0% DV)

For more depth of flavor, toast the slivered almonds in a small skillet over medium heat, stirring constantly, for 2 to 3 minutes or until golden brown.

Add 1 to 2 tsp (5 to 10 mL) teriyaki sauce if more flavor is desired in this dish, but note that the sodium will also increase.

If you are watching your sodium intake, do not add the salt in step 2, and use only 1 tbsp (15 mL) or less soy sauce.

If preparing this recipe for one person, cut all of the ingredients in half. Or simply prepare the full recipe up to the end of step 3, let cool and store in an airtight container in the refrigerator for up to 2 days. Reheat in the microwave on High for 1 to 2 minutes, or until heated through, and continue with step 4.

3. In the same skillet (no need to wash it), combine the remaining oil, garlic, celery, carrots, red cabbage and onion over medium heat. Cook, stirring, for 3 to 5 minutes or until vegetables are tender-crisp. Stir cornstarch mixture and pour into skillet; cook, stirring, for about 1 minute or until liquid is thickened and vegetables are coated. Transfer to the bowl with the chicken and stir to combine.

4. Divide lettuce between two plates and top with chicken and vegetable mixture. Arrange edamame, mandarin oranges, wonton strips and almonds over top.

Health Bite

Compared to other beans, edamame is lower in carbohydrates and higher in protein, which makes for a great bean choice when you're keeping the carbs in check.

Pulled Chicken Tacos

Taco Tuesday, anyone? Simply toss the ingredients into the slow cooker and let the magic happen!

TIPS

Top tacos with minced fresh cilantro, raw onions and/or jalapeño peppers for added flavor.

If preparing this recipe for one person, cut all of the ingredients in half. Or simply prepare the full recipe up to the end of step 2 and store leftovers in an airtight container in the refrigerator for up to 2 days. Reheat in the microwave on High for 1 to 2 minutes, or until heated through, and assemble tacos just before serving.

Health Bite

Also known as alligator pear, avocado is high in monounsaturated fat and is a good source of lutein.

- 4-quart slow cooker

2	boneless skinless chicken breasts (each 4 oz/125 g)	2
2 tsp	chili powder	10 mL
$\frac{1}{2}$ tsp	freshly ground black pepper	2 mL
$\frac{1}{2}$ cup	julienned red bell pepper	125 mL
$\frac{1}{4}$ cup	sliced onion	60 mL
2 tbsp	diced tomato	30 mL
1 cup	ready-to-use low-sodium chicken broth	250 mL
1 cup	salsa verde	250 mL
4	4-inch (10 cm) hard corn taco shells	4
$\frac{1}{2}$	avocado, sliced	$\frac{1}{2}$

1. Season chicken breasts with chili powder and pepper and add to slow cooker stoneware. Add red pepper, onion and tomato. Pour broth and salsa verde into slow cooker; stir to mix thoroughly. Cover and cook on Low for 8 hours or on High for 4 hours, until chicken is no longer pink inside.

2. Transfer chicken to a cutting board and use two forks to shred meat. Return chicken to slow cooker, increase heat to High (if needed) and continue cooking for 10 minutes.

3. Use a slotted spoon to transfer chicken and vegetable mixture to taco shells, dividing evenly, and top with slices of avocado.

NUTRIENTS PER SERVING			
Calories	385	Fiber	5 g (20% DV)
Fat	15 g	Protein	29 g
Saturated fat	4 g	Calcium	35 mg (4% DV)
Sodium	839 mg (35% DV)	Iron	2 mg (11% DV)
Carbohydrate	32 g	Vitamin D	0 IU (0% DV)

"It's Greek to Me" Burgers

MAKES 2 SERVINGS

I scream, you scream, we all scream: "It's Greek to me!" Feed your taste buds with flavors from the Mediterranean. Serve the burger in your favorite whole wheat pita with a side of cucumber salad or green beans in a light tomato sauce.

TIPS

The sliced tomato adds vitamin C, for easy absorption of iron.

If preparing this recipe for one person, cut all of the ingredients in half. Or simply prepare the full recipe up to the end of step 3, let the leftover patty cool and store in an airtight container in the refrigerator for up to 2 days. Reheat in the microwave on High for 1 to 2 minutes, or until heated through, and assemble burger just before serving.

1/2 cup	frozen chopped spinach	125 mL
8 oz	lean ground turkey, preferably white meat	250 g
3 oz	feta cheese, crumbled	90 g
2 tbsp	finely chopped onion	30 mL
	Canola oil nonstick cooking spray	
2	6 1/2-inch (16 cm) whole wheat pita pockets	2
2 tbsp	olive tapenade	30 mL
2 tbsp	plain hummus (or Spicy Sun-Dried Tomato Hummus, page 201)	30 mL
2	thick slices tomato	2

1. In a ramekin or small bowl, microwave spinach on High for about 45 seconds or until no longer frozen. Pour off any excess liquid.

2. In a medium bowl, combine turkey, feta, onion and spinach. Mix together and form 2 patties, each about 3/4 inch (2 cm) thick.

3. Spray a medium skillet with cooking spray and place over medium-high heat. Add patties and cook, turning once, for about 5 minutes per side or until patties are lightly browned on the outside and a thermometer inserted in the center registers 165°F (74°C).

4. Separate the two layers of each pita. Top each bottom half with a burger, tapenade, hummus and tomato, dividing evenly. Replace each top half of pita.

Health Bite

Olives, like olive oil, are a great source of heart-friendly monounsaturated fatty acids. Research suggests that replacing dietary saturated fat and trans fat with monounsaturated fats may help improve insulin sensitivity. For burger toppings, we love olive tapenades and avocado.

NUTRIENTS PER SERVING			
Calories	442	Fiber	5 g (20% DV)
Fat	21 g	Protein	35 g
Saturated fat	9 g	Calcium	281 mg (28% DV)
Sodium	1008 mg (42% DV)	Iron	4 mg (22% DV)
Carbohydrate	32 g	Vitamin D	7 IU (2% DV)

Old Bay Turkey Topas

MAKES 1 SERVING

This is your new version of the twice-baked potato — the turkey twice-baked potato — made hip, healthy and spicy with Old Bay seasoning. "Topa" is a play on "pota" in "potato." Switch the "p" and the "t" to get "topa." The "t" represents the turkey!

TIPS

A mini food processor makes mincing easy, but feel free to use a knife and cutting board instead.

Add in 3 tbsp (45 mL) plain Greek yogurt with the red pepper for a moist and creamy texture.

To reduce your sodium intake, skip the store-bought salsa and instead top each serving with 1 tbsp (15 mL) diced tomato.

- Preheat oven to 400°F (200°C)
- Baking sheet, lined with foil
- Mini food processor (see tip, at left)

1	medium russet potato, halved lengthwise	1
1/4 cup	fresh flat-leaf (Italian) parsley leaves	60 mL
1/4 cup	fresh oregano leaves	60 mL
1	clove garlic	1
2 tsp	olive oil	10 mL
1/2 cup	chopped onion	125 mL
4 oz	lean ground turkey, preferably white meat	125 g
1 tbsp	finely chopped red bell pepper	15 mL
1/4 tsp	Old Bay seasoning	1 mL
2 tbsp	salsa	30 mL

1. Microwave potato halves on High for 4 minutes or until softened.

2. Place potato halves cut side up on prepared baking sheet. Bake in preheated oven for about 10 minutes or until the skin is crispy.

3. Meanwhile, in food processor, pulse parsley, oregano and garlic until minced.

4. In a medium skillet, heat oil over medium heat. Add onion and cook, stirring, for 2 minutes. Add turkey and cook, breaking it up with a spoon, for 5 minutes or until no longer pink. Remove from heat and add herb mixture to skillet; stir to combine.

NUTRIENTS PER SERVING			
Calories	492	Fiber	11 g (44% DV)
Fat	12 g	Protein	42 g
Saturated fat	2 g	Calcium	281 mg (28% DV)
Sodium	539 mg (23% DV)	Iron	9 mg (50% DV)
Carbohydrate	56 g	Vitamin D	11 IU (3% DV)

TIPS

■ ■ ■ ■ ■ ■ ■ ■ ■ ■ ■ ■ ■ ■ ■ ■

Serve with a chilled cucumber salad or chilled Avocado Cucumber Soup (page 102) to cool the heat in your mouth.

If preparing this recipe for two people, simply double all of the ingredients.

5. Scoop out the inner flesh of potato halves and transfer to a medium bowl (reserving skins). Add turkey mixture, red pepper and Old Bay seasoning to potato flesh; stir to combine. Divide mixture evenly between potato skins and top with salsa.

Health Bite

■ ■

The protein and fat in this recipe help to delay the absorption of the carbohydrate (the potato). The high fiber content provides for a lower total carb count. Refer to chapter 2 for more information on subtracting fiber from total carbohydrates.

Baked Pasta

MAKES 2 SERVINGS

No need to fret over calculating carbohydrates here, because the work is done for you. This comfort-food classic provides 57 grams of carbohydrate per serving.

TIPS

If you prefer a meatless meal, replace the turkey with 2 cups (500 mL) diced tofu.

If desired, garnish with 2 tbsp (30 mL) chopped fresh basil.

Balance the warm and cheesy penne pasta dish with a side of leafy green vegetables.

If preparing this recipe for one person, cut all of the ingredients in half. Or simply prepare the full recipe and save half for leftovers. Store leftovers in an airtight container in the refrigerator for up to 2 days. Reheat in the microwave on High for 1 to 2 minutes or until heated through.

Health Bite

Tomatoes contain the antioxidant lycopene. This plant compound is more easily absorbed from cooked tomato than from raw. Lycopene may be protective for cardiovascular disease and prostate cancer.

- Preheat oven to 350°F (180°C)
- 8-inch (20 cm) square glass or ceramic baking dish, lightly sprayed with canola oil nonstick cooking spray

4 oz	whole wheat penne pasta	125 g
1 tsp	olive oil	5 mL
8 oz	lean ground turkey breast	250 g
1/2 cup	ricotta cheese	125 mL
1/4 cup	shredded mozzarella cheese	60 mL
1/4 cup	grated Parmesan cheese	60 mL
1 tsp	dried oregano	5 mL
1 tsp	garlic powder	5 mL
1 tsp	dried basil	5 mL
1 tsp	dried parsley	5 mL
1/4 cup	low-sodium tomato sauce	60 mL
1	can (14 oz/398 mL) no-salt-added diced tomatoes, drained	1

1. In a large pot of boiling water, cook penne according to package directions. Drain and set aside.

2. Meanwhile, in a medium skillet, heat oil over medium-high heat. Add turkey and cook, breaking it up with a spoon, for 8 to 10 minutes or until no longer pink. Remove from heat and set aside.

3. In a medium bowl, combine ricotta, mozzarella, Parmesan, oregano, garlic powder, basil and parsley.

4. In prepared baking dish, combine noodles, tomato sauce, tomatoes, turkey and cheese mixture.

5. Bake in preheated oven for 25 minutes or until cheese is bubbling.

NUTRIENTS PER SERVING			
Calories	640	Fiber	9 g (36% DV)
Fat	26 g	Protein	45 g
Saturated fat	12 g	Calcium	414 mg (41% DV)
Sodium	780 mg (33% DV)	Iron	5 mg (28% DV)
Carbohydrate	57 g	Vitamin D	24 IU (6% DV)

Grilled Pork Chops with Brown Sugar, Cinnamon and Ginger Apples

A 1950s dish gets a modern spin. This elegant version of pork chops and applesauce has become a classic in our homes. Complement this dish with a mustard green salad on the side.

TIPS

If desired, omit the raisins.

For a sophisticated presentation, ladle sauce onto plates and top with chops, then apples.

If preparing this recipe for one person, cut all of the ingredients in half. Or simply prepare the full recipe and save half for leftovers. Store leftovers in an airtight container in the refrigerator for up to 2 days. Reheat in the microwave on High for 1 to 2 minutes or until heated through.

Health Bite

Cinnamon has been linked to helping maintain a healthy blood sugar level.

- 4-quart slow cooker

2 tsp	butter	10 mL
2	boneless pork loin chops (each 5 oz/150 g)	2
1/2 tsp	freshly ground black pepper	2 mL
Pinch	salt	Pinch
1	large tart apple (such as Granny Smith; unpeeled), chopped (about 2 cups/500 mL)	1
1 tsp	brown sugar	5 mL
1 tsp	ground cinnamon	5 mL
1 tsp	ground ginger	5 mL
2 tbsp	golden raisins	30 mL
1/2 cup	sliced red onion	125 mL
1 cup	ready-to-use low-sodium chicken broth	250 mL
1 cup	water	250 mL

1. In a medium skillet, melt butter over medium-high heat. Season pork chops on both sides with pepper and salt. Add pork chops to skillet and sear, turning once, for about 3 minutes per side or until browned. Place pork chops in slow cooker.

2. In a small bowl, toss apple with brown sugar, cinnamon and ginger until evenly coated. Add apple, raisins and onion to slow cooker. Pour broth and water over top. Cover and cook on Low for 5 to 6 hours or on High for 3 to 4 hours, until apple is tender, onion is translucent and just a hint of pink remains in pork.

NUTRIENTS PER SERVING			
Calories	426	Fiber	4 g (16% DV)
Fat	14 g	Protein	46 g
Saturated fat	6 g	Calcium	54 mg (5% DV)
Sodium	196 mg (8% DV)	Iron	3 mg (17% DV)
Carbohydrate	30 g	Vitamin D	41 IU (10% DV)

Herbed Pork Tenderloin with Smashed Potatoes

Eat French restaurant–style food in your own kitchen. Learn how to dress up your pork and smash your potatoes. Serve with steamed thin green beans, also known as haricots verts.

TIPS

If you don't have two roasting pans, use a baking dish for the potatoes instead.

If you can't find fingerling potatoes, choose small roasting potatoes. The goal is to be able to smash each potato with the back of a fork.

To make your own herbes de Provence seasoning, combine ¼ cup (60 mL) dried thyme, ¼ cup (60 mL) dried rosemary, 2 tbsp (30 mL) dried savory, 1 tbsp (15 mL) dried marjoram and 2¼ tsp (11 mL) dried culinary lavender (lavender is optional). Store the seasoning blend in an airtight glass container for up to 3 months.

- Preheat oven to 400°F (200°C)
- 2 small roasting pans (see tip, at left), lined with foil or sprayed with canola oil nonstick cooking spray

8 oz	fingerling potatoes	250 g
3 tbsp	herbes de Provence	45 mL
8 oz	pork tenderloin (1 small)	250 g
1	clove garlic, minced	1
2 tsp	olive oil	10 mL
Pinch	salt	Pinch

1. Use a fork to poke holes in each potato. Arrange in a prepared roasting pan and bake in preheated oven for 5 minutes.

2. Meanwhile, sprinkle herbes de Provence on the bottom of a large plate or shallow baking dish. Roll and coat the pork tenderloin with the seasoning. Place pork tenderloin in the second prepared roasting pan and put in the oven alongside the potatoes. Set timer for 15 minutes.

3. After the potatoes have baked for 20 minutes and the pork for 15 minutes, remove both from oven and check the meat to make sure it is cooked to at least medium-rare (145°F/63°C). If needed, continue to cook the pork until it reaches the desired doneness. Transfer pork to a cutting board and let rest while you continue with step 4.

NUTRIENTS PER SERVING			
Calories	290	Fiber	3 g (12% DV)
Fat	9 g	Protein	32 g
Saturated fat	7 g	Calcium	22 mg (2% DV)
Sodium	71 mg (3% DV)	Iron	2 mg (11% DV)
Carbohydrate	20 g	Vitamin D	11 IU (3% DV)

TIPS

If you love garlic, use 2 cloves instead of 1 in this recipe.

If preparing this recipe for one person, cut all of the ingredients in half. Or simply prepare the full recipe up to the end of step 4, let cool, and store leftover pork and potatoes in separate airtight containers in the refrigerator for up to 2 days. Reheat in the microwave on High for 1 to 2 minutes or until heated through.

4. In a small bowl, combine garlic, oil and salt. In roasting pan, smash each potato once with the back of a fork (do not mash). Brush garlic mixture onto the potatoes, covering all sides. Return pan to the oven and roast for about 15 minutes or until crispy.

5. Slice pork. Divide pork and potatoes between two plates and serve.

Health Bite

According to the National Institutes of Health, garlic is used to treat several conditions associated with the blood system and heart, such as high cholesterol, atherosclerosis, heart attack and hypertension.

Pork Lo Mein

Chinese food was a regular Saturday night dinner outing when we were growing up. Here is a new version made to meet your carb range and, of course, treat your taste buds.

TIPS

If you don't have fresh gingerroot, use ¼ tsp (1 mL) ground ginger.

We've used a reduced-sodium soy sauce with 550 mg sodium per tablespoon (15 mL) for the nutrient analysis for this recipe. If you wish to reduce the sodium further, look for a "Lite" product with even lower sodium (about 50% less than regular). If the soy sauce you have has more sodium listed on the label, reduce the amount you add to the recipe, or factor in the increase in sodium to your meal.

8 oz	whole wheat spaghetti	250 g
2 tsp	cornstarch	10 mL
1 tsp	minced fresh gingerroot	5 mL
1 tbsp	reduced-sodium soy sauce	15 mL
2 tsp	unseasoned rice vinegar	10 mL
2 tsp	sesame oil	10 mL
1 tsp	Sriracha	5 mL
1 tsp	olive oil	5 mL
6 oz	pork tenderloin, cubed	175 g
1	clove garlic, minced	1
1	red bell pepper, julienned	1
1	small carrot, shredded	1
1 cup	lightly packed trimmed baby spinach	250 mL
½ cup	snow peas, trimmed	125 mL
½ cup	sliced mushrooms	125 mL
½	red onion, thinly sliced	½

1. In a large pot of boiling water, cook spaghetti according to package directions. Drain and set aside.

2. Meanwhile, in a small bowl, whisk together cornstarch, ginger, soy sauce, vinegar, sesame oil and Sriracha.

3. In a large skillet, heat olive oil over medium heat. Add pork and cook, stirring occasionally, for 10 minutes or until browned on all sides. Add garlic, red pepper, carrot, spinach, snow peas, mushrooms and onion. Cook, stirring, for 4 minutes.

NUTRIENTS PER SERVING			
Calories	366	Fiber	6 g (24% DV)
Fat	10 g	Protein	27 g
Saturated fat	2 g	Calcium	66 mg (7% DV)
Sodium	422 mg (18% DV)	Iron	3 mg (17% DV)
Carbohydrate	45 g	Vitamin D	8 IU (2% DV)

TIPS

Swap the spaghetti for buckwheat soba noodles or even rice noodles for a different taste and texture.

If preparing this recipe for one person, cut all of the ingredients in half.

4. Add soy sauce mixture and cook, stirring, for 1 minute or until vegetables are tender-crisp, sauce is slightly thickened and just a hint of pink remains inside pork.

5. Add spaghetti to skillet and toss to combine. Serve immediately.

Health Bite

Spinach contains the antioxidant alphalipoic acid, which is associated with lower glucose levels and increased insulin sensitivity in individuals with diabetes.

Pork Green Chili

Here's a Southwestern classic that won't disappoint. Nicknamed "PGC" in Lisa's kitchen, this dish will have you saying: "Y-U-M!"

TIPS

Tomatillos can be found in the produce section next to the tomatoes. They are essential to many sauces of Central American and Mexican cuisine. After removing the husk, wash the tomatillo in lukewarm water to remove the sticky layer.

If fresh tomatillos are unavailable, use 2 whole tomatillos from a can and dice them.

8 oz	pork tenderloin, cut into 1-inch (2.5 cm) cubes	250 g
2 tbsp	yellow cornmeal (preferably stone-ground), divided	30 mL
1 tbsp	chili powder	15 mL
1 tsp	olive oil	5 mL
2	tomatillos, husks removed, diced (see tips, at left)	2
1	can (4$\frac{1}{2}$ oz/127 mL) diced green chiles, with juice	1
1	small jalapeño pepper, seeded and minced	1
$\frac{1}{2}$ cup	chopped onion	125 mL
1 cup	ready-to-use low-sodium chicken broth	250 mL
2	6-inch (15 cm) corn tortillas	2
2 tbsp	sour cream	30 mL
2 tbsp	chopped fresh cilantro	30 mL

1. In a bowl, toss pork in 1 tbsp (15 mL) cornmeal and the chili powder.

2. In a large skillet, heat oil over medium-high heat. Add pork and cook, stirring, for 3 minutes or until browned on all sides. Add tomatillos, green chiles, jalapeño, onion and broth to the skillet; stir to combine.

NUTRIENTS PER SERVING			
Calories	395	Fiber	5 g (20% DV)
Fat	14 g	Protein	39 g
Saturated fat	5 g	Calcium	67 mg (7% DV)
Sodium	470 mg (20% DV)	Iron	4 mg (22% DV)
Carbohydrate	25 g	Vitamin D	32 IU (8% DV)

Always wear kitchen gloves when handling jalapeños and avoid touching your skin and eyes.

If preparing this recipe for one person, cut all of the ingredients in half. Or simply prepare the full recipe up to the end of step 3 and store leftovers in an airtight container in the refrigerator for up to 2 days. Reheat in the microwave on High for 1 to 2 minutes, or until heated through, and proceed with step 4.

3. Reduce heat to medium. Sprinkle in the remaining cornmeal and stir to combine. Cover, reduce heat to medium-low and simmer, stirring occasionally, for 8 to 10 minutes or until sauce has thickened and just a hint of pink remains inside pork.

4. Place each tortilla in a bowl. Divide pork green chili between bowls. Top with sour cream and garnish with cilantro.

Health Bite

Because of its antioxidant content, the oil extracted from cilantro leaves has been shown to slow unwanted oxidation when added to other foods, which prevents their spoilage.

Marinated Beef Tenderloin and Grilled Corn Salad

Bring summer to dinner with this tender cut of beef partnered with grilled corn salad — it will call your name after a long day at the beach.

TIPS

We've used a reduced-sodium soy sauce with 550 mg sodium per tablespoon (15 mL) for the nutrient analysis for this recipe. If you wish to reduce the sodium further, look for a "Lite" product with even lower sodium (about 50% less than regular). If the soy sauce you have has more sodium listed on the label, reduce the amount you add to the recipe, or factor in the increase in sodium to your meal.

If desired, marinate the beef for up to 24 hours. Cover and store in the refrigerator.

If fresh corn cobs are not available, substitute 1 1/2 cups (375 mL) rinsed drained canned corn kernels.

- Preheat oven to 350°F (180°C)
- 9-inch (23 cm) square glass baking dish

8 oz	beef tenderloin	250 g
2	cloves garlic, minced	2
1 tsp	freshly ground black pepper	5 mL
1/2 cup	balsamic vinegar	125 mL
2 tbsp	reduced-sodium soy sauce	30 mL

GRILLED CORN SALAD

2	ears of corn, husks and silk removed (about 1 1/2 cups/375 mL kernels)	2
2 tsp	olive oil	10 mL
1 tsp	lemon pepper seasoning salt	5 mL
1	avocado, sliced	1
1/2	medium onion, finely chopped	1/2
1/2 cup	halved cherry tomatoes	125 mL
1 tbsp	chopped fresh cilantro	15 mL
1/4 cup	freshly squeezed lime juice	60 mL

1. In baking dish, rub beef with garlic and pepper, spreading evenly. Pour vinegar and soy sauce over beef and roll meat in liquids to coat.

2. Roast in preheated oven for 15 minutes, then turn beef and roast for another 15 minutes, spooning liquid over beef occasionally, until an instant-read thermometer inserted in the thickest part of the tenderloin registers 145°F (63°C) for medium-rare, or until desired doneness is reached.

3. *Grilled Corn Salad:* Meanwhile, preheat barbecue grill to medium.

NUTRIENTS PER SERVING			
Calories	579	Fiber	12 g (48% DV)
Fat	32 g	Protein	37 g
Saturated fat	7 g	Calcium	30 mg (3% DV)
Sodium	611 mg (26% DV)	Iron	7 mg (39% DV)
Carbohydrate	40 g	Vitamin D	7 IU (2% DV)

Two large limes yields $\frac{1}{4}$ cup (60 mL) juice, enough for this recipe.

If preparing this recipe for one person, cut all of the ingredients in half. Or simply prepare the full recipe and save half for leftovers. Store corn salad and beef in separate airtight containers in the refrigerator for up to 2 days.

4. In a large bowl, submerge the ears of corn in cold water for 15 minutes.

5. Brush corn with oil and sprinkle with lemon pepper seasoning salt. Arrange corn on grill and cook, rotating every 2 to 3 minutes, until slightly charred all over, about 10 minutes. Transfer to a plate to cool, then cut kernels off cobs.

6. In a medium bowl, combine corn, avocado, onion, tomatoes and cilantro. Pour lime juice over mixture and toss until thoroughly coated.

Health Bite
■ ■

Starchy vegetables, such as sweet potatoes, potatoes, corn and squash, affect your blood sugar almost equally. One-third of a cup (75 mL) sweet potato, $\frac{1}{2}$ cup (125 mL) mashed potato, $\frac{1}{2}$ cup (125 mL) corn and $\frac{3}{4}$ cup (175 mL) winter squash each provide approximately 15 grams of carbs per serving, according to the American Diabetes Association's Diabetic Exchange List.

Steak with Chimichurri

Meat eaters, and even picky eaters, delight. This Argentinian sauce is so addictive that it will get your flavor-fussy friends to clean their plates. If you have the time, prepare the chimichurri the night before to let the flavors mingle.

TIPS

This steak can also be prepared on the barbecue. Preheat greased barbecue grill to high (or 400°F/200°C) and grill steak for 3 minutes per side or until an instant-read thermometer inserted in the thickest part of the steak registers 145°F (63°C) for medium-rare, or until desired doneness is reached.

A thin steak will cook more quickly. Reduce the heat and cooking time for thin cuts of meat and poultry.

Serve steak over arugula greens and a carb of your choice.

If preparing this recipe for one person, cut all of the ingredients in half. Or simply prepare the full recipe and save half for leftovers. Store leftovers in an airtight container in the refrigerator for up to 2 days. Reheat in the microwave on High for 1 to 2 minutes or until heated through.

- Food processor

½ cup	firmly packed fresh parsley leaves	125 mL
½ cup	firmly packed fresh cilantro leaves	125 mL
1 tbsp	chopped red bell pepper	15 mL
2	cloves garlic	2
5 tbsp	extra virgin olive oil, divided	75 mL
½ tsp	freshly squeezed lemon juice	2 mL
9 oz	hangar steak (preferably 1 inch/2.5 cm thick)	275 g
¼ tsp	sea salt	1 mL

1. In food processor, combine parsley, cilantro, red pepper, garlic, 2 tbsp (30 mL) oil and lemon juice. Process until smooth. Add the remaining oil, 1 tbsp (15 mL) at a time, pulsing in between and using a spatula to wipe down the sides. Pour chimichurri into a small bowl, cover and refrigerate for at least 30 minutes or for up to 24 hours.

2. Meanwhile, preheat oven to 400°F (200°C).

3. Place steak on a broiler pan or baking sheet. Bake, turning once, for 3 minutes per side or until an instant-read thermometer inserted in the thickest part of the steak registers 145°F (63°C) for medium-rare, or until desired doneness is reached. Let steak rest for 3 minutes to let the juices reintegrate into the meat. Season steak with salt. Slice steak and brush with chimichurri.

Health Bite

Parsley contains the flavonol myricetin, which may lower blood sugar by decreasing the body's resistance to insulin, as demonstrated in animal research.

NUTRIENTS PER SERVING			
Calories	531	Fiber	1 g (4% DV)
Fat	40 g	Protein	39 g
Saturated fat	7 g	Calcium	35 mg (4% DV)
Sodium	356 mg (15% DV)	Iron	6 mg (33% DV)
Carbohydrate	2 g	Vitamin D	36 IU (9% DV)

Hearty Beef Stew

Meals like this seem impossible to make on a weeknight, but the slow cooker does all the work for you! Sear the beef, then stick it in the slow cooker with the other traditional stew vegetables.

TIPS

Look for low-sodium Worcestershire-style sauce in natural foods stores and online. It should contain 20 mg sodium per teaspoon (5 mL).

This stew can be stored in an airtight container in the freezer for up to 3 months. Thaw overnight in the refrigerator or defrost in the microwave before reheating.

If preparing this recipe for one person, cut all of the ingredients in half. Or simply prepare the full recipe and save half for leftovers. Store leftovers in an airtight container in the refrigerator for up to 2 days. Reheat in the microwave on High for 1 to 2 minutes or until heated through.

Health Bite

There is early research that suggests that enjoying onions as part of your diet may help prevent bone loss and osteoporosis.

- 4-quart slow cooker

8 oz	boneless beef chuck, cut into 2-inch (5 cm) cubes	250 g
1 tsp	freshly ground black pepper	5 mL
1 tsp	dried thyme	5 mL
Pinch	salt	Pinch
2 tbsp	all-purpose flour	30 mL
2 tsp	olive oil	10 mL
2	small onions, finely chopped	2
2	stalks celery, chopped	2
2	cloves garlic, minced	2
2	small potatoes (unpeeled), cut into 1-inch (2.5 cm) cubes	2
1	small carrot, cut into chunks	1
1	bay leaf	1
2 cups	ready-to-use low-sodium beef broth	500 mL
2 tbsp	low-sodium Worcestershire sauce (such as Robbie's Worcestershire Pure & Mild Sauce)	30 mL

1. In a bowl, season beef with pepper, thyme and salt. Sprinkle beef with flour until evenly coated.

2. In a medium skillet, heat oil over medium-high heat. Add beef and cook, turning, until browned on all sides, about 6 minutes. Transfer to slow cooker.

3. Add onions, celery, garlic, potatoes, carrot, bay leaf, broth and Worcestershire sauce to slow cooker; stir to combine thoroughly. If beef is not fully submerged in liquid, add water. Cover and cook on Low for 8 hours or on High for 4 hours, until meat is tender. Discard bay leaf and serve.

NUTRIENTS PER SERVING			
Calories	652	Fiber	7 g (28% DV)
Fat	35 g	Protein	39 g
Saturated fat	13 g	Calcium	83 mg (8% DV)
Sodium	512 mg (21% DV)	Iron	7 mg (39% DV)
Carbohydrate	49 g	Vitamin D	32 IU (8% DV)

Great-Grandma's Italian Meatballs and Sauce

Great-grandparents don't write down their recipes. Instead, they *make* their recipes — and recipes for the entire family, not just one or two people. Here is a version of Laura's great-grandmother's meatballs and sauce (a.k.a. gravy) made from memory and just for two. It is the perfect Sunday dinner to eat without the chaos of the whole family around.

TIPS

If you don't have an ice cream scooper, use a large spoon and shape the meatballs by hand by rolling the mixture in your palm.

Wash your hands and remove jewelry before making meatballs.

Partner each serving with 1 oz (30 g) of your favorite pasta to keep the dish under 60 grams of carbs.

- Ice cream scooper (see tip, at left)

SAUCE

1	can (28 oz/796 mL) whole tomatoes (preferably San Marzano)	1
2 tbsp	olive oil	30 mL
1	shallot, chopped	1
1	clove garlic, minced	1
½ cup	pitted black olives, sliced into thirds	125 mL
¼ cup	chopped fresh flat-leaf (Italian) parsley	60 mL
¼ cup	chopped fresh basil	60 mL
1 tsp	freshly ground black pepper	5 mL
Pinch	sea salt	Pinch

MEATBALLS

8 oz	lean ground beef	250 g
1	clove garlic, minced	1
1	large egg, beaten	1
⅓ cup	Italian-seasoned dry bread crumbs	75 mL
¼ cup	grated Parmesan cheese	60 mL
2 tbsp	chopped fresh parsley	30 mL
2 tsp	dried oregano	10 mL

1. *Sauce:* Set a colander over a large bowl and pour whole tomatoes and juice through colander. Reserve the juices. Crush tomatoes by hand or using a potato masher.

continued on page 193

NUTRIENTS PER SERVING			
Calories	652	Fiber	7 g (28% DV)
Fat	36 g	Protein	41 g
Saturated fat	12 g	Calcium	465 mg (47% DV)
Sodium	1336 mg (56% DV)	Iron	11 mg (61% DV)
Carbohydrate	41 g	Vitamin D	57 IU (14% DV)

Chicken Burrito Bowl (page 167)

Pork Lo Mein (page 184)

Steak with Chimichurri (page 190)

Salted Fig and Pine Nut Parfait (page 203)

"Crave No More" Cupcakes (page 218)

No-Bake Key Lime Pie (page 221)

Mom's Pumpkin Bread (page 250)

**Rosemary Roasted
Cashews and
Walnuts (page 262)**

TIPS

To decrease the sodium in this recipe, choose low-sodium or no-added-salt tomatoes and bread crumbs.

If preparing this recipe for one person, cut all of the ingredients in half. Or simply prepare the full recipe and save half for leftovers. Store leftovers in an airtight container in the refrigerator for up to 2 days. Reheat in the microwave on High for 1 to 2 minutes or until heated through.

2. In a large saucepan, heat oil over medium-high heat. Add shallot and cook, stirring, for 2 minutes. Add garlic and cook, stirring, for 2 minutes. Add tomatoes, olives, parsley, basil, pepper and salt; stir to combine. Pour in tomato juice and stir; bring a simmer. Reduce heat to low, cover and simmer while you prepare the meatballs, about 10 minutes.

3. *Meatballs:* Meanwhile, in a medium bowl, use your hands to combine ground beef, garlic, egg, bread crumbs, cheese, parsley and oregano.

4. Using the ice cream scooper, scoop out about 1 heaping tablespoon (15 mL) meat mixture and form a meatball. Add to the saucepan. Repeat with the remaining meat mixture. When the meatballs are all formed and simmering in the sauce, cover, increase heat to medium-high and boil gently for 15 to 20 minutes or until meatballs are no longer pink inside.

Health Bite

When purchasing ground meat and poultry, the terminology on labels differs by country. In the U.S., "lean" contains less than 10% fat (or 90% lean), and "extra-lean" contains less than 5% fat (95% lean). In Canada, "lean" contains 17% fat or less, and "extra-lean" contains 10% fat or less. The nutrient analysis for these recipes has been calculated based on the U.S. fat content, so choose your ground meat accordingly or factor in the different amount of fat to your daily intake.

Meatloaf with Sweet Potato Fries

This is everyday living with diabetes made healthy and delicious. Choose either lean ground turkey or lean ground beef. Both are equally healthy, so it is truly up to your taste buds to decide.

TIPS

Wash your hands and remove any jewelry before mixing meatloaf.

You can cut your sweet potato into long wedges or thin chips. If you choose to make wedges, add an extra 10 minutes to the baking time.

- Preheat oven to 400°F (200°C)
- 8- by 4-inch (20 by 10 cm) metal loaf pan or two mini (5½- by 3-inch/14 by 8 cm) loaf pans, sprayed with canola oil nonstick cooking spray
- Baking sheet, lined with foil and sprayed with canola oil nonstick cooking spray

8 oz	lean ground beef or turkey	250 g
½	orange bell pepper, finely chopped	½
1 cup	diced zucchini	250 mL
½ cup	finely chopped red onion	125 mL
¼ cup	quinoa, rinsed	60 mL
1	large egg, beaten	1
2 tbsp	unsweetened tomato sauce	30 mL
1 tbsp	low-sodium Worcestershire sauce	15 mL
2 tsp	coarse-ground Dijon mustard	10 mL
¼ cup	barbecue sauce	60 mL
1	large sweet potato (6 oz/175 g), cut into ¼-inch (0.5 cm) slices (see tip, at left)	1
1 tsp	olive oil	5 mL
Pinch	sea salt	Pinch

1. In a medium bowl, using your hands, mix together ground beef, orange pepper, zucchini, onion, quinoa, egg, tomato sauce, Worcestershire sauce and mustard. Mold the meat mixture into a loaf shape and transfer to the prepared loaf pan, molding it to fit evenly. Brush barbecue sauce on top of the loaf. Set aside.

NUTRIENTS PER SERVING			
Calories	547	Fiber	6 g (24% DV)
Fat	19 g	Protein	40 g
Saturated fat	6 g	Calcium	109 mg (11% DV)
Sodium	676 mg (28% DV)	Iron	6 mg (33% DV)
Carbohydrate	51 g	Vitamin D	24 IU (6% DV)

If preparing this recipe for one person, cut all of the ingredients in half. Or simply prepare the full recipe and save half for leftovers. Store leftovers in an airtight container in the refrigerator for up to 2 days. Reheat in the microwave on High for 1 to 2 minutes or until heated through.

2. Arrange sweet potato slices on prepared baking sheet and brush both sides with oil. Sprinkle with salt.

3. Place loaf pan and baking sheet side by side in preheated oven and bake for 20 minutes. Flip sweet potato slices over. Bake for another 10 minutes or until meatloaf is pulling away from the sides of the pan and a thermometer inserted in the center registers 165°F (74°C), and the sweet potato slices are tender and browned.

Health Bite

▪ ▪

The USA's Food and Drug Administration advises you to wash your hands for at least 20 seconds with soap and warm water before and after handling raw food.

Browned Beef Chili

This nourishing, diabetes-friendly dinner is ideal for a cool fall evening. Don't be intimidated by the long ingredient list; it's a snap to prepare.

TIPS

Easily substitute diced fresh tomatoes for the canned in this recipe.

If you want a spicier version, top with 1 chopped jalapeño in step 3. Leave a few seeds in for added heat.

If preparing this recipe for one person, cut all of the ingredients in half. Or simply prepare the full recipe and save half for leftovers. Store leftovers in an airtight container in the refrigerator for up to 2 days. Reheat in the microwave on High for 1 to 2 minutes or until heated through.

Health Bite

Using quinoa rather than white rice as the base for this chili is a higher-protein option.

1 tsp	olive oil	5 mL
8 oz	lean ground beef	250 g
1/4 tsp	garlic powder	1 mL
1/4 tsp	chili powder	1 mL
1/4 tsp	ground paprika	1 mL
1/4 tsp	onion powder	1 mL
1/2	medium onion, chopped	1/2
2/3 cup	canned diced tomatoes, with juice	150 mL
1/4 cup	rinsed drained canned pinto beans	60 mL
1/4 cup	rinsed drained canned kidney beans	60 mL
1/2 cup	ready-to-use low-sodium beef broth	125 mL
1 cup	hot cooked quinoa	250 mL
1/2 cup	shredded Cheddar cheese	125 mL
2 tbsp	sour cream	30 mL
1 tbsp	chopped green onions	15 mL

1. In a large skillet, heat oil over medium-high heat. Add ground beef, garlic powder, chili powder, paprika and onion powder; cook, breaking up beef with a spoon and stirring ingredients together, for 5 to 8 minutes or until beef is no longer pink.

2. Add onion and tomatoes; stir to combine. Cook, stirring, for about 3 minutes or until onion is translucent.

3. Add pinto beans, kidney beans and broth; bring to a simmer. Cover, reduce heat to medium-low and simmer for 5 to 7 minutes or until onion is tender and flavors are blended.

4. Divide cooked quinoa between two bowls. Scoop chili over quinoa and top with cheese, sour cream and green onions.

NUTRIENTS PER SERVING			
Calories	581	Fiber	7 g (28% DV)
Fat	29 g	Protein	45 g
Saturated fat	13 g	Calcium	305 mg (31% DV)
Sodium	454 mg (19% DV)	Iron	5 mg (28% DV)
Carbohydrate	32 g	Vitamin D	11 IU (3%DV)

SAVORY SNACKS AND SIDES

Spicy Sweet Potato Chips and Creamy Onion Dip

This recipe is great for beginner chip bakers. The smoky sweet potato chips lend a great contrast to this smooth onion dip. Always a crowd-pleaser, this recipe is modified for you or two!

TIPS

It is important to prepare thin, uniform slices for the chips so that they cook evenly. A mandoline is the best tool for this task. If you don't have one, you can use a sharp knife.

If preparing this recipe for one person, cut all of the ingredients in half. Or simply prepare the full dip recipe (steps 3 and 4) and save half for leftovers. (The chips don't store well.) Store leftover dip in an airtight container in the refrigerator for up to 2 days.

Health Bite

Sweet potatoes are an awesome source of the fat-soluble vitamin A and the antioxidant vitamin C. Sweet potatoes and yams are related but are from different plant sources.

- Preheat oven to 400°F (200°C)
- Large baking sheet, lined with parchment paper

1	medium sweet potato (unpeeled), thinly sliced (see tip, at left)	1
2 tbsp	freshly squeezed lime juice	30 mL
2 tsp	olive oil, divided	10 mL
1 tsp	paprika	5 mL
1 tsp	chipotle chile powder	5 mL
Pinch	salt	Pinch
1	clove garlic, minced	1
1/2	medium onion, finely chopped	1/2
1 tsp	granulated sugar	5 mL
1/2 cup	mayonnaise	125 mL
1/4 cup	plain 2% Greek yogurt	60 mL
1 tsp	freshly ground black pepper	5 mL

1. In a medium bowl, toss sweet potato with lime juice, 1 tsp (5 mL) oil, paprika and chipotle powder.

2. Arrange slices on prepared baking sheet. Bake in preheated oven for 20 to 30 minutes or until lightly browned. Flip the slices, turn the baking sheet and bake for 15 minutes or until crispy. Slide the sheet of parchment paper off the baking sheet onto a wire rack. Let cool at room temperature for up to 3 hours.

3. Meanwhile, in a small skillet, heat the remaining oil over medium-high heat. Add garlic, onion and sugar; cook, stirring often, for 10 minutes or until onion is caramelized.

4. In a small bowl, combine onion mixture, mayonnaise, yogurt and pepper. Cover and refrigerate for 1 hour or until chilled. Serve with sweet potato chips.

NUTRIENTS PER SERVING			
Calories	507	Fiber	3 g (12% DV)
Fat	46 g	Protein	5 g
Saturated fat	9 g	Calcium	62 mg (6% DV)
Sodium	470 mg (20% DV)	Iron	1 mg (6% DV)
Carbohydrate	21 g	Vitamin D	4 IU (1% DV)

Personal Artichoke and Spinach Party Dip

Whether you are hosting a small party or recovering the day after the party, this dip will meet your taste buds' needs. It's filled with flavor, fun for the fingers and, of course, fresh!

TIPS

You can also bake this dip. In a baking dish, combine spinach, artichoke hearts, garlic, water and cream cheese; bake in a preheated 350°F (180°C) oven for 5 minutes or until melted and creamy. Stir in sour cream, Parmesan, black pepper and hot pepper flakes; bake for 8 minutes or until bubbling.

Dip raw vegetables — such as broccoli, cauliflower and cucumbers — into this savory snack to keep carbs curbed.

If preparing this recipe for one person, cut all of the ingredients in half. Or simply prepare the full recipe and save half for leftovers. Store leftovers in an airtight container in the refrigerator for up to 2 days. Reheat in the microwave on High for 1 to 2 minutes or until heated through.

- 2-cup (500 mL) microwave-safe dish

1/2 cup	chopped fresh or thawed frozen spinach	125 mL
1/2 cup	chopped drained canned artichoke hearts	125 mL
1 tsp	minced garlic	5 mL
2 tbsp	water	30 mL
1/4 cup	cream cheese (2 oz/60 g), softened	60 mL
2 tbsp	sour cream	30 mL
2 tbsp	grated Parmesan cheese (1 oz/30 g)	30 mL
1/4 tsp	freshly ground black pepper	1 mL
1/4 tsp	hot pepper flakes	1 mL

1. In microwave-safe dish, combine spinach, artichoke hearts, garlic and water. Microwave on High for 30 seconds. Add cream cheese, stir to combine and microwave on High for 30 seconds. Add sour cream, Parmesan, black pepper and hot pepper flakes; stir to combine. Microwave on High for 45 seconds or until bubbling. Stir again. Serve warm.

Health Bite

Spinach, liver, yeast, asparagus and Brussels sprouts are the best sources of folate. Folate is helpful in reducing levels of homocysteine and may be protective against stroke.

NUTRIENTS PER SERVING			
Calories	231	Fiber	5 g (20% DV)
Fat	17 g	Protein	9 g
Saturated fat	10 g	Calcium	226 mg (23% DV)
Sodium	491 mg (21% DV)	Iron	1 mg (6% DV)
Carbohydrate	11 g	Vitamin D	5 IU (1% DV)

Limelight Guacamole

MAKES 2 SERVINGS

Tick-tock, it's time for guac! Mash to your desired consistency. Lisa likes to leave some avocado chunks in the mix for added texture.

TIPS

A ripe avocado yields slightly when squeezed. To pit the avocado, sink the blade of a chef's knife into the side of the pit, then twist it out.

Always wear kitchen gloves when handling jalapeños and avoid touching your skin and eyes.

For a spicier guacamole, increase the jalapeño to 1 jalapeño pepper, minced, and leave in a few seeds.

If preparing this recipe for one person, cut all of the ingredients in half. Or simply prepare the full recipe and save half for leftovers. To limit oxygen exposure, pour 1 tsp (5 mL) additional lime juice over leftovers and cover tightly with plastic wrap. Store in the refrigerator for up to 24 hours.

1	large avocado	1
1	plum (Roma) tomato, diced	1
1/2	small jalapeño pepper, seeded and minced	1/2
1/2	small onion, minced	1/2
1 tbsp	chopped fresh cilantro	15 mL
1/2 tsp	ground cumin	2 mL
1/2 tsp	garlic powder	2 mL
2 tbsp	freshly squeezed lime juice	30 mL
Pinch	salt	Pinch

1. Cut avocado in half, remove the pit and scoop flesh from skins into a bowl. Add tomato, jalapeño, onion, cilantro, cumin, garlic powder and lime juice. Mash with two forks until desired consistency is reached. Season with salt.

Health Bite

The avocado is a fruit (yes, fruit), as identified by its huge seed. An avocado contains almost twice as much potassium as a banana.

NUTRIENTS PER SERVING			
Calories	165	Fiber	7 g (28% DV)
Fat	14 g	Protein	3 g
Saturated fat	2 g	Calcium	21 mg (2% DV)
Sodium	88 mg (4% DV)	Iron	1 mg (6% DV)
Carbohydrate	12 g	Vitamin D	0 IU (0% DV)

Spicy Sun-Dried Tomato Hummus

MAKES 2 SERVINGS

Did you know you can make your own hummus in under 5 minutes? Whip out your food processor or blender and say good-bye to store-bought hummus. The trick to making this bean-based dip taste authentic is the tahini. Enjoy with veggies, like sliced peppers or cucumbers. If more carbohydrates are needed, consider dipping whole wheat pita chips or Roasted Garlic Pita Points (page 205).

TIPS

If a smokier flavor is desired, increase the chipotle chile powder to 1 tsp (5 mL).

If a spicier hummus is desired, substitute ½ tsp (2 mL) cayenne pepper for the chipotle chile powder.

If preparing this recipe for one person, cut all of the ingredients in half. Or simply prepare the full recipe and save half for leftovers. Store leftovers in an airtight container in the refrigerator for up to 4 days.

- Food processor or high-power blender

2	cloves garlic	2
¾ cup	rinsed drained canned no-salt-added chickpeas	175 mL
2 tbsp	dry-packed sun-dried tomatoes (about 4)	30 mL
2 tbsp	freshly squeezed lemon juice	30 mL
2 tbsp	tahini	30 mL
1 tbsp	water	15 mL
1 tbsp	extra virgin olive oil	15 mL
½ tsp	ground cumin	2 mL
½ tsp	chipotle chile powder	2 mL
Pinch	salt	Pinch
1 tsp	paprika	5 mL

1. Add garlic to the food processor and pulse until minced. Add chickpeas, sun-dried tomatoes, lemon juice, tahini, water, oil, cumin, chipotle powder and salt. Process until puréed.

2. Transfer hummus to a serving bowl and sprinkle with paprika.

Health Bite

Lemons are an excellent source of antioxidant vitamin C, which means they can help fight cancer-causing free radicals.

NUTRIENTS PER SERVING			
Calories	269	Fiber	7 g (28% DV)
Fat	16 g	Protein	9 g
Saturated fat	2 g	Calcium	13 mg (1% DV)
Sodium	252 mg (11% DV)	Iron	6 mg (33% DV)
Carbohydrate	26 g	Vitamin D	0 IU (0% DV)

Olive Tapenade

MAKES 2 SERVINGS

With only 3 grams of carbohydrates per serving, this dip allows room for more carbs. Consider enjoying it with Roasted Garlic Pita Points (page 205).

TIPS

Spread tapenade on whole wheat crackers or on pita points.

If preparing this recipe for one person, cut all of the ingredients in half. Or simply prepare the full recipe and save half for leftovers. Store leftovers in an airtight container in the refrigerator for up to 4 days.

- Small food processor or blender

12	pitted kalamata olives (about 1 oz/30 g)	12
1	clove garlic	1
1 tsp	drained capers	5 mL
2 tsp	olive oil	10 mL
½ tsp	freshly ground black pepper	2 mL
1 tsp	dried Italian seasoning	5 mL
1 tsp	chopped fresh parsley	5 mL

1. In food processor, combine olives, garlic, capers, oil, pepper and Italian seasoning; pulse until minced and combined.
2. Transfer tapenade to a bowl and garnish with parsley.

Health Bite

The Greek kalamata olive contains monounsaturated fat, which has been shown to support cardiovascular health.

NUTRIENTS PER SERVING			
Calories	95	Fiber	0 g (0% DV)
Fat	10 g	Protein	0 g
Saturated fat	1 g	Calcium	5 mg (1% DV)
Sodium	520 mg (22% DV)	Iron	0 mg (0% DV)
Carbohydrate	3 g	Vitamin D	0 IU (0% DV)

Salted Fig and Pine Nut Parfait

Figs, one of the most versatile fruits, are trending at many restaurants. For the person with a more refined palate, this snack will satisfy your inner foodie.

TIPS

Substitute chopped walnuts for the pine nuts.

Substitute basil for the rosemary.

If you want to prepare this snack ahead of time, leave out the figs until ready to serve, to prevent them from becoming soggy. Also use this technique if you're planning on saving the second serving for leftovers, storing in an airtight container in the refrigerator for up to 2 days.

If preparing this recipe for one person, cut all of the ingredients in half.

- Preheat oven to 400°F (200°C)
- 2 small parfait glasses or tall thin glasses

4	figs (preferably Mission), stemmed and diced	4
2 tsp	liquid honey	10 mL
2 tsp	olive oil	10 mL
Pinch	sea salt	Pinch
2 tbsp	pine nuts	30 mL
1/2 tsp	dried rosemary	2 mL
1/4 cup	whole-milk ricotta cheese	60 mL
1/4 cup	plain 2% Greek yogurt	60 mL

1. Arrange diced figs on a baking sheet. In a small bowl, combine honey and oil. Brush figs with honey mixture. Bake in preheated oven for 8 to 10 minutes or until shiny and glossy. Let cool. Season with salt.

2. Meanwhile, in a small skillet, toast pine nuts and rosemary over medium heat, stirring constantly, for 1 minute or until fragrant. Set aside and let cool.

3. In each parfait dish, layer one-third ricotta, one-third figs, one-third yogurt and one-third pine nuts mixture. Repeat with the remaining ingredients until all have been used.

Health Bite

Figs are considered to be a false fruit. The tiny fruits are actually located on the inside of the purple-tinged skin. Figs contain calcium, phosphorus and iron.

NUTRIENTS PER SERVING			
Calories	229	Fiber	3 g (12% DV)
Fat	13 g	Protein	8 g
Saturated fat	4 g	Calcium	120 mg (12% DV)
Sodium	230 mg (10% DV)	Iron	1 mg (6% DV)
Carbohydrate	21 g	Vitamin D	3 IU (1% DV)

Balsamic Avocado

Spoon this smooth snack right into your mouth. The acidity of the balsamic perfectly balances the creamy fat from the avocado.

TIPS

A ripe avocado yields slightly when squeezed. To pit the avocado, sink the blade of a chef's knife into the side of the pit, then twist it out.

If preparing this recipe for one person, cut all of the ingredients in half. You can prepare the full recipe of balsamic syrup and refrigerate leftovers in an airtight container in the refrigerator for up to 2 weeks.

½ cup	balsamic vinegar	125 mL
1 tsp	granulated sugar	5 mL
1	avocado	1

1. In a small saucepan, heat vinegar over medium heat and add sugar while whisking continuously. Increase heat to high and bring to a boil. Reduce heat to medium and boil gently, whisking constantly, until vinegar is reduced by about half and the syrup is sticking to the whisk.

2. Cut the avocado in half and remove the pit. Arrange each half on a plate or in a bowl and pour the balsamic syrup over top.

Health Bite

Remember: fat does not make you fat. Fat is needed to absorb fat-soluble vitamins like vitamins A, D, E and K.

NUTRIENTS PER SERVING			
Calories	178	Fiber	5 g (20% DV)
Fat	10 g	Protein	2 g
Saturated fat	1 g	Calcium	26 mg (3% DV)
Sodium	20 mg (1% DV)	Iron	1 mg (6% DV)
Carbohydrate	19 g	Vitamin D	0 IU (0% DV)

Roasted Garlic Pita Points

Four ingredients. Ten minutes. Two servings. One delicious recipe. These pita points pair perfectly with Spicy Sun-Dried Tomato Hummus (page 201), Olive Tapenade (page 202) and Limelight Guacamole (page 200).

TIPS

If you like a bit of spice, sprinkle 1 tsp (5 mL) chili powder on the pita points with the garlic powder in step 1.

If preparing this recipe for one person, cut all of the ingredients in half. Or simply prepare the full recipe and save half for leftovers. Store leftovers in an airtight container for up to 1 week.

- Preheat oven to 400°F (200°C)

1	6½-inch (16 cm) whole wheat pita pocket	1
2 tsp	olive oil	10 mL
2 tsp	garlic powder	10 mL
Pinch	sea salt	Pinch

1. Using a pizza cutter or sharp knife, cut pita pocket into 8 wedges as if you were slicing a pizza. Separate the tops and bottoms of each triangle so you have 16 triangular pieces. Lightly brush both sides of each pita point with oil and sprinkle with garlic powder and salt.

2. Arrange pita points on a baking sheet and bake in preheated oven, turning once halfway through, for 10 minutes or until crispy.

Health Bite

Be mindful of your sodium intake if you have high blood pressure. The American Heart Association encourages individuals to moderate their sodium levels to less than 2300 mg daily.

NUTRIENTS PER SERVING			
Calories	135	Fiber	3 g (12% DV)
Fat	6 g	Protein	4 g
Saturated fat	1 g	Calcium	7 mg (1% DV)
Sodium	269 mg (11% DV)	Iron	1 mg (6% DV)
Carbohydrate	20 g	Vitamin D	0 IU (0% DV)

Becca's Baked Brie with Apple Dippers

MAKES 2 SERVINGS

This warm appetizer is ideal for a girls' night in. Lisa's friend Becca makes this whenever Lisa visits, so grab your gal pal and get on with the gab! Use the apple slices for dipping into the baked Brie.

TIPS

If you have high LDL (low-density lipoprotein, or "bad") cholesterol or need to be mindful of calories, omit the butter in step 1 and choose Brie made from partly skimmed cow's milk. Brie varieties range in percentage of fat and therefore overall calories. Double-cream and triple-cream cheese will contain more than 60% and 75% butterfat.

If preparing this recipe for one person, cut all of the ingredients in half. Or simply prepare the full recipe up to the end of step 2 and save half for leftovers. Store leftovers in an airtight container for up to 3 days. Reheat in the microwave on High for 1 to 2 minutes, or until heated through, and proceed with step 3.

- Preheat oven to 350°F (180°C)
- Small shallow baking dish, about 5 inches (12.5 cm) in diameter

1/4 cup	sliced almonds	60 mL
2 tbsp	unsweetened dried cranberries	30 mL
1 tsp	packed brown sugar	5 mL
1 tsp	ground cinnamon	5 mL
1/2 tsp	ground cloves	2 mL
1 tbsp	melted butter	15 mL
1/2 tsp	vanilla extract	2 mL
4 oz	wedge Brie cheese, cut into four 1-oz (30 g) pieces	125 g
1	medium tart apple (such as Granny Smith; unpeeled), sliced	1

1. In a small bowl, combine almonds, cranberries, brown sugar, cinnamon, cloves, butter and vanilla until thoroughly combined.

2. In baking dish, arrange Brie pieces in a single layer. Pour almond mixture over top. Bake in preheated oven for 10 minutes or until Brie is bubbling.

3. Use apple slices to dip into Brie mixture.

Health Bite

Almonds contain many micronutrients, including calcium, iron, magnesium and riboflavin.

NUTRIENTS PER SERVING			
Calories	370	Fiber	5 g (20% DV)
Fat	26 g	Protein	15 g
Saturated fat	14 g	Calcium	171 mg (17% DV)
Sodium	399 mg (17% DV)	Iron	1 mg (6% DV)
Carbohydrate	21 g	Vitamin D	12 IU (3% DV)

Tropical Piña Colada Muffins

MAKES 4 SMALL MUFFINS (2 MUFFINS PER SERVING)

Grab your apron as well as your lei! Diced pineapple, shredded coconut and lime zest create a trifecta of taste that will have you baking this recipe again and again. Serve fresh out of the oven for the best flavor.

TIPS

You can use either fresh or drained canned unsweetened pineapple in this recipe.

If preparing this recipe for one person, cut all of the ingredients in half. Or simply prepare the full recipe and save half for leftovers. Store leftover muffins in an airtight container for up to 4 days.

- Preheat oven to 350°F (180°C)
- Muffin pan, 4 cups sprayed with canola oil nonstick cooking spray

1/4 cup	yellow cornmeal (preferably stone-ground)	60 mL
1/4 cup	all-purpose flour	60 mL
1/4 tsp	baking powder	1 mL
1	large egg	1
2 tbsp	coconut milk	30 mL
1 tbsp	canola oil	15 mL
2 tsp	grated lime zest	10 mL
1 tbsp	freshly squeezed lime juice	15 mL
1 tsp	vanilla extract	5 mL
1 tbsp	unsweetened shredded coconut	15 mL
1 tbsp	diced pineapple	15 mL

1. In a medium bowl, combine cornmeal, flour and baking powder.
2. In another medium bowl, whisk together egg, coconut milk, oil, lime zest, lime juice and vanilla.
3. Add egg mixture to cornmeal mixture; stir to mix thoroughly. Fold in coconut and pineapple. Divide batter evenly among prepared muffin cups.
4. Bake in preheated oven for about 30 minutes or until a tester inserted in the center of a muffin comes out clean.

Health Bite

One lime contains about 20 mg of vitamin C. This is about 30% of the recommended daily intake.

NUTRIENTS PER SERVING			
Calories	246	Fiber	2 g (8% DV)
Fat	12 g	Protein	6 g
Saturated fat	3 g	Calcium	44 mg (4% DV)
Sodium	77 mg (3% DV)	Iron	2 mg (11% DV)
Carbohydrate	28 g	Vitamin D	29 IU (7% DV)

Vodka-Infused Watermelon Topped with Whipped Ricotta and Honey Basil Vinaigrette

MAKES 2 SERVINGS

This popular summer picnic recipe is polished by adding a dollop of fluffy ricotta with a drizzle of sweet honey and balsamic vinegar on top. As always, be sure to check your blood sugar before enjoying this snack.

TIP

If preparing this recipe for one person, cut all of the ingredients in half. Or simply prepare the full recipe and save half for leftovers. Store leftovers in an airtight container in the refrigerator for up to 2 days.

2 cups	cubed watermelon	500 mL
1 tbsp	vodka	15 mL
1/4 cup	whole-milk ricotta cheese	60 mL
2 tsp	liquid honey	10 mL
1 tsp	balsamic vinegar	5 mL
1 tbsp	chopped fresh basil	15 mL

1. Arrange watermelon cubes in a single layer in a shallow storage container. Sprinkle vodka over top. Cover and refrigerate for at least 1 hour.

2. Divide watermelon between two bowls.

3. In a small bowl, using a fork or small whisk, quickly whisk ricotta for about 1 minute or until it reaches a light, whipped consistency.

4. In another small bowl, combine honey and vinegar until thoroughly combined.

5. Top watermelon with ricotta and drizzle with vinegar mixture. Garnish with basil.

Health Bite

Watermelon, like other red fruits, contains carotenoids, which are phytochemicals that act as antioxidants to help fight free radicals.

NUTRIENTS PER SERVING			
Calories	132	Fiber	1 g (4% DV)
Fat	4 g	Protein	4 g
Saturated fat	3 g	Calcium	77 mg (8% DV)
Sodium	31 mg (1% DV)	Iron	1 mg (6% DV)
Carbohydrate	21 g	Vitamin D	3 IU (1% DV)

Shredded Brussels Sprouts with Cranberries

Never doubt the power of a Brussels sprout. It's one of the most nutrient-dense vegetables. This colorful side salad offers high-quality nutrition and a snappy texture.

TIP

If preparing this recipe for one person, cut all of the ingredients in half. Or simply prepare the full recipe and save half for leftovers. Store leftovers in an airtight container in the refrigerator for up to 2 days.

LEMON AND ROSEMARY VINAIGRETTE

1/4 tsp	grated lemon zest	1 mL
2 tbsp	freshly squeezed lemon juice	30 mL
2 tbsp	olive oil	30 mL
1 tsp	spicy brown mustard	5 mL
1 tsp	dried rosemary	5 mL
1 cup	shredded or thinly sliced Brussels sprouts (about 6 large)	250 mL
1/4 cup	unsweetened dried cranberries	60 mL
1/4 cup	coarsely chopped walnuts	60 mL

1. *Lemon and Rosemary Vinaigrette:* In a small bowl, whisk together lemon zest, lemon juice, oil, mustard and rosemary until thoroughly emulsified.

2. In another small bowl, combine Brussels sprouts, cranberries and walnuts. Pour vinaigrette over top and toss until evenly coated. Cover and refrigerate for 1 hour before serving.

Health Bite

Brussels sprouts are really little cabbages from the cruciferous family, a family of vegetables that also includes broccoli, kale and cauliflower. Cruciferous vegetables are considered anti-inflammatory.

NUTRIENTS PER SERVING			
Calories	269	Fiber	4 g (16% DV)
Fat	24 g	Protein	4 g
Saturated fat	3 g	Calcium	25 mg (3% DV)
Sodium	50 mg (2% DV)	Iron	0 mg (0% DV)
Carbohydrate	11 g	Vitamin D	0 IU (0% DV)

Beet and Goat Cheese Salad

MAKES 2 SERVINGS

Beets and goat cheese go marvelously together. This sweet yet tart snack will keep you fueled until dinnertime.

TIPS

Use any leftover beets to make homemade beet hummus or add them to Shredded Brussels Sprouts with Cranberries (page 209).

If preparing this recipe for one person, cut all of the ingredients in half. Or simply prepare the full recipe and save half for leftovers. Store leftovers in an airtight container in the refrigerator for up to 2 days.

1 tbsp	olive oil	15 mL
2 tsp	white wine vinegar	10 mL
1/2 tsp	dried Italian seasoning	2 mL
1 cup	lightly packed baby kale	250 mL
1/2 cup	cubed cooked golden beets	125 mL
1/2 cup	cubed cooked red beets	125 mL
2 oz	soft goat cheese, crumbled	60 g
2 tbsp	chopped walnuts	30 mL

1. In a small bowl, whisk together oil, vinegar and Italian seasoning.
2. In a medium bowl, gently toss together kale, golden beets, red beets, goat cheese and walnuts. Pour vinaigrette over mixture and toss to coat.

Health Bite

The anti-inflammatory properties of beets may decrease your risk of heart disease, diabetes and Alzheimer's disease. A half cup (125 mL) of sliced beets contains 9 grams of carbohydrates and 2 grams of fiber.

NUTRIENTS PER SERVING			
Calories	224	Fiber	5 g (20% DV)
Fat	19 g	Protein	8 g
Saturated fat	6 g	Calcium	92 mg (9% DV)
Sodium	267 mg (11% DV)	Iron	3 mg (17% DV)
Carbohydrate	9 g	Vitamin D	4 IU (1% DV)

Olive and Feta Salad

MAKES 2 SERVINGS

Let's get Mediterranean! This snack is super-simple and pairs well with soft pita.

TIPS

If you had cheese earlier in the day, replace the feta with diced cooked beets or serve over arugula.

If preparing this recipe for one person, cut all of the ingredients in half. Or simply prepare the full recipe and save half for leftovers. Store leftovers in an airtight container in the refrigerator for up to 2 days.

½ cup	rinsed drained mixed pitted olives (such as kalamata, Lucques, Mission and/or Cerignola)	125 mL
1	clove garlic, minced	1
2 tbsp	olive oil	30 mL
1 tsp	grated lemon zest	5 mL
1 tbsp	freshly squeezed lemon juice	15 mL
¼ tsp	freshly ground black pepper	1 mL
¼ tsp	hot pepper flakes	1 mL
1	plum (Roma) tomato, diced	1
1	small cucumber, peeled and diced	1
1 tbsp	finely chopped red onion	15 mL
2 tbsp	crumbled feta cheese	30 mL

1. In an airtight container, combine olives, garlic, oil, lemon zest, lemon juice, pepper and hot pepper flakes. Cover and shake well until thoroughly combined. Refrigerate overnight or for up to 1 week.

2. In a small bowl, combine tomato, cucumber and onion. Pour marinated olives over vegetable mixture. Top with crumbled cheese.

Health Bite

Olives are fruits that are about 85% fat. They are high in the monounsaturated fat oleic acid, which is associated with being protective against heart disease.

NUTRIENTS PER SERVING			
Calories	218	Fiber	2 g (8% DV)
Fat	21 g	Protein	3 g
Saturated fat	4 g	Calcium	85 mg (9% DV)
Sodium	608 mg (25% DV)	Iron	1 mg (6% DV)
Carbohydrate	8 g	Vitamin D	2 IU (0% DV)

Edamame with Pickled Ginger

This is Laura's clients' favorite snack to choose when meal planning. Sometimes snacks become repetitive, but this one will keep you interested in eating well and managing your blood sugar.

TIPS

Keep frozen edamame on hand for quick protein. One cup (250 mL) shelled edamame contains about 15 grams of carbohydrates.

If preparing this recipe for one person, cut all of the ingredients in half. Or simply prepare the full recipe and save half for leftovers. Store leftovers in an airtight container in the refrigerator for up to 24 hours.

1	clove garlic, minced	1
1 tbsp	chopped green onions	15 mL
1 tbsp	unseasoned rice vinegar	15 mL
1 tsp	reduced-sodium soy sauce (see tip, page 188)	5 mL
1 tsp	toasted sesame oil	5 mL
1 cup	thawed frozen shelled edamame	250 mL
1/3 cup	drained pickled ginger slices	75 mL

1. In a small bowl, whisk together garlic, green onion, vinegar, soy sauce and sesame oil until thoroughly combined. Add edamame and stir until coated with sauce. Serve with pickled ginger on the side.

Health Bite

Soybeans are a great source of protein and fiber, while ginger offers anti-inflammatory properties and aids in digestion.

NUTRIENTS PER SERVING			
Calories	138	Fiber	2 g (8% DV)
Fat	6 g	Protein	8 g
Saturated fat	1 g	Calcium	77 mg (8% DV)
Sodium	211 mg (9% DV)	Iron	1 mg (6% DV)
Carbohydrate	9 g	Vitamin D	0 IU (0% DV)

SWEET SNACKS

Oatmeal Chocolate Chip Cookies

Here is your very own
personalized cookie
recipe that keeps you
in your carb range and
yields just enough so
that any morsels don't
call your name all night
long. Eat mindfully to
savor every bite.

TIPS
∙ ∙ ∙ ∙ ∙ ∙ ∙ ∙ ∙ ∙ ∙ ∙ ∙ ∙ ∙ ∙ ∙

If you don't have a small egg,
use half a large egg white,
which equals 1 tbsp + 2 tsp
(25 mL).

Use higher-protein flours, such
as almond flour, to keep your
carbohydrates within a snack
range of 15 to 30 grams.

This recipe doesn't work well
if halved to a single serving.
Instead, choose a lucky
friend or family member and
share the recipe. Or simply
prepare the full recipe and
save half for leftovers. Store
leftover cookies in an airtight
container in the refrigerator
for up to 1 week.

Health Bite
∙ ∙ ∙ ∙ ∙ ∙ ∙ ∙ ∙ ∙ ∙ ∙ ∙ ∙

Oats are rich in beta-
gluten fiber, which helps
lower levels of low-
density lipoprotein (LDL,
or "bad") cholesterol.

- Preheat oven to 350°F (180°C)
- Baking sheet, lined with parchment paper

2 tbsp	almond flour (almond meal)	30 mL
1/4 tsp	ground cinnamon	1 mL
1/8 tsp	baking powder	0.5 mL
1 tbsp	granulated sugar	15 mL
1	small egg white (see tip, at left)	1
1 1/2 tsp	canola oil	7 mL
1/4 tsp	vanilla extract	1 mL
1/4 cup	large-flake (old-fashioned) rolled oats	60 mL
1 tbsp	mini semisweet chocolate chips	15 mL

1. In a small bowl, using a wooden spoon, whisk together flour, cinnamon and baking powder.

2. In a medium bowl, whisk together sugar, egg white, oil and vanilla until smooth and fluffy.

3. Gradually add the flour mixture to the egg mixture and stir until thoroughly combined. Stir in oats and chocolate chips.

4. Using an ice cream scooper or a tablespoon (15 mL) measure, scoop out batter for each of 4 cookies, spacing them at least 1 inch (2.5 cm) apart on prepared baking sheet.

5. Bake in preheated oven for 8 to 10 minutes or until cookies are golden brown and firm in the center. Let cool on pan on a wire rack for 5 minutes, then transfer cookies to the rack to cool.

NUTRIENTS PER SERVING			
Calories	178	Fiber	2 g (8% DV)
Fat	10 g	Protein	5 g
Saturated fat	2 g	Calcium	38 mg (4% DV)
Sodium	60 mg (3% DV)	Iron	1 mg (6% DV)
Carbohydrate	19 g	Vitamin D	0 IU (0% DV)

Quinoa Raisin Cookies

There's no reason to pay for expensive healthy cookies at the store when you can simply bake your own! Save your carbs at snack time for these cool cookies.

TIP

This recipe doesn't work well if halved to a single serving. Instead, find a friend or family member to share it with. Or simply prepare the full recipe and save half for leftovers. Store leftover cookies in an airtight container in the refrigerator for up to 1 week.

Health Bite

You may call quinoa a super-grain, but this Incan nutritional treasure is actually a seed. It comes from the same plant family as spinach and the sugar beet. Quinoa is sometimes called a psuedocereal because it is a nonlegume (not a bean, nut or pea) that is grown for grain (versus cereal grains, which come from grassy plants). Buckwheat and amaranth are also known as pseudocereals.

- Preheat oven to 350°F (180°C)
- Baking sheet, lined with parchment paper

1/4 cup	quinoa, rinsed	60 mL
1/2 cup	water	125 mL
2 tbsp	almond flour (almond meal)	30 mL
1/4 tsp	ground cinnamon	1 mL
1/8 tsp	baking powder	0.5 mL
1 tbsp	granulated sugar	15 mL
1	small egg white (see tip, page 214)	1
1 1/2 tsp	canola oil	7 mL
1/4 tsp	vanilla extract	1 mL
1 tbsp	raisins	15 mL

1. In a small saucepan, combine quinoa and water; bring to a boil over high heat. Reduce heat to low, cover and simmer for 15 minutes or until quinoa has absorbed water.

2. In a small bowl, using a wooden spoon, whisk together flour, cinnamon and baking powder.

3. In a medium bowl, whisk together sugar, egg white, oil and vanilla until smooth and fluffy.

4. Gradually add the flour mixture to the egg mixture, stirring until thoroughly combined. Stir in quinoa and raisins.

5. Using an ice scream scooper or a tablespoon (15 mL) measure, scoop out batter for each of 4 cookies, spacing them at least 1 inch (2.5 cm) apart on prepared baking sheet.

6. Bake in preheated oven for 8 to 10 minutes or until cookies are golden brown and firm in the center. Let cool on pan on a wire rack for 5 minutes, then transfer cookies to the rack to cool.

NUTRIENTS PER SERVING			
Calories	195	Fiber	3 g (12% DV)
Fat	8 g	Protein	6 g
Saturated fat	1 g	Calcium	51 mg (5% DV)
Sodium	54 mg (2% DV)	Iron	1 mg (6% DV)
Carbohydrate	25 g	Vitamin D	0 IU (0% DV)

S'mores

This dessert is reminiscent of summer camp and even winter campfires alongside the ski slopes. To make this dish work for your healthy lifestyle, we have created a meringue marshmallow.

TIPS

Don't get any yolk in the cream of tartar mixture; yolk will prevent peaks from forming.

The egg white in this recipe is not thoroughly cooked, so if the food safety of raw eggs is a concern for you, use a pasteurized egg white or 1½ tbsp (22 mL) pasteurized liquid egg white.

Be sure to use real maple syrup and follow the recipe to a "t" for a s'more that is less than 30 grams of carbohydrate.

If you have type 1 diabetes, consider spreading 1 tbsp (15 mL) natural peanut butter on one graham cracker for a source of protein and fat to slow the breakdown of this sweet snack.

This recipe doesn't work well if halved to a single serving. Instead, choose a lucky friend or family member and share the recipe.

- Preheat oven to 250°F (120°C)
- Baking sheet, lined with parchment paper

1	large egg white (see tips, at left), at room temperature	1
⅛ tsp	cream of tartar	0.5 mL
2 tbsp	pure maple syrup	30 mL
2	milk chocolate kisses (such as Hershey Kisses, or 2½ tbsp/37 mL finely chopped milk chocolate)	2
2	rectangular graham crackers (each 5- by 2½ inches/12.5 by 6 cm), split in half	2

1. In a small bowl, using an electric mixer on high speed, beat egg white and cream of tartar for 4 minutes or until soft peaks form. Gradually pour in maple syrup while continuing to beat, making the peaks firm and glossy.

2. Using a spoon, divide egg white mixture into two dollops on prepared baking sheet. These will be your "marshmallows." Transfer baking sheet to preheated oven, turn off the heat and let stand for 1 hour without opening the oven door.

3. Just before "marshmallows" are ready, in a small microwave-safe bowl, microwave chocolate on High for 10 to 15 seconds or until melted.

4. Top 1 graham cracker with half the chocolate and one "marshmallow," then top with a second graham cracker. Repeat with the remaining ingredients.

Health Bite

There is preliminary research on the neuroprotective affects of the penolic compounds found in pure maple syrup from Canada.

NUTRIENTS PER SERVING			
Calories	144	Fiber	1 g (4% DV)
Fat	3 g	Protein	3 g
Saturated fat	1 g	Calcium	33 mg (3% DV)
Sodium	100 mg (4% DV)	Iron	1 mg (6% DV)
Carbohydrate	27 g	Vitamin D	0 IU (0% DV)

Peanut Butter Energy Balls

Need an energy-dense snack before spin class? These vegetarian power-packed balls provide protein and carbohydrates to help support your exercise routine. Remember, always check your blood sugar before, during and after working out.

TIPS

You can substitute chopped walnuts for the almonds.

If preparing this recipe for one person, cut all of the ingredients in half. Or simply prepare the full recipe and save half for leftovers. Store these balls in an airtight container lined with parchment paper in the refrigerator for up to 4 days or in the freezer for up to 1 month.

- Shallow sealable storage container, lined with parchment paper

1 tbsp	chia seeds	15 mL
¼ cup	creamy natural peanut butter	60 mL
1 tbsp	water	15 mL
2	pitted dates, diced	2
¼ cup	large-flake (old-fashioned) rolled oats	60 mL
2 tbsp	slivered almonds	30 mL
1 tbsp	ground cinnamon	15 mL

1. In a medium microwave-safe bowl, microwave chia seeds, peanut butter and water on High for about 30 seconds or until melted. Add dates, oats, almonds and cinnamon; stir to combine.

2. Using your hands, shape the mixture into 8 balls and arrange in prepared shallow container. Freeze overnight.

Health Bite

Dates contain a good amount of fiber and energy, as well as essential nutrients such as zinc, vitamins A and K, and some B vitamins.

NUTRIENTS PER SERVING			
Calories	340	Fiber	7 g (28% DV)
Fat	22 g	Protein	10 g
Saturated fat	3 g	Calcium	109 mg (11% DV)
Sodium	141 mg (6% DV)	Iron	6 mg (33% DV)
Carbohydrate	29 g	Vitamin D	0 IU (0% DV)

"Crave No More" Cupcakes

When eating consistent carbohydrates throughout the day, dessert is actually part of your meal plan. Black bean brownie cupcakes are perfect for managing your blood sugar while fulfilling any chocolate cravings.

TIPS

Save extra black beans for use in the salad in Citrus Fish Fajitas (page 142).

Serve hot with vanilla bean ice cream or as a side with an après-dinner drink.

This recipe doesn't work well if halved to a single serving. Instead, find a friend or family member to share it with. Or simply prepare the full recipe and save half for leftovers. Store leftover cupcakes in an airtight container in the refrigerator for up to 1 week. Alternatively, wrap cooled cupcakes individually in foil and store in a sealable plastic freezer bag in the freezer for up to 1 month.

- Preheat oven to 350°F (180°C)
- Food processor
- Muffin pan, 4 cups lined with paper liners

1/3 cup	unsweetened cocoa powder	75 mL
2 tbsp	almond flour (almond meal)	30 mL
2 tbsp	semisweet or bittersweet (dark) chocolate chips	30 mL
1 tsp	baking powder	5 mL
3/4 cup	rinsed drained canned black beans	175 mL
1	large egg	1
1 tbsp	pure maple syrup	15 mL
2 tsp	canola oil	10 mL

1. In a large bowl, combine cocoa powder, flour, chocolate chips and baking powder.

2. In food processor, combine black beans, egg, maple syrup and oil; process until smooth.

3. Scrape black bean mixture into flour mixture and stir gently until thoroughly combined. Scoop batter into prepared muffin cups.

4. Bake in preheated oven for 18 to 20 minutes or until a tester inserted in the center of a cupcake comes out clean. Let cool in pan on a wire rack for 5 minutes, then transfer to the rack to cool for another 10 minutes before serving.

Health Bite

The iron, calcium, magnesium, manganese, copper and zinc in black beans can help to keep bones strong and healthy.

NUTRIENTS PER SERVING			
Calories	309	Fiber	11 g (44% DV)
Fat	17 g	Protein	12 g
Saturated fat	5 g	Calcium	223 mg (22% DV)
Sodium	443 mg (19% DV)	Iron	4 mg (22% DV)
Carbohydrate	38 g	Vitamin D	22 IU (6% DV)

Lemon Ginger Cupcakes

Diabetes-friendly cupcakes are tonight's snack! Bake and serve with a dollop of lemon-flavored Greek yogurt or ginger-flavored goat's milk yogurt for a bite of bitter sweetness.

TIP

This recipe doesn't work well if halved to a single serving. Instead, find a friend or family member to share it with. Or simply prepare the full recipe and save half for leftovers. Store leftover cupcakes in an airtight container in the refrigerator for up to 1 week. Alternately, wrap cooled cupcakes individually in foil and store in a sealable plastic freezer bag in the freezer for up to 1 month.

- Preheat oven to 350°F (180°C)
- Muffin pan, 4 cups lined with paper liners

1/2 cup	almond flour (almond meal)	125 mL
1/4 cup	whole wheat flour	60 mL
1 tbsp	wheat germ	15 mL
1/2 tsp	ground ginger	2 mL
1/4 tsp	baking soda	1 mL
1	large egg	1
1 tsp	grated lemon zest	5 mL
1/2 cup	unsweetened almond milk	125 mL

1. In a medium bowl, whisk together almond flour, whole wheat flour, wheat germ, ginger and baking soda.
2. In a small bowl, combine egg, lemon zest and almond milk.
3. Add egg mixture to flour mixture and stir to combine. Scoop batter into prepared muffin cups.
4. Bake in preheated oven for about 20 minutes or until a tester inserted into the center of a cupcake comes out clean. Let cool in pan on a wire rack for 5 minutes, then transfer to the rack to cool for another 10 minutes before serving.

Health Bite

Lemon zest contains polyphenols, which may, when eaten often, improve insulin resistance by suppressing the accumulation of fat around the belly.

NUTRIENTS PER SERVING			
Calories	275	Fiber	6 g (24% DV)
Fat	18 g	Protein	12 g
Saturated fat	2 g	Calcium	140 mg (14% DV)
Sodium	309 mg (13% DV)	Iron	2 mg (11% DV)
Carbohydrate	19 g	Vitamin D	47 IU (12% DV)

Grapefruit Olive Oil Cakes

MAKES 2 SERVINGS

Usually found on menus at high-end restaurants (you know, the kind that don't list prices), this cake can now be created in the comfort of your home and at a reduced cost. Grapefruit is extremely high in vitamin C and is one of the most hydrating fruits. Its bold citrus flavor balances the olive oil.

TIPS

One grapefruit will yield more than enough zest and juice for this recipe; refrigerate or freeze extra for another use.

This recipe doesn't work well if halved to a single serving. Instead, find a friend or family member to share it with. Or simply prepare the full recipe and save half for leftovers. Store leftover cake in an airtight container in the refrigerator for up to 2 days.

- Preheat oven to 350°F (180°C)
- Two ³/₄-cup (175 mL) ramekins, sprayed with canola oil nonstick cooking spray

¹/₂ cup	all-purpose flour	125 mL
¹/₄ tsp	baking powder	1 mL
Pinch	salt	Pinch
2 tsp	granulated sugar	10 mL
1	large egg	1
¹/₃ cup	olive oil	75 mL
¹/₃ cup	unsweetened almond milk	75 mL
2 tsp	grated grapefruit zest	10 mL
2 tbsp	freshly squeezed grapefruit juice	30 mL
1	sprig mint, halved	1

1. In a medium bowl, whisk together flour, baking powder and salt.

2. In a small bowl, whisk together sugar, egg, oil, almond milk, grapefruit zest and grapefruit juice.

3. Add egg mixture to flour mixture and stir to combine thoroughly. Divide batter between prepared ramekins.

4. Bake in preheated oven for 15 to 20 minutes or until edges are golden brown and a tester inserted in the center of a cake comes out clean. Let cool for 10 minutes, garnish with mint and serve in ramekins.

Health Bite

A list of added sugars by the American Heart Association includes (but is not limited to) agave nectar, molasses, maple syrup, raw sugar, sucrose cane sugar, corn sweetener, brown sugar and evaporated cane juice.

NUTRIENTS PER SERVING			
Calories	459	Fiber	1 g (4% DV)
Fat	36 g	Protein	6 g
Saturated fat	6 g	Calcium	110 mg (11% DV)
Sodium	180 mg (8% DV)	Iron	2 mg (11% DV)
Carbohydrate	30 g	Vitamin D	38 IU (10% DV)

No-Bake Key Lime Pie

Wander into a tropical haven of limes, coconut and cashews. You are not on an island, but it will taste like you are.

TIPS

If you can't find Key limes, regular lime zest and juice will work in this recipe.

If preparing this recipe for two people, simply double all of the ingredients.

Health Bite

Cashews are rich in monounsaturated fatty acids, with are part of a heart-healthy Mediterranean diet.

- ¾-cup (175 mL) ramekin

5	cashews	5
1	graham cracker square (2½ by 2½ inches/6 by 6 cm)	1
1 tsp	coconut oil	5 mL
2 tbsp	unsweetened shredded coconut	30 mL
1 tsp	granulated sugar	5 mL
¾ cup + 2 tbsp	plain 2% Greek yogurt (7 oz/210 g)	205 mL
1½ tsp	grated Key lime zest, divided	7 mL
1 tbsp	freshly squeezed Key lime juice	15

1. In a sealable plastic bag, using a mallet, hammer or rolling pin, crush cashews and graham cracker to the consistency of sand.

2. In a small bowl, combine crushed graham cracker mixture and coconut oil; press into bottom of ramekin.

3. In another small bowl, combine shredded coconut, sugar, yogurt, 1 tsp (5 mL) lime zest and lime juice. Scoop mixture onto graham cracker crust, smooth top and sprinkle with the remaining lime zest. Cover and refrigerate for at least 1 hour, until chilled, or for up to 24 hours.

NUTRIENTS PER SERVING			
Calories	368	Fiber	2 g (8% DV)
Fat	19 g	Protein	23 g
Saturated fat	13 g	Calcium	215 mg (22% DV)
Sodium	105 mg (4% DV)	Iron	1 mg (6% DV)
Carbohydrate	27 g	Vitamin D	2 IU (0% DV)

Ambrosia

Traditionally, coconut and oranges flavored this recipe. Laura loved this dish as a child. She made it with her mom, adding a combination of sour cream, mandarin oranges, pineapple and marshmallows. Here is today's *Everyday Diabetes* version just for you.

TIPS

You can use fresh or canned oranges and pineapple in this recipe. But be sure to drain and rinse canned fruit to remove any syrup.

If you choose flavored Greek yogurt, be mindful of the additional carbohydrates.

Make this recipe immediately before serving to prevent the fruit juices from decreasing the yogurt's thick, creamy texture.

If preparing this recipe for two people, simply double all of the ingredients.

$1/_3$ cup	mini marshmallows	75 mL
2 tbsp	diced mandarin oranges (see tip, at left)	30 mL
1 tbsp	diced pineapple	15 mL
$1/_2$ cup	plain 2% Greek yogurt	125 mL
1 tsp	vanilla extract	5 mL

1. In a small bowl, stir together marshmallows, mandarin oranges, pineapple, yogurt and vanilla. Serve immediately.

Health Bite

Research has shown that bromelain, an enzyme found in pineapples, can reduce swelling, bruising and pain following an injury.

NUTRIENTS PER SERVING			
Calories	165	Fiber	1 g (4% DV)
Fat	3 g	Protein	12 g
Saturated fat	1 g	Calcium	124 mg (12% DV)
Sodium	53 mg (2% DV)	Iron	0 mg (0% DV)
Carbohydrate	18 g	Vitamin D	1 IU (0% DV)

Chocolate Mousse

It doesn't take a pastry chef to master this silky and sweet mousse recipe. Even better, this chocolate mousse has only 23 grams of carbohydrate.

TIPS

You can use any kind of chocolate chips in this recipe.

To get the most volume when whipping cream, chill a metal or glass bowl and the beaters for your mixer in the refrigerator and make sure the cream is very cold.

This recipe doesn't work well if halved to a single serving. Instead, find a friend or family member to share it with. Or simply prepare the full recipe and save half for leftovers. Store leftover mousse in an airtight container in the refrigerator for up to 2 days.

1	large egg yolk	1
1 tbsp	granulated sugar	15 mL
1/2 cup	heavy or whipping (35%) cream	125 mL
1/4 cup	milk chocolate chips	60 mL
1/3 cup	heavy or whipping (35%) cream	75 mL

1. In a medium bowl, using an electric mixer on high speed, beat egg yolk for 30 seconds. Gradually pour in sugar and beat for 1 minute, until pale and thick.

2. In a small saucepan, heat 1/2 cup (125 mL) cream over medium heat for 5 minutes or until almost hot. Pour half of warmed cream into egg mixture and stir to combine.

3. Reduce heat to medium-low and pour egg and cream mixture back into saucepan with remaining warmed cream. Cook, stirring, for 2 to 3 minutes or until well blended and smooth. Add chocolate chips and stir until all of the chips are melted. Transfer to another medium bowl with a lid and refrigerate for at least 2 hours, until chilled, or for up to 3 days.

4. Before serving, using an electric mixer on high speed, beat 1/3 cup (75 mL) cream for 5 minutes or until light and fluffy. Fold into chilled chocolate mixture.

Health Bite

While many know that chocolate has several healthy components from the cocoa (flavenoids, flavenols and antioxidants), there is newer research noted by the Cleveland Clinic suggesting that the saturated fat stearic acid found in cocoa butter (which is a naturally occurring fat in chocolate) may be neutral on heart health. This fatty acid doesn't increase or decrease cholesterol levels. More evidence that fat is not "bad."

NUTRIENTS PER SERVING			
Calories	490	Fiber	1 g (4% DV)
Fat	45 g	Protein	5 g
Saturated fat	28 g	Calcium	84 mg (8% DV)
Sodium	33 mg (1% DV)	Iron	1 mg (6% DV)
Carbohydrate	23 g	Vitamin D	89 IU (22% DV)

Cinnamon Chia Peach Pudding

MAKES 1 SERVING

You will just love this tasty textured pudding. Your friends will ask you to make them a single serving of this trendy sweet.

TIPS

You can substitute unsweetened soy milk for the almond milk.

This pudding will taste best after 24 hours (the chia seeds will have time to absorb the liquid) and will stay fresh for up to 3 days in the refrigerator.

If preparing this recipe for two people, simply double all of the ingredients.

- Wide-mouth mason jar (16 oz/500 mL) or bowl with lid

¼ cup	chopped peaches	60 mL
2 tbsp	chia seeds	30 mL
1 tsp	ground cinnamon	5 mL
⅔ cup	unsweetened almond milk	150 mL
2 tsp	vanilla extract	10 mL
1 tsp	pure maple syrup	5 mL

1. In mason jar (or bowl), combine peaches, chia seeds, cinnamon, almond milk, vanilla and maple syrup. Secure the lid and shake well. Refrigerate for at least 1 hour or until pudding-like in consistency (see tip, at left).

Health Bite

Peaches contain vitamin C, fiber, choline and potassium — all of which support heart health.

NUTRIENTS PER SERVING			
Calories	187	Fiber	9 g (36% DV)
Fat	8 g	Protein	5 g
Saturated fat	1 g	Calcium	296 mg (30% DV)
Sodium	125 mg (5% DV)	Iron	4 mg (22% DV)
Carbohydrate	21 g	Vitamin D	67 IU (17% DV)

Avocado Ice Cream

Avocado is a fruit. Just like any other fruit, it can be a great flavor for ice cream, especially with chocolate. Dare your senses and delight in this dish created just for you.

TIPS

If you have overripe bananas, remove the peel, slice into quarters and freeze in a sealable plastic bag for up to 3 months for baking and ice cream recipes.

A ripe avocado yields slightly when squeezed. To pit the avocado, sink the blade of a chef's knife into the side of the pit, then twist it out.

If preparing this recipe for one person, cut all of the ingredients in half. Or simply prepare the full recipe and save half for leftovers. Store leftover ice cream in an airtight container in the freezer for up to 3 months.

- Food processor

¾ cup	sliced banana (about 1)	175 mL
1	medium avocado	1
2 tbsp	cacao nibs	30 mL

1. Place banana in sealable freezer bag; freeze overnight.
2. In food processor, process banana and avocado until smooth. Add cacao nibs and pulse a few times, until evenly distributed.
3. Transfer mixture to a small bowl, cover and freeze for 1 to 2 hours or until frozen.

Health Bite

Also known as alligator pear, avocado is high in monounsaturated fat and is a good source of lutein.

NUTRIENTS PER SERVING			
Calories	253	Fiber	11 g (44% DV)
Fat	17 g	Protein	4 g
Saturated fat	5 g	Calcium	23 mg (2% DV)
Sodium	6 mg (0% DV)	Iron	1 mg (6% DV)
Carbohydrate	30 g	Vitamin D	0 IU (0% DV)

Salted Cocoa Strawberries

Craving something both salty and sweet? These berries will help you meet your needs without opening an oven! Serve alongside a plate of hard and soft cheeses.

TIPS

If you prefer to use a different fruit, choose one that is wet to the touch when sliced or chopped, like cantaloupe or apples, to help the cocoa stick to the fruit.

If preparing this recipe for one person, cut all of the ingredients in half. Or simply prepare the full recipe and save half for leftovers. Store leftovers in an airtight container in the refrigerator for up to 24 hours.

2 tbsp	unsweetened cocoa powder	30 mL
1/4 tsp	sea salt	1 mL
8	strawberries (do not dry after washing)	8

1. In a small bowl, combine cocoa powder and salt.
2. Using your fingers, dip each strawberry in salted cocoa. Arrange dusted strawberries on a plate and enjoy.

Health Bite

One cup (250 mL) strawberries provides 3 grams of fiber, 220 milligrams of potassium and 85 milligrams of vitamin C.

NUTRIENTS PER SERVING			
Calories	28	Fiber	3 g (12% DV)
Fat	1 g	Protein	12 g
Saturated fat	0.4 g	Calcium	15 mg (2% DV)
Sodium	294 mg (12% DV)	Iron	1 mg (6% DV)
Carbohydrate	7 g	Vitamin D	0 IU (0% DV)

Baked Cardamom Apple

Feeling a bit spicy? Indulge in an aromatic baked apple.

TIPS

To avoid a sticky mess, place the apple in a paper muffin liner within the baking dish.

To prepare this recipe in the microwave, complete the recipe up to the end of step 2, then place the apple on a microwave-safe dish and microwave on High for 3 minutes or until softened. Fill the apple with the oat mixture and microwave on High for 2 minutes or until the mixture is bubbly. Let cool for 5 minutes before serving.

If preparing this recipe for two people, simply double all of the ingredients.

- Preheat oven to 350°F (180°C)
- Small baking dish, lined with parchment paper

1	small apple (such as McIntosh)	1
2 tbsp	large-flake (old-fashioned) rolled oats	30 mL
1 tbsp	crushed pecans	15 mL
2 tsp	coconut oil	10 mL
1/4 tsp	ground cinnamon	1 mL
1/4 tsp	ground cardamom	1 mL

1. Using a small paring knife, cut a circle the size of a dime around the apple's stem. Cut into the apple's center, pushing about halfway down, and remove the stem. Turn the apple upside down and cut down into the center to reach the hollowed-out area. Remove the remaining core. Using the knife, scrape the sides of the apple's interior center and smooth out.

2. In a small bowl, combine oats, pecans, coconut oil, cinnamon and cardamom.

3. Place apple in prepared baking dish and fill apple with oats mixture.

4. Bake in preheated oven for 35 to 40 minutes or until apple is soft with wilting skin.

Health Bite

Oats are rich in beta-gluten fiber, which helps lower levels of low-density lipoprotein (LDL, or "bad") cholesterol.

NUTRIENTS PER SERVING			
Calories	243	Fiber	6 g (24% DV)
Fat	15 g	Protein	2 g
Saturated fat	8 g	Calcium	22 mg (2% DV)
Sodium	2 mg (0% DV)	Iron	1 mg (6% DV)
Carbohydrate	29 g	Vitamin D	0 IU (0% DV)

Chocolate Nut Butter Banana Kebab

Get decadent with this kebab. Slather a banana with chocolate peanut butter to experience a mouthwatering dessert made by you!

TIPS

If preparing this recipe ahead of time, remove kebab from freezer after 15 minutes and transfer to a sealable plastic freezer bag or glass dish with cover. Store frozen kebab in the freezer for up to 2 weeks.

We used Peanut Butter & Co's Dark Chocolate Dreams to keep this sweet snack in target carbohydrate range (1 tbsp/15 mL equals 6 grams of carbohydrate).

If preparing this recipe for two people, simply double all of the ingredients.

- One 12-inch (30 cm) wooden skewer
- Baking sheet, lined with parchment paper

1/2	medium banana	1/2
1 tbsp	chocolate peanut butter	15 mL
5	unsalted cashews	5

1. Cut banana half into 6 slices. Spread one side of each slice with chocolate peanut butter.

2. In a sealable plastic bag, using a mallet, hammer or rolling pin, crush cashews until a coarse consistency is reached. Sprinkle crushed cashews over chocolate peanut butter on banana slices.

3. Slide the skewer through the center of each banana slice with the flat, cut sides parallel to the skewer and place the banana kebab on the prepared baking sheet. Freeze on baking sheet for 15 minutes or until chilled.

Health Bite

Bananas support heart health, thanks to their fiber, potassium and vitamins C and B_6.

NUTRIENTS PER SERVING			
Calories	183	Fiber	3 g (12% DV)
Fat	11 g	Protein	5 g
Saturated fat	2 g	Calcium	13 mg (1% DV)
Sodium	20 mg (1% DV)	Iron	3 mg (17% DV)
Carbohydrate	24 g	Vitamin D	0 IU (0% DV)

BONUS SECTION 1
HUNGRY FOR THE HOLIDAYS

Cinnamon and Nutmeg Acorn Squash

MAKES 2 SERVINGS

Christmas is a time to spend with loved ones — not bent over the stove, stirring dinner. This four-ingredient recipe is seriously simple and will leave you with time to spend with your special someone on this winter holiday.

TIPS

Save those seeds! Clean the acorn squash seeds and season with your favorite flavors, such as paprika, chipotle chile powder, dried rosemary and sea salt, or ground cinnamon. Arrange on a baking sheet and roast in a 375°F (190°C) oven for 15 minutes or until golden brown, toasted and brown around the edges.

If preparing this recipe for one person, cut all of the ingredients in half. Or simply prepare the full recipe and save half for leftovers. Store leftovers in an airtight container for up to 2 days. Reheat in the microwave on High for 1 to 2 minutes or until heated through.

- Preheat oven to 375°F (190°C)
- 13- by 9-inch (33 by 23 cm) glass baking dish

1	medium acorn squash	1
1 tbsp	butter, melted	15 mL
1 tsp	ground nutmeg	5 mL
1 tsp	ground cinnamon	5 mL

1. Cut acorn squash in half. Using a spoon, scoop out seeds (see tip, at left). Place squash halves, cut side up, in baking dish. Pour water into the bottom of the baking dish, around the squash halves, up to 1 inch (2.5 cm) depth.

2. Drizzle each squash half with butter and season with nutmeg and cinnamon.

3. Bake in preheated oven for 50 minutes or until squash is easily pierced with a fork.

Health Bite

Squash is a good source of carotenoids, which are important for eye health.

NUTRIENTS PER SERVING			
Calories	148	Fiber	8 g (32% DV)
Fat	6 g	Protein	2 g
Saturated fat	4 g	Calcium	86 mg (9% DV)
Sodium	7 mg (0% DV)	Iron	2 mg (11% DV)
Carbohydrate	24 g	Vitamin D	4 IU (1% DV)

Strawberry Quinoa Salad

MAKES 1 SERVING

Moms need rest and relaxation. This is an easy salad to make Mom feel loved while keeping her healthy. This salad is perfect poolside because it's easy to digest and pairs nicely with a white wine or prosecco.

TIPS

If you want to choose a different grain or seed, try ½ cup (125 mL) cooked wheat berries or farro.

If preparing this recipe for two people, simply double all of the ingredients.

- **Preheat oven to 350°F (180°C)**

20	unsalted shelled pistachios	20
1 tbsp	olive oil	15 mL
2 tsp	red wine vinegar	10 mL
1 tsp	liquid honey	5 mL
½ cup	lightly packed watercress	125 mL
½ cup	packed trimmed spinach	125 mL
¼ cup	finely chopped red onion	60 mL
5	strawberries, thinly sliced	5
½ cup	cooked quinoa, cooled	125 mL

1. Spread pistachios on a baking sheet and bake in preheated oven for 5 to 10 minutes or until lightly browned. Transfer pistachios to a sealable plastic bag and, using a mallet, hammer or rolling pin, coarsely crush pistachios.

2. In a small bowl, whisk together crushed pistachios, oil, vinegar and honey until thoroughly combined.

3. In a large bowl, combine watercress, spinach, onion, strawberries and quinoa. Pour in vinaigrette and toss to coat. Serve immediately.

Health Bite

You may call quinoa a super-grain, but this Incan nutritional treasure is actually a seed. It comes from the same plant family as spinach and the sugar beet. Quinoa is sometimes called a psuedocereal because it is a nonlegume (not a bean, nut or pea) that is grown for grain (versus cereal grains, which come from grassy plants). Buckwheat and amaranth are also known as pseudocereals.

NUTRIENTS PER SERVING			
Calories	378	Fiber	6 g (24% DV)
Fat	22 g	Protein	9 g
Saturated fat	3 g	Calcium	92 mg (9% DV)
Sodium	29 mg (1% DV)	Iron	3 mg (17% DV)
Carbohydrate	40 g	Vitamin D	0 IU (0% DV)

Haroset

Celebrate your seder meal with this carb-friendly haroset. This meal has been modified to reduce the grams of carbohydrate with the understanding that haroset is traditionally eaten with matzo.

TIPS

For a sweeter apple, choose a Fuji or Gala apple; for a more tart flavor, use a McIntosh or Granny Smith apple.

If preparing this recipe for one person, cut all of the ingredients in half. Or simply prepare the full recipe and save half for leftovers. Store leftovers in an airtight container in the refrigerator for up to 2 days.

2	pitted dates, diced	2
1	apple (unpeeled), finely diced	1
1/4 cup	chopped walnuts	60 mL
1/4 cup	chopped almonds	60 mL
1/2 tsp	ground cinnamon	2 mL
1/2 tsp	ground ginger	2 mL
2 tbsp	kosher sweet red wine	30 mL
2 tsp	liquid honey	10 mL

1. In a medium bowl, combine dates, apple, walnuts, almonds, cinnamon, ginger, wine and honey; stir to coat thoroughly.

Health Bite

Apples are excellent sources of fiber, flavonoids and antioxidants.

NUTRIENTS PER SERVING			
Calories	283	Fiber	4 g (16% DV)
Fat	18 g	Protein	3 g
Saturated fat	2 g	Calcium	72 mg (7% DV)
Sodium	3 mg (0% DV)	Iron	6 mg (33% DV)
Carbohydrate	27 g	Vitamin D	0 IU (0% DV)

Texas Caviar

MAKES 2 SERVINGS

Ring in the New Year with this effortless Southern appetizer. The rumor has it that eating black-eyed peas on New Year's Day will bring you prosperity in the new year. At the least, this recipe will leave you rich in fiber, protein and vitamins!

TIPS

Always wear kitchen gloves when handling jalapeños and avoid touching your skin and eyes.

If you prefer a spicier dip, add some of the seeds from the jalapeño.

Add 1 tbsp (15 mL) freshly squeezed lime juice with the vinegar for a kick of citrus.

If preparing this recipe for one person, cut all of the ingredients in half. Or simply prepare the full recipe and save half for leftovers. Store leftovers in an airtight container in the refrigerator for up to 4 days.

2 tbsp	olive oil	30 mL
1 tbsp	white vinegar	15 mL
1 tsp	dried Italian seasoning	5 mL
1/3 cup	rinsed drained canned black-eyed peas	75 mL
1	clove garlic, minced	1
1/4 cup	finely chopped bell pepper (any color)	60 mL
1/4 cup	finely chopped green onions	60 mL
1/4 cup	diced tomatoes	60 mL
1 tsp	chopped fresh cilantro	5 mL
1 tsp	minced seeded jalapeño pepper	5 mL

1. In a small bowl, whisk together oil, vinegar and Italian seasoning.

2. In a medium bowl, combine black-eyed peas, garlic, bell pepper, green onions, tomatoes, cilantro and jalapeño. Pour dressing over black-eyed pea mixture and toss to coat.

Health Bite

Black-eyed peas are a low-fat, low-calorie food and help to keep you feeling sated.

NUTRIENTS PER SERVING			
Calories	172	Fiber	3 g (12% DV)
Fat	14 g	Protein	3 g
Saturated fat	2 g	Calcium	46 mg (5% DV)
Sodium	142 mg (6% DV)	Iron	2 mg (11% DV)
Carbohydrate	11 g	Vitamin D	0 IU (0% DV)

Small-Batch Sauerkraut

MAKES 4 SERVINGS

Every guy we know loves sauerkraut, especially when it's made from scratch and served on Father's Day. Make this jar of tart cabbage at least 1 week in advance, allowing time for the fermentation process. (Plus, it will give you time to make a second batch, if your first efforts fall short.) No vinegar or yeast is needed for this fermentation process; instead, the cabbage has its own natural source of bacteria, coating the cabbage leaves and providing for the right environment when mixed with salt.

TIPS

To shred cabbage for this recipe, use half a small cabbage, remove the outer leaves and cut out the core. Cut the half into three wedges and then slice each third crosswise into thin strips.

Red (purple) cabbage will also work in this recipe.

- 1-pint (500 mL) mason jar with lid
- Shot glass filled with a small weight or clean rock
- Cheesecloth or clean, lint-free tea towel and elastic

3 cups	shredded green cabbage	750 mL
1¹⁄₂ tbsp	sea salt (see tip, opposite)	22 mL
1 tsp	caraway seeds (optional)	5 mL

1. In a large bowl, combine cabbage and salt; let stand for about 10 minutes or until cabbage starts to release water.

2. Use your fingers to massage the salt into the cabbage leaves for 10 minutes. The cabbage will slowly release juices into the bowl. (Your hands and fingers may get tired, so take a break but do not rush the process.) Continue massaging until you have at least ¹⁄₄ cup (60 mL) liquid. If desired, add caraway seeds and stir to combine.

3. Fill mason jar one-quarter full with cabbage mixture; using a wooden spoon, push the cabbage down firmly. Repeat until the cabbage mixture is 2 inches (5 cm) from the top of the jar. Push cabbage mixture down firmly, ensuring the liquid rises to the top. The cabbage should not be exposed to the air.

4. Press the prepared glass shot into the jar to ensure the cabbage stays submerged. Cover the jar with cheesecloth and secure with an elastic; store jar in a dark, cool place to ferment.

NUTRIENTS PER SERVING			
Calories	15	Fiber	2 g (8% DV)
Fat	0 g	Protein	1 g
Saturated fat	0 g	Calcium	29 mg (3% DV)
Sodium	1763 mg (74% DV)	Iron	8 mg (44% DV)
Carbohydrate	4 g	Vitamin D	0 IU (0 % DV)

TIPS

It's important to use salt with no additives for fermenting. Check the label and make sure you are using pure salt. Kosher salt or pickling/canning salt can be used in place of sea salt.

To reduce the sodium, drain off liquid from sauerkraut when serving.

Serve on your favorite hot dog or hamburger.

5. For the first 24 hours, press the cabbage down every 3 to 4 hours (don't worry about following this schedule during your sleeping hours). The amount of juice in the jar should increase over time (although sometimes it does not). If the cabbage is not completely submerged after 24 hours, dissolve 1 tsp (5 mL) salt into 1 cup (250 mL) warm water and pour in just enough of this homemade brine to cover the cabbage completely. Return to cool, dark place to ferment.

6. Let cabbage ferment undisturbed for 3 days, then taste your cabbage. If you like the taste, remove cloth and elastic, and seal jar with the lid. If you prefer a stronger sauerkraut, replace cloth and elastic and return to cool, dark place to ferment for up to 7 more days. If at any time mold starts to form or you notice any off or foul odors, discard contents of the jar and recycle jar or sanitize thoroughly. Store sauerkraut in the refrigerator for up to 2 months.

Health Bite

Many studies have shown a connection between the consumption of plant foods like cabbage and a decrease in the risk for obesity, diabetes and heart disease.

Pumpkin Beef Stew

MAKES 2 SERVINGS

Chunks of pumpkin, beef, kale and white beans in a simmering broth make this the most inviting, aromatic stew for Halloween. When you turn off your porch light, you can relax and warm yourself with this savory soup.

TIPS

If desired, use canola oil in both steps 1 and 2.

If you can't find a pie pumpkin, choose butternut squash.

Feel free to use frozen butternut squash and kale instead of the fresh pumpkin and kale. Add thawed frozen veggies in step 4 with the cannellini beans.

If a 15-oz (425 mL) can of cannellini beans is not available, you can use a 14-oz (398 mL) can, or measure 1²/₃ cups (400 mL) drained rinsed cannellini beans from a larger can.

2 tsp	canola oil	10 mL
8 oz	beef chuck stew meat, cut into bite-size chunks	250 g
¼ tsp	hot pepper flakes	1 mL
1 tbsp	olive oil	15 mL
½	onion, finely chopped	½
1	clove garlic, minced	1
2 cups	water	500 mL
2 cups	ready-to-use low-sodium vegetable broth	500 mL
2 tsp	chopped fresh parsley	10 mL
2 tsp	chopped fresh rosemary	10 mL
2 cups	shredded trimmed kale leaves	500 mL
1 cup	cubed pie pumpkin or squash	250 mL
1	can (15 oz/425 mL) no-salt-added cannellini (white kidney) beans, drained and rinsed (see tip, at left)	1

1. In a medium skillet, heat canola oil over high heat for 30 seconds. Quickly sear the beef chuck on each side for about 15 seconds per side. Remove from heat and set aside.

2. In a large stockpot, toast hot pepper flakes over medium heat for 1 minute. Add olive oil, onion and garlic; cook, stirring, for 5 minutes or until onion is soft.

NUTRIENTS PER SERVING			
Calories	568	Fiber	11 g (44% DV)
Fat	26 g	Protein	42 g
Saturated fat	8 g	Calcium	162 mg (16% DV)
Sodium	280 mg (12% DV)	Iron	6 mg (33% DV)
Carbohydrate	42 g	Vitamin D	32 IU (8% DV)

TIP

■ ■ ■ ■ ■ ■ ■ ■ ■ ■ ■ ■ ■ ■

If preparing this recipe for one person, cut all of the ingredients in half. Or simply prepare the full recipe and save half for leftovers. Store cooled leftovers in an airtight container in the refrigerator for up to 2 days or in the freezer for up to 1 month. On the morning you plan to enjoy the stew for dinner, transfer frozen stew to the refrigerator to thaw. Reheat in the microwave on High for 1 to 2 minutes or until heated through.

3. Add water, broth, parsley and rosemary to the onion mixture. Bring to a boil over high heat, then reduce heat to low. Stir in beef, kale and pumpkin. Cover and simmer over low heat for 15 minutes or until beef is cooked halfway through but still pink in the center.

4. Add cannellini beans, stir to combine and cook for another 10 to 15 minutes or until pumpkin and beef are tender. Serve immediately.

Health Bite

■ ■

Kale, like some other green leafy vegetables, contains some calcium. But because the fiber and oxalates may prevent your body from absorbing the calcium, it's important to eat a variety of foods to meet all of your micronutrient needs.

Nanny's Macaroni Salad

Every Easter, Lisa's great-grandmother's macaroni salad is on the table for their huge family dinner. After a few modifications, this recipe is now ready for you and another. Maybe one day it will become one of your holiday traditions, too.

TIPS

If you have leftover cooked macaroni noodles, use 1 cup (250 mL) in place of the dried.

To hard-cook eggs, place eggs in a medium pot of cold water. Bring to a boil over high heat. Watch closely! When you begin to see tiny bubbles (light boil), cover the pot and remove from heat. Let eggs stand for 15 minutes. To stop the cooking, plunge eggs into a bowl filled with ice and water for 10 minutes or until chilled.

If preparing this recipe for one person, cut all of the ingredients in half. Or simply prepare the full recipe and save half for leftovers. Store leftovers in an airtight container in the refrigerator for up to 2 days.

2 oz	whole wheat elbow macaroni	60 g
4	hard-cooked large eggs (see tip, at left), diced	4
¼ cup	finely chopped onion	60 mL
½ cup	sliced drained pimiento-stuffed green olives	125 mL
2 tbsp	plain 2% Greek yogurt	30 mL
2 tbsp	mayonnaise	30 mL
1 tsp	smoked paprika	5 mL

1. In a large pot of boiling water, cook pasta according to package directions. Drain, rinse under cold water and set aside.

2. In a medium bowl, combine eggs, onion, olives and macaroni; stir to combine. Add yogurt and mayonnaise; stir to combine. Sprinkle with paprika. Cover and refrigerate for at least 1 hour or for up to 2 days.

Health Bite

According to the Mayo Clinic, eating 7 eggs a week significantly increases the risk of heart disease in people who have diabetes, so this recipe should be consumed in moderation.

NUTRIENTS PER SERVING			
Calories	376	Fiber	3 g (12% DV)
Fat	22 g	Protein	19 g
Saturated fat	6 g	Calcium	90 mg (9% DV)
Sodium	486 mg (20% DV)	Iron	3 mg (17% DV)
Carbohydrate	26 g	Vitamin D	88 IU (22% DV)

Red Lentil Soup

MAKES 2 SERVINGS

This is lentil soup for the soul. The puréed consistency makes the soup easier to digest when breaking your fast. Serve with lean lamb, roast chicken or a white fish to make this an unforgettable meal.

TIPS

To toast walnuts, place a small skillet over medium-low heat. Add walnuts and cook, stirring constantly, until fragrant and toasted, about 3 minutes.

If preparing this recipe for one person, cut all of the ingredients in half. Or simply prepare the full recipe and save half for leftovers. Store leftovers in an airtight container in the refrigerator for up to 5 days or in the freezer for up to 2 months. If frozen, let thaw overnight in the refrigerator or defrost in the microwave. Reheat in the microwave on High for 1 to 2 minutes or until heated through.

- Food processor or blender

2 tbsp	olive oil	30 mL
1/2 cup	diced carrot	125 mL
1/2 cup	finely chopped onion	125 mL
1/2 tsp	ground cumin	2 mL
1/2 tsp	ground allspice	2 mL
3 cups	ready-to-use low-sodium chicken or vegetable broth	750 mL
3/4 cup	dried red lentils	175 mL
1 tsp	freshly squeezed lemon juice	5 mL
2 tbsp	chopped walnuts, toasted (see tip, at left)	30 mL
1 tsp	chopped fresh parsley	5 mL

1. In a medium saucepan, heat oil over medium heat. Add carrot and onion; cook, stirring, for 4 to 5 minutes or until onion is golden. Add cumin and allspice; cook, stirring, for 2 minutes.

2. Pour in broth and stir well. Add red lentils and reduce heat to low. Cover the saucepan, leaving lid ajar, and simmer for about 30 minutes or until lentils are soft.

3. Remove from heat and let cool for 10 minutes. Stir in lemon juice.

4. Using food processor or blender, purée the soup. Divide soup between two bowls and garnish with walnuts and parsley. Serve warm.

Health Bite

A mixed macronutrient meal like this one is best for your blood sugar and your entire gastrointestinal system.

NUTRIENTS PER SERVING			
Calories	523	Fiber	10 g (40% DV)
Fat	22 g	Protein	27 g
Saturated fat	3 g	Calcium	88 mg (9% DV)
Sodium	216 mg (9% DV)	Iron	7 mg (39% DV)
Carbohydrate	60 g	Vitamin D	0 IU (0% DV)

Matzo Ball Soup

Matzo ball soup is on the menu! Here is your grandmother's recipe made diabetes-friendly. Be sure you have time to spare. The matzo meal needs to sit in the refrigerator for 1 to 2 hours before cooking, and the matzo balls need 1 hour of cooking before they are added to the soup. This soup is incredibly delicious and worth every minute of preparation. It is perfect for college students or couples celebrating the holiday season on a smaller scale.

TIP

You can use 1 tsp (5 mL) of reduced-sodium Better Than Bouillon if you cannot find low-sodium bouillon cubes at your local grocery store, though the sodium content of each serving of soup will increase by about 250 mg.

MATZO BALLS

1/2 cup	matzo meal	125 mL
1/2 tsp	baking powder	2 mL
Pinch	salt	Pinch
1 tbsp	olive oil	15 mL
1	large egg	1
5 cups	water	1.25 L

CHICKEN SOUP BROTH

4 cups	water	1 L
1	cube low-sodium chicken bouillon	1
8 oz	skinless bone-in chicken breast (1 breast)	250 g
1 1/2 cups	baby carrots, chopped	375 mL
2/3 cup	finely chopped white onion	150 mL
1/2 cup	chopped parsnip	125 mL
1/2 cup	chopped celery	125 mL
1 1/2 tsp	dried parsley	7 mL
Pinch	salt	Pinch

1. *Matzo Balls:* In a medium bowl, combine matzo meal, baking powder and salt. Stir in oil and egg; do not overmix. Cover bowl and refrigerate for 1 to 2 hours or until the matzo meal has absorbed all the liquid.

2. In a large pot, bring 5 cups (1.25 L) water to a boil over high heat. Using your hands, roll the matzo mixture into 6 small or 4 larger balls and drop them into the boiling water. When all the matzo balls have risen to the top, cover, reduce heat to a simmer and cook for 1 hour.

NUTRIENTS PER SERVING			
Calories	360	Fiber	6 g (24% DV)
Fat	12 g	Protein	18 g
Saturated fat	2 g	Calcium	162 mg (16% DV)
Sodium	480 mg (20% DV)	Iron	3 mg (17% DV)
Carbohydrate	44 g	Vitamin D	23 IU (6% DV)

TIP

∎ ∎ ∎ ∎ ∎ ∎ ∎ ∎ ∎ ∎ ∎ ∎ ∎ ▪

If preparing this recipe for one person, cut all of the ingredients in half. Or simply prepare the full recipe and save half for leftovers. Store leftovers in an airtight container in the refrigerator for up to 2 days. Reheat in the microwave on High for 1 to 2 minutes or until heated through.

3. *Chicken Soup Broth:* Meanwhile, in a large stockpot, bring 4 cups (1 L) water to a boil. Add bouillon cube, chicken, carrots, onion, parsnip, celery and parsley. Return to a boil, then reduce heat to low and simmer for 1 hour or until parsnip is soft and chicken is no longer pink inside.

4. Transfer chicken to a shallow dish and use two forks to shred the meat. Discard bone. Return chicken and accumulated juices to the stockpot. Using a slotted spoon, transfer matzo balls to the soup. Stir in salt.

Health Bite

∎ ▪

Parsnips are a good source of fiber, folate and vitamin C.

Slow Cooker Corned Beef, Potatoes and Cabbage

MAKES 2 SERVINGS

Not Irish? Not a problem. If you'd rather celebrate Saint Patrick's day at home instead of at a bustling bar, this recipe is for you. This traditionally time-consuming meal is made simple with the help of a slow cooker. Come home to the rich smell of spiced corned beef and celebrate Saint Patrick's Day the relaxing way.

TIP

For a richer flavor, use ready-to-use low-sodium beef broth instead of water, but note that the sodium level will increase.

- **4-quart slow cooker**

3	cloves garlic, minced	3
1	onion, sliced	1
8 oz	corned beef brisket	250 g
4	whole black peppercorns	4
4	whole allspice	4
2	whole cloves	2
2	bay leaves, crumbled	2
1 tsp	granulated sugar	5 mL
1/2 tsp	freshly ground black pepper	2 mL
1/2 tsp	coriander seeds	2 mL
1/4 tsp	yellow mustard seeds	1 mL
1/4 tsp	hot pepper flakes	1 mL
2 cups	water	500 mL
1 tsp	apple cider vinegar	5 mL
2	small red potatoes, cubed	2
1/2	head green cabbage, cut into 4 wedges (about 2 lbs/1 kg)	1/2

1. In slow cooker, combine garlic and onion, spreading out to cover bottom. Add corned beef brisket, fat side up, on top. Make sure beef isn't touching the bottom of the slow cooker.

2. Add peppercorns, allspice, cloves, bay leaves, sugar, pepper, coriander seeds, mustard seeds and hot pepper flakes. Pour in water and vinegar. Stir to combine. Make sure meat is covered by liquid. If not, add more water. Cover and cook on Low for 2$\frac{1}{2}$ hours.

NUTRIENTS PER SERVING			
Calories	510	Fiber	11 g (44% DV)
Fat	23 g	Protein	27 g
Saturated fat	7 g	Calcium	184 mg (18% DV)
Sodium	1169 mg (49% DV)	Iron	7 mg (39% DV)
Carbohydrate	53 g	Vitamin D	5 IU (1% DV)

Serve with brown or spicy mustard for some added heat!

If preparing this recipe for one person, cut all of the ingredients in half. Or simply prepare the full recipe and save half for leftovers. Store leftovers in an airtight container in the refrigerator for up to 2 days. Reheat in the microwave on High for 1 to 2 minutes or until heated through.

3. After $2\frac{1}{2}$ hours, turn beef over and add potatoes. Make sure meat is covered by liquid. If not, add more water. Cover, increase heat to High and cook for 1 hour. Add cabbage in the last 20 minutes of cooking.

4. Drain off liquid, transfer brisket to a cutting board, trim fat and slice. Serve with potatoes and cabbage.

Health Bite

Cabbage contains vitamin K, vitamin C and folate.

Cajun Catfish and Spicy Sautéed Okra Salad

MAKES 2 SERVINGS

It's no surprise that Kwanzaa, a festivity of culture and family, is celebrated with comfort foods. The catfish is jazzed up with a savory spice mix, and the gorgeous green okra salad adds crisp balance.

TIPS

If you prefer a milder dish, reduce the cayenne pepper to 1/2 tsp (2 mL) or less.

Always wear kitchen gloves when handling jalapeños and avoid touching your skin and eyes.

2 tsp	cayenne pepper	10 mL
1/2 tsp	freshly ground black pepper	2 mL
1/2 tsp	ground white pepper	2 mL
1/2 tsp	garlic powder	2 mL
1/2 tsp	onion powder	2 mL
1/8 tsp	paprika	0.5 mL
2	skinless catfish fillets (each 4 oz/125 g)	2
2 tsp	olive oil, divided	10 mL
1	clove garlic, minced	1
1 cup	thawed frozen cut okra	250 mL
1/2 cup	finely chopped onion	125 mL
1/4 cup	diced tomatoes	60 mL
1/4 cup	canned diced green chiles	60 mL
1 tsp	minced seeded jalapeño pepper	5 mL
1/4 tsp	hot pepper flakes	1 mL

1. In a small bowl, combine cayenne, black pepper, white pepper, garlic powder, onion powder and paprika. Season catfish on both sides with spice blend.

2. In a medium skillet, heat 1 tsp (5 mL) oil over medium-high heat. Add catfish to skillet and cook, flipping once during cooking, for about 5 minutes or until fish is opaque and flakes easily when tested with a fork. Transfer catfish to a plate and tent with foil to keep warm.

NUTRIENTS PER SERVING			
Calories	278	Fiber	4 g (16% DV)
Fat	14 g	Protein	24 g
Saturated fat	3 g	Calcium	110 mg (11% DV)
Sodium	734 mg (31% DV)	Iron	2 mg (11% DV)
Carbohydrate	17 g	Vitamin D	11 IU (3% DV)

TIPS

If more carbohydrates are desired, consider serving ½ cup (125 mL) roasted sweet potatoes or a piece of cornbread on the side.

If preparing this recipe for one person, cut all of the ingredients in half. Or simply prepare the full recipe and save half for leftovers. Store catfish and okra salad in separate airtight containers in the refrigerator for up to 2 days. Reheat vegetables in the microwave on High for 1 to 2 minutes or until heated through, and reheat fish on Medium (50%) power for 1 to 2 minutes or until heated through.

3. Add the remaining oil to skillet (no need to wash it). Add garlic, okra, onion, tomatoes, green chiles, jalapeño and hot pepper flakes; stir to combine. Cook, stirring occasionally, for 10 to 12 minutes or until vegetables are softened. Serve alongside catfish.

Health Bite

Okra is high in folate, a water-soluble B vitamin.

Crepes with a Strawberry Balsamic Reduction

**MAKES 2 SERVINGS
(1 CREPE PER SERVING)**

Regardless of your home country, freedom is cherished by all. Celebrate with these red and white crepes. Of course, you can add blueberries, too.

TIPS

If you want to make this a red-white-and-blue-themed snack, use ½ cup (125 mL) strawberries and add ½ cup (125 mL) blueberries to keep the carbs as low as possible.

Serve this as a meal with 1 cup (250 mL) cottage cheese or plain Greek yogurt to ensure carbs stay within your target range.

½ cup	all-purpose flour	125 mL
5 tsp	beaten egg (half a large egg)	25 mL
½ cup	unsweetened soy milk or other plant-based milk	125 mL
1 tbsp	butter, melted	15 mL
Pinch	salt	Pinch
1 cup	quartered hulled strawberries	250 mL
½ cup	raspberry-flavored balsamic vinegar	125 mL
	Canola oil nonstick cooking spray	

1. In a medium bowl, whisk together flour, egg, soy milk, butter and salt. Transfer bowl to the refrigerator to let bubbles disperse while making the strawberry sauce.

2. In a small saucepan, heat strawberries and vinegar over medium heat, stirring constantly for 5 minutes. Increase heat to high and bring to a boil. Reduce heat to medium and boil gently, stirring constantly, for about 20 minutes or until vinegar is reduced by half and sauce is thick enough to coat the spoon. Remove from heat.

3. Meanwhile, remove the batter from the refrigerator and stir for 10 seconds.

NUTRIENTS PER SERVING			
Calories	302	Fiber	3 g (12% DV)
Fat	10 g	Protein	9 g
Saturated fat	5 g	Calcium	123 mg (12% DV)
Sodium	147 mg (6% DV)	Iron	3 mg (17% DV)
Carbohydrate	42 g	Vitamin D	56 IU (14% DV)

TIP

■ ■ ■ ■ ■ ■ ■ ■ ■ ■ ■ ■ ■ ■

This recipe doesn't work well if halved to a single serving. Instead, choose a lucky friend or family member and share the recipe. Or simply prepare the full recipe up to the end of step 4, let cool, and store sauce and crepes in separate airtight containers in the refrigerator for up to 2 days. Reheat in the microwave on Medium (50%) power for about 1 minute, or until heated through, and proceed with step 5.

4. Spray a medium skillet with cooking spray and place over medium-high heat until pan is hot. Using a $\frac{1}{4}$-cup (60 mL) measure, scoop batter onto the skillet. Tilt the skillet to create a thin layer of batter over the bottom. When the batter bubbles around the edges, after about 30 seconds, use a spatula to quickly flip the crepe over. Cook for another 30 seconds or until the crepe is cooked through; transfer to a plate. Repeat with the remaining batter, adjusting heat and spraying skillet as necessary between crepes.

5. Drizzle strawberry balsamic reduction down the center of each crepe. Fold, roll or serve crepes as is.

Health Bite

■ ■

Strawberries are high in vitamin C and potassium.

Tagliatelle with Pork Ragù

Stay home this Valentine's Day. Make yourself and your special someone a pasta dish to remember. Your love life will thank you!

TIP

Chew on some fresh mint after dinner for fresh breath!

2 tsp	canola oil	10 mL
10 oz	pork tenderloin	300 g
1/2 cup	diced carrot	125 mL
1/2 cup	red wine	125 mL
1	can (28 oz/796 mL) crushed tomatoes	1
1/2 cup	minced shallots	125 mL
1 tsp	garlic powder	5 mL
1/4 tsp	ground cinnamon	1 mL
1/4 tsp	freshly ground black pepper	1 mL
1 cup	ready-to-use low-sodium vegetable broth (approx.)	250 mL
4 oz	whole wheat tagliatelle	125 g

1. In a Dutch oven or large pot, heat oil over medium-high heat. Sear pork on each side for 2 to 3 minutes or until lightly browned on all sides. Transfer to a bowl and set aside.

2. Add carrot and red wine to the pot; cook over medium heat, stirring, for about 5 minutes or until carrot starts to soften. Add tomatoes, shallots, garlic powder, cinnamon and pepper; stir to combine. Add broth and stir well.

3. Return pork to the pot, making sure it is fully submerged in the sauce. (If not fully submerged, add more broth.) Cover, reduce heat to low and simmer, stirring occasionally, for about 45 minutes or until pork is tender and falling apart.

NUTRIENTS PER SERVING			
Calories	613	Fiber	10 g (40% DV)
Fat	21 g	Protein	49 g
Saturated fat	6 g	Calcium	191 mg (19% DV)
Sodium	215 mg (9% DV)	Iron	8 mg (44% DV)
Carbohydrate	50 g	Vitamin D	41 IU (10% DV)

If preparing this recipe for one person, cut all of the ingredients in half. Or simply prepare the full recipe and save half for leftovers. Store tagliatelle and pork ragù in separate airtight containers in the refrigerator for up to 2 days. Reheat in the microwave on High for 1 to 2 minutes or until heated through.

4. Meanwhile, in a medium pot of boiling water, cook tagliatelle according to package directions or until al dente. Drain and set aside.

5. Remove pork from the pot and transfer to a bowl. Using two forks, shred pork into small pieces. Return pork to the sauce and stir well, scraping down the sides and bottom of the pot.

6. Divide tagliatelle between bowls and top with pork ragù.

Health Bite

The protein and fiber in this dish will help prevent the pasta from being rapidly absorbed and causing a sugar boost.

Mom's Pumpkin Bread

MAKES 2 SERVINGS

In Texas, there aren't really four seasons. The weather is consistently hot and humid, no matter what month it is. Growing up, Lisa knew it was the start of fall when she smelled cinnamon and nutmeg wafting through the house. She always ran to the kitchen to confirm that her mom had just baked her famous pumpkin bread.

TIPS

You can use leftover unseasoned cooked pumpkin in place of canned in this recipe.

Enjoy this loaf at breakfast with a side of high-protein Greek yogurt, or spread with nut butter for a more filling snack.

If preparing this recipe for one person, cut all of the ingredients in half. Or simply prepare the full recipe and save half for leftovers. Store leftovers wrapped in foil in the refrigerator for up to 2 weeks.

Health Bite

Both canned and fresh pumpkin contain beneficial nutrients, such as vitamin A, iron and potassium.

- Preheat oven to 350°F (180°C)
- 8- by 4-inch (20 by 10 cm) metal loaf pan or 2 mini 4- by 2¼-inch (10 by 5.5 cm) metal loaf pans, sprayed with canola oil nonstick cooking spray

¾ cup	almond flour (almond meal)	175 mL
1 tsp	baking soda	5 mL
1 tsp	ground cinnamon	5 mL
½ tsp	ground nutmeg	2 mL
1	large egg	1
1	large egg white	1
2 tbsp	granulated sugar	30 mL
⅓ cup	pumpkin purée (not pie filling)	75 mL
¼ cup	water	60 mL
1 tbsp	canola oil	15 mL

1. In a small bowl, whisk together flour, baking soda, cinnamon and nutmeg.

2. In another small bowl, whisk together egg, egg white and sugar.

3. In a medium bowl, whisk together pumpkin, water and oil until thoroughly combined. Add egg mixture; stir to combine. Add flour mixture; stir to combine thoroughly. Transfer batter to prepared loaf pan, smoothing top.

4. Bake in preheated oven for 25 minutes or until a tester inserted in the center of the loaf comes out clean. Transfer loaf pan to a wire rack and let cool for 30 minutes before serving.

NUTRIENTS PER SERVING			
Calories	428	Fiber	8 g (32% DV)
Fat	31 g	Protein	15 g
Saturated fat	3 g	Calcium	144 mg (14% DV)
Sodium	972 mg (41% DV)	Iron	2 mg (11% DV)
Carbohydrate	28 g	Vitamin D	22 IU (6% DV)

BONUS SECTION 2
EVERYDAY OCCASIONS

Fennel Sweet Potato Salad

MAKES 2 SERVINGS

Your friends will want to come to your kitchen for some of this most amazing, mouthwatering salad. Plus, you get to spend the night enjoying your friend rather than cooking. Make this salad before your guest arrives and serve warm or cold, when hungry. Serve with roasted chicken and greens to make a complete meal. Laura's friend, certified sommelier Michelle Erland, recommends pairing this dish with a light-bodied wine such as Beaujolais or Pinot Noir.

TIPS

Plain balsamic vinegar also works in this recipe.

To prepare fennel, peel off damaged and tough outer layers and cut the trimmed bulb in half lengthwise. Cut the halves into quarters, then thinly slice the fennel crosswise.

- Preheat oven to 400°F (200°C)
- Baking sheet, lined with foil and sprayed with canola oil nonstick cooking spray

VINAIGRETTE

2 tbsp	olive oil	30 mL
2 tbsp	berry-flavored balsamic vinegar	30 mL
1 tsp	anise seeds	5 mL

SALAD

2	sweet potatoes (unpeeled; about 8 oz/ 250 g), cubed	2
1 tbsp	olive oil	15 mL
Pinch	salt	Pinch
1	small bulb fennel, cored and thinly sliced (about 2 cups/500 mL)	1
¼ cup	sweetened dried cranberries	60 mL
1 cup	arugula	250 mL

1. *Vinaigrette:* In a small bowl, whisk together oil, vinegar and anise seeds.

2. *Salad:* On prepared baking sheet, drizzle sweet potatoes with oil and sprinkle with salt; toss to evenly coat, then spread out, leaving space between cubes. Roast in preheated oven for 45 minutes or until golden brown and tender.

NUTRIENTS PER SERVING			
Calories	366	Fiber	8 g (32% DV)
Fat	21 g	Protein	4 g
Saturated fat	3 g	Calcium	111 mg (11% DV)
Sodium	90 mg (4% DV)	Iron	2 mg (11% DV)
Carbohydrate	45 g	Vitamin D	0 IU (0% DV)

TIP
∎ ∎ ∎ ∎ ∎ ∎ ∎ ∎ ∎ ∎ ∎ ∎ ∎ ∎

If preparing this recipe for one person, cut all of the ingredients in half. Or simply prepare the full recipe up to the end of step 2 and save half for leftovers. Store vinaigrette and salad ingredients in separate airtight containers in the refrigerator for up to 2 days. Reheat sweet potatoes in the microwave on High for 1 to 2 minutes, or until heated through, and proceed with step 3.

3. In a medium bowl, combine sweet potatoes, fennel and cranberries. Stir vinaigrette and pour over salad; toss to combine.

4. Divide arugula between bowls and top with the sweet potato mixture.

Health Bite
∎ ∎

When comparing 1 cup (250 mL) white potato with an equal volume of sweet potato, both contain equal amounts of carbohydrates — about 30 grams. Although the sweet potato is highly nutritious, the *Cochrane Database of Systematic Review* found insufficient evidence connecting the sweet potato with improved glycemic control.

Traditional Cucumber and Cream Cheese Tea Sandwich

MAKES 2 SERVINGS

Get your good china out for these pretty little sandwiches. Your food environment — from place settings to placemats — is just as important as the food you eat. Make eating an experience. Tea time is the perfect meal to practice mindfulness.

TIPS

You can also spread this cream cheese mixture into the hollow of celery stalks or onto carrots sliced in half lengthwise.

If preparing this recipe for one person, cut all of the ingredients in half. Or simply prepare the full recipe and save half for leftovers. Store leftovers in an airtight container in the refrigerator for up to 2 days.

1 oz	cream cheese, at room temperature	30 g
1 tsp	grated lemon zest	5 mL
1 tbsp	freshly squeezed lemon juice	15 mL
1/4 tsp	dried Italian seasoning	1 mL
1/8 tsp	garlic powder	0.5 mL
2	slices whole wheat bread, crusts removed	2
1	small cucumber, peeled and thinly sliced	1

1. In a small bowl, combine cream cheese, lemon zest, lemon juice, Italian seasoning and garlic powder.

2. Divide the cream cheese mixture between bread slices, spreading to coat to edges. Arrange cucumber over one slice and top with the remaining bread slice. Cut sandwich into four quarters.

Health Bite

Cucumbers are made up of 95% water and are low in calories, fat and sodium.

NUTRIENTS PER SERVING			
Calories	136	Fiber	3 g (12% DV)
Fat	6 g	Protein	5 g
Saturated fat	3 g	Calcium	74 mg (7% DV)
Sodium	177 mg (7% DV)	Iron	1 mg (6% DV)
Carbohydrate	15 g	Vitamin D	0 IU (0% DV)

Branzino with Capers

MAKES 2 SERVINGS

This recipe tastes better than cake! But eat it with the expectation that you will be eating birthday cake immediately after this no-carb fish dish, to keep your total carbohydrate count between 45 and 60 grams.

TIPS

If you can't find branzino, choose another white fish, such as tilapia, sole or trout.

Nonpareil capers are considered to be the best for cooking purposes in terms of flavor and texture.

Serve with roasted broccoli or steamed greens.

If preparing this recipe for one person, cut all of the ingredients in half. Or simply prepare the full recipe and save half for leftovers. Store leftovers in an airtight container in the refrigerator for up to 2 days. Reheat in the microwave on Medium (50%) power for 1 to 2 minutes or until heated through.

3 tsp	olive oil, divided	15 mL
1	clove garlic, minced	1
10 oz	deboned branzino (European sea bass) fillet	300 g
2 tbsp	drained capers (preferably nonpareil)	30 mL
¼ tsp	grated lemon zest	1 mL
1 tbsp	freshly squeezed lemon juice	15 mL

1. In a medium skillet, heat 2 tsp (10 mL) oil over medium heat. Add garlic and cook, stirring, for about 1 minute or until golden. Arrange branzino on top of garlic, cover and cook for about 5 minutes or until almost opaque. Remove from heat.

2. Meanwhile, in a small bowl, whisk together the remaining oil, capers, lemon zest and lemon juice.

3. Drizzle lemon mixture evenly over the branzino in the skillet. Cover and let stand for 3 to 5 minutes or until fish is opaque and flakes easily when tested with a fork.

Health Bite

Lemons are an excellent source of antioxidant vitamin C, which means they can help prevent the formation of cancer-causing free radicals.

NUTRIENTS PER SERVING			
Calories	252	Fiber	1 g (4% DV)
Fat	16 g	Protein	27 g
Saturated fat	3 g	Calcium	43 mg (4% DV)
Sodium	311 mg (13% DV)	Iron	1 mg (6% DV)
Carbohydrate	2 g	Vitamin D	250 IU (63% DV)

Prosciutto Flatbread

MAKES 2 SERVINGS

This flatbread will have your guest wanting more! Make date night anxiety-free by enjoying this sexy flatbread entrée. Serve with a naturally lower-carbohydrate option, such as oysters on the half shell or mussels in a white wine broth.

TIPS

■ ■ ■ ■ ■ ■ ■ ■ ■ ■ ■ ■ ■ ■ ■ ■

Most frozen pizza dough comes in a package of 16 oz (464 g). If you don't have a kitchen scale to weigh out a portion, divide the dough in half, then cut off one-quarter of one half and you'll be left with your 6-oz (175 g) portion. Place extra dough in an oiled resealable plastic bag or covered bowl and refrigerate for up to 2 days. The extra dough can be used to make Margherita Flatbread (page 140) or baked as a plain crust and frozen for later.

Roll your dough into whatever shape you desire. Make it a classic round pizza or even a square. Monitor for doneness, as shape and thickness of the crust will affect the cooking time.

- Preheat oven to 400°F (200°C)
- Baking sheet, sprayed with canola oil nonstick cooking spray

6 oz	thawed frozen whole-grain pizza dough (see tip, at left)	175 g
	All-purpose flour (optional)	
1 tbsp	olive oil	15 mL
1/4 tsp	dried rosemary	1 mL
Pinch	sea salt	Pinch
2 tbsp	part-skim ricotta cheese	30 mL
3/4 cup	arugula	175 mL
4 oz	thinly sliced prosciutto	125 g
4 tbsp	shaved Parmesan cheese	60 mL
1 tbsp	freshly squeezed lemon juice	15 mL
Pinch	freshly ground black pepper	Pinch

1. On a work surface, roll out pizza dough into a long, thin rectangular shape, about 12 by 5 inches (30 by 12.5 cm), dusting with flour, if necessary, to prevent sticking. Transfer to prepared baking sheet. Brush oil over the dough and sprinkle with rosemary and salt.

2. Bake in preheated oven for about 15 minutes or until golden brown and crispy. Transfer flatbread to a large cutting board and let cool for 5 minutes.

NUTRIENTS PER SERVING			
Calories	456	Fiber	6 g (24% DV)
Fat	22 g	Protein	24 g
Saturated fat	8 g	Calcium	367 mg (37% DV)
Sodium	1242 mg (52% DV)	Iron	3 mg (17% DV)
Carbohydrate	41 g	Vitamin D	16 IU (4% DV)

3. Spread ricotta over flatbread and then top with arugula. Using a pizza cutter or serrated knife, cut flatbread in half. Arrange prosciutto and Parmesan over each half, dividing evenly. Drizzle with lemon juice and season with pepper.

Health Bite

Arugula, like other leafy greens, contains a high concentration of nitrate, which has been shown to lower blood pressure and enhance athletic performance by reducing the amount of oxygen needed during exercise.

Grilled Zucchini, Mushroom and Feta Salad

MAKES 2 SERVINGS

Aaah, summer. The time of the year when relaxation is encouraged. Use this season to your advantage by enjoying this zippy recipe. Grilling the zucchini and mushrooms adds a well-rounded flavor that is contrasted by the tangy feta cheese.

TIPS

Use a damp paper towel to scrub dirt from mushrooms (do not clean with water, as mushrooms will absorb excess water). Use a spoon to remove the gills.

If preparing this recipe for one person, cut all of the ingredients in half. Or simply prepare the full recipe and save half for leftovers. Store leftovers in an airtight container in the refrigerator for up to 2 days.

Health Bite

Zucchini contains a good amount of potassium, which can help control blood pressure because it decreases the effects of salt on your body.

• **Preheat barbecue grill to medium-high**

2	large zucchini, sliced lengthwise into ½-inch (1 cm) thick slices	2
2	large portobello mushrooms, stemmed and gills removed	2
3 tbsp	olive oil, divided	45 mL
½ tsp	salt	2 mL
½ tsp	freshly ground black pepper	2 mL
1 tbsp	balsamic vinegar	15 mL
1 tsp	Dijon mustard	5 mL
2 tsp	chopped fresh thyme	10 mL
2 oz	feta cheese, crumbled (½ cup/125 mL)	60 g

1. Brush zucchini slices and mushrooms with 1 tbsp (15 mL) oil. Season with salt and pepper.

2. Arrange zucchini and mushrooms on preheated grill and grill, turning once, for 2 to 3 minutes per side or until char marks are visible and vegetables are tender-crisp. Transfer to a cutting board. When cool enough to handle, chop zucchini and mushrooms.

3. Meanwhile, whisk together the remaining oil, vinegar, mustard and thyme.

4. In a medium bowl, combine zucchini and mushrooms. Pour in vinaigrette and toss to coat. Top with cheese. Serve warm or cover and refrigerate for 1 hour before serving.

NUTRIENTS PER SERVING			
Calories	337	Fiber	5 g (20% DV)
Fat	28 g	Protein	10 g
Saturated fat	7 g	Calcium	208 mg (21% DV)
Sodium	945 mg (39% DV)	Iron	3 mg (17% DV)
Carbohydrate	16 g	Vitamin D	12 IU (3% DV)

Chilled Gazpacho

Skip the heavy salads and deli meats that can spoil in the beach heat. Freeze this dish and let it thaw in your beach bag so you have a perfectly cool soup ready to help you chill out.

TIPS

If you're planning to enjoy this soup quite soon after preparing it but still need it to go, simply store in an insulated water bottle or Thermos to keep it chilled.

If preparing this recipe for one person, cut all of the ingredients in half. Or simply prepare the full recipe and save half for leftovers. Store leftovers in an airtight container in the refrigerator for up to 3 days or in the freezer for up to 3 months.

• Blender

2	small tomatoes, cut into chunks	2
1	cucumber, peeled and cut into chunks	1
1	clove garlic	1
1	medium red bell pepper, cut into chunks	1
1/2	medium onion, cut into chunks	1/2
1/4 cup	red wine vinegar	60 mL
2 tbsp	olive oil	30 mL
1/4 tsp	freshly ground black pepper	1 mL
Pinch	salt	Pinch

1. In blender, combine tomatoes, cucumber, garlic, red pepper, onion, vinegar, oil, pepper and salt. Blend until fairly smooth, or to desired consistency. Transfer to a bowl or airtight container, cover and refrigerate for at least 1 hour, until chilled, or for up to 3 days before serving.

Health Bite

Lycopene, which gives tomatoes their red color, is an antioxidant that may help prevent cancer and cardiovascular disease. Choose ripe tomatoes for the highest levels of this powerful antioxidant.

NUTRIENTS PER SERVING			
Calories	186	Fiber	4 g (16% DV)
Fat	14 g	Protein	3 g
Saturated fat	2 g	Calcium	40 mg (4% DV)
Sodium	274 mg (11% DV)	Iron	1 mg (6% DV)
Carbohydrate	13 g	Vitamin D	0 IU (0% DV)

Trail Mix "GRAM"

MAKES 2 SERVINGS

If hiking for longer than 2 hours, you'll need extra nutrition to make up for the calories you've burned. Feed your muscles with Laura's version of GORP (granola, oats, raisins and peanuts). This snack is higher in carbs than the other snacks in this cookbook. Spread the snack out during your hike or plan accordingly with your insulin dosage. Or throw it in your school bag or gym bag and snack on it all week.

TIPS

GORP is also known as "good old raisins and peanuts." The "G" in this "GRAM" recipe is whole-*grain* pretzels.

To decrease the carb count, replace the candy-coated chocolate pieces with macadamia nuts. To reduce the calories, swap the pretzels with whole-grain popcorn.

If preparing this recipe for one person, cut all of the ingredients in half. Or simply prepare the full recipe and save half for leftovers. Store leftovers in an airtight container or sealable bag for up to 1 week.

1 cup	whole-grain pretzels	250 mL
¼ cup	raisins	60 mL
¼ cup	roasted unsalted almonds	60 mL
¼ cup	candy-coated chocolate pieces (such as M&Ms)	60 mL

1. In a sealable bag (or jar), combine pretzels, raisins, almonds and chocolate-covered peanuts. Seal bag (or jar) and shake to combine.

Health Bite

It's important to keep your body fueled with water and snacks before and during exercise. This will be helpful in preventing dehydration and can keep you from feeling fatigued and from developing cramps. A good rule of thumb is to drink 2 cups (500 mL) water at least 2 hours before your activity, and drink another 2 cups for every hour you are active.

If you're an athlete participating in an event lasting more than 1 hour, you should also think about replenishing electrolytes (such as sodium and potassium), which can be depleted through sweating, a process that can adversely affect your performance. To replace lost electrolytes, consider choosing a sports drink, such as Gatorade.

NUTRIENTS PER SERVING			
Calories	360	Fiber	5 g (20% DV)
Fat	15 g	Protein	7 g
Saturated fat	4 g	Calcium	92 mg (9% DV)
Sodium	125 mg (5% DV)	Iron	2 mg (11% DV)
Carbohydrate	52 g	Vitamin D	0 IU (0% DV)

Parmesan and Paprika Popcorn

MAKES 2 SERVINGS

You won't miss movie popcorn after tasting this refined version of an American classic. Think of popcorn as a blank canvas and yourself as a flavor artist. At only 15 grams of carbs per serving, this recipe enables you to eat anxiety-free while watching your favorite flick.

TIPS

If you buy kernels and pop them on the stovetop, use 1 tbsp (15 mL) canola oil with 2 tbsp (30 mL) kernels, keeping in mind that the fat content will increase.

You can easily substitute for the spices in this recipe. Experiment with ground cumin, garlic powder or dried oregano, starting with 1/4 tsp (1 mL) increments.

If preparing this recipe for one person, cut all of the ingredients in half. Or simply prepare the full recipe and save half for leftovers. Store leftovers in an airtight container for up to 2 days. Reheat in the microwave on High for 20 seconds or until heated through.

4 cups	hot air-popped popcorn	1 L
1 tbsp	butter, melted	15 mL
2 tbsp	grated Parmesan cheese	30 mL
2 tsp	smoked paprika	10 mL
1/2 tsp	chipotle chile powder (or to taste)	2 mL

1. Place popcorn in a medium bowl and pour butter over top. Sprinkle with cheese, paprika and chipotle powder. Toss until popcorn is fully coated.

Health Bite

Popcorn is a whole grain and is ideal as a high-volume, low-calorie snack.

NUTRIENTS PER SERVING			
Calories	148	Fiber	4 g (16% DV)
Fat	9 g	Protein	5 g
Saturated fat	5 g	Calcium	80 mg (8% DV)
Sodium	166 mg (7% DV)	Iron	2 mg (11% DV)
Carbohydrate	15 g	Vitamin D	5 IU (1% DV)

Rosemary Roasted Cashews and Walnuts

MAKES 2 SERVINGS

Pull out the poker chips, dust off the dominoes and preheat your oven! This simple game-night favorite will keep your hands full between turns. The dried rosemary adds an unexpected earthy flavor to the crunchy cashew and walnut combo.

TIPS

Buy raw, unsalted cashews and walnuts for this recipe, not the roasted nuts sold in the snack aisle. Raw nuts are often available in the produce section or bulk section and at natural foods stores.

If preparing this recipe for one person, cut all of the ingredients in half. Or simply prepare the full recipe and save half for leftovers. Store leftovers in an airtight container for up to 3 days.

- Preheat the oven to 450°F (230°C)
- Baking sheet, lined with parchment paper

18	whole cashews	18
14	walnut halves	14
1 tbsp	olive oil	15 mL
½ tsp	salt	2 mL
2 tsp	dried rosemary, crumbled	10 mL

1. In a small bowl, combine cashews and walnuts. Add oil and season with rosemary and salt; toss until evenly coated.

2. Spread nuts on prepared baking sheet. Bake in preheated oven, stirring once during baking, for 5 minutes or until golden brown. Let cool for 5 minutes and serve warm, or let cool completely and serve at room temperature.

Health Bite

Cashews provide zinc and protein, which are key nutrients for cell growth and repair.

NUTRIENTS PER SERVING			
Calories	330	Fiber	3 g (12% DV)
Fat	32 g	Protein	7 g
Saturated fat	4 g	Calcium	49 mg (5% DV)
Sodium	593 mg (25% DV)	Iron	2 mg (11% DV)
Carbohydrate	9 g	Vitamin D	0 IU (0% DV)

Turkey Chili with Corn Chips

MAKES 2 SERVINGS

You'll score big with this fan favorite. Kick off your Super Bowl Sunday with a bowl of this spicy southern chili. The lean ground turkey will still satisfy anyone craving a hearty meal. Trust us, you won't fumble with this recipe.

TIPS

Add a few slices of pickled jalapeño peppers on top of this dish, if desired.

If preparing this recipe for one person, cut all of the ingredients in half. Or simply prepare the full recipe up to the end of step 2 and save half for leftovers. Store leftovers in an airtight container in the refrigerator for up to 2 days or in the freezer for up to 2 weeks. If frozen, let thaw overnight in the refrigerator or defrost in the microwave. Reheat in the microwave on High for 2 minutes, or until heated through, and proceed with step 3.

8 oz	lean ground turkey	250 g
1 tsp	chili powder	5 mL
1	clove garlic, minced	1
1/2	onion, chopped	1/2
1 tsp	garlic powder	5 mL
1 tsp	ground cumin	5 mL
1	can (10 oz/284 mL) diced tomatoes with green chiles, with juice	1
1/4 cup	rinsed drained canned pinto beans	60 mL
1/4 cup	shredded Cheddar cheese	60 mL
1 cup	corn chips (2 oz/60 g)	250 mL
2 tbsp	sour cream	30 mL

1. In a medium skillet, combine turkey and chili powder; heat over medium-high heat until sizzling. Add garlic, onion, garlic powder and cumin; stir to combine. Cook turkey mixture, breaking the turkey up with a spoon, for 6 to 9 minutes or until no longer pink.

2. Reduce heat to medium, add diced tomatoes with green chiles and pinto beans; cook for 3 to 5 minutes or until simmering.

3. Divide mixture between two bowls. Top evenly with cheese, corn chips and sour cream.

Health Bite

Pinto beans support healthy red blood cell production with their iron content, and heart health with their potassium.

NUTRIENTS PER SERVING			
Calories	468	Fiber	6 g (24% DV)
Fat	23 g	Protein	31 g
Saturated fat	8 g	Calcium	186 mg (19% DV)
Sodium	1181 mg (49% DV)	Iron	4 mg (22% DV)
Carbohydrate	35 g	Vitamin D	25 IU (6% DV)

Dark Hot Chocolate

MAKES 2 SERVINGS

Before you head to the ski slopes, the snow hill for sledding or the fort for a snowball fight, fuel yourself with quick-acting sugar. Later you can snuggle up with your book and put on some slippers without worrying about a sugar low. (This drink is sweet, creamy and high in carbs for a snack. Be sure to account for the grams by playing in the snow to keep your sugar within your ideal range.)

TIPS

To keep carbs curbed, choose any variety of unsweetened plant milk, such as hemp milk or almond milk.

If preparing this recipe for one person, cut all of the ingredients in half. Or simply prepare the full recipe and save half for leftovers. Store leftovers in an airtight container in the refrigerator for up to 2 days. Reheat in the microwave on High for 1 minute or until heated through.

2 tbsp	finely chopped bittersweet (dark) chocolate (1 oz/30 g)	30 mL
2 cups	unsweetened soy milk	500 mL
2 tsp	agave nectar	10 mL
1 tsp	vanilla extract	5 mL
Pinch	salt	Pinch

1. In a small saucepan, combine chocolate, soy milk, agave nectar, vanilla and salt over medium-high heat. Cook, whisking often, for 5 minutes or until blended and almost boiling. Ladle into mugs and serve immediately.

Health Bite

We used unsweetened soy milk in this recipe as it adds more protein than almond milk to help prevent a blood sugar spike.

NUTRIENTS PER SERVING			
Calories	172	Fiber	4 g (16% DV)
Fat	8 g	Protein	8 g
Saturated fat	4 g	Calcium	300 mg (30% DV)
Sodium	90 mg (4% DV)	Iron	2 mg (11% DV)
Carbohydrate	19 g	Vitamin D	120 IU (30% DV)

BONUS SECTION 3
14-DAY MEAL PLANS

To make the *Everyday Diabetes Meals* a lifestyle, just follow this 14-day meal plan. All meals average between 45 and 60 grams of carbohydrate, while all snacks range between 15 and 30 grams. All meals combine the three macronutrients: carbohydrates, proteins and fats, and most snacks contain two of the three macronutrients. When trying new foods and new recipes, Laura and Lisa recommend testing your blood sugar immediately before your meal and then 2 hours after your meal. Everyone absorbs foods at a different rate and in a different way, depending on your sleep, stress and activity level. Blood sugar management should be individualized just for you. Now go on and enjoy every day of your journey with diabetes. Each day includes at least one snack and sometimes two. The nighttime snack may be combined with the dinner meal to help with carbohydrate distribution and to allow for a more realistic eating style.

Week 1

Breakfast

²/₃ cup (150 mL) plain 2% Greek
    yogurt
¼ cup (60 mL) cooked farro
1 small pear, diced
2 tbsp (30 mL) walnuts

Snack

¼ cup (60 mL) almonds
1 orange

Lunch

Avocado Cucumber Soup (page 102)
Whole wheat wrap filled with 4 oz
    (125 g) grilled steak and 2 cups
    (500 mL) cooked vegetables
    (½ cup/125 mL sliced onion;
    1½ cups/375 mL red, orange and
    yellow bell peppers; 1 clove garlic,
    minced; and 2 tsp/10 mL canola oil
    cooked, stirring, over medium heat)

Dinner

Stir-Fried Peppered Shrimp with
    Cockles (page 154)
2 Quinoa Raisin Cookies (page 215)

Breakfast

Blueberry Boost Parfait (page 70)

Lunch

Pesto Grilled Cheese (page 117)
1 cup (250 mL) broccoli roasted
    with 2 tsp (10 mL) olive oil

Snack

12 olives
5 high-fiber crackers (1 oz/30 g total)

Dinner

1 roasted skinless chicken breast
    (5 oz/150 g)
1 steamed small sweet potato
    (topped with 2 tsp/10 mL butter)
2 cups (250 mL) arugula tossed with
    1 tbsp (15 mL) vinaigrette

Snack

1 small apple
1 tbsp (15 mL) almond butter

TUESDAY

Breakfast

2 Power Pumpkin Pancakes (page 89)

Lunch

Salad of 1 cup (250 mL) lightly
packed spinach tossed with
1 tbsp (15 mL) sweetened dried
cranberries, 4 large grilled peeled
deveined shrimp, ¾ cup (175 mL)
cooked orzo and 1 tbsp (15 mL)
vinaigrette

Snack

⅔ cup (150 mL) plain 2% Greek
yogurt with 1 small cookie
crumbled on top

Dinner

"It's Greek to Me" Burgers (page 177)
1 cup (250 mL) arugula tossed with
1 tbsp (15 mL) olive oil dressing
2 small clementines

WEDNESDAY

Breakfast

1 cup (250 mL) higher-fiber (5 g),
moderate-carbohydrate (less than
25 g) cereal mixed with ¾ cup
(175 mL) blueberry-flavored 2% or
0% Greek yogurt

Lunch

Tuscan Sausage and Polenta
(page 127)

Snack

2 tbsp (30 mL) pecans
1 small banana

Dinner

Citrus Fish Fajitas (page 142)
½ cup (125 mL) steamed spinach
2 Lemon Ginger Cupcakes (page 219)

Breakfast

Italian Baked Eggs with Ciabatta
Toast (page 76)

Lunch

Peanut butter and jam sandwich
(2 slices sprouted bread
sandwiching 4 tsp/20 mL natural
peanut butter and 2 tsp/10 mL
jam)

²⁄₃ cup (150 mL) plain 2% Greek
yogurt

Snack

Chocolate Mousse (page 223)

Dinner

Meatloaf with Sweet Potato Fries
(page 194)

1½ cups (375 mL) sliced cucumbers
and tomatoes

Snack

1 higher-fiber, lower-carbohydrate,
higher-protein bar (about 5 grams
fiber, 15 grams carbohydrate, 7 to
14 grams protein)

Breakfast

English muffin (halved and toasted),
¼ cup (60 mL) steamed spinach
and 2 eggs cooked any style; top
each muffin half with half the
spinach and 1 egg

Lunch

CABB Salad (page 112)
Roasted Garlic Pita Points (page 205)

Snack

²⁄₃ cup (150 mL) plain 2% Greek
yogurt

½ cup (125 mL) berries

Dinner

Pasta Bolognese: 2 oz (60 g) sprouted
grain pasta, cooked until al dente,
topped with sauce (½ cup/125 mL
unsweetened tomato sauce,
preferably made with olive oil;
4 oz/125 g browned ground
turkey; ¼ cup/60 mL diced
cooked carrots; 8 sliced olives;
1 cup/250 mL steamed spinach)

Snack

½ cup (125 mL) unsweetened non-
dairy milk

2 Oatmeal Chocolate Chip Cookies
(page 214)

Week 2

Breakfast

Fiesta Eggs Benedict (page 80)

Lunch

No Skimpy Shrimp Salad Sandwich (page 116)

Snack

1 small apple

1 oz (30 g) cheese

Dinner

5 oz (150 g) roast turkey (discard skin after roasting)

1 small baked sweet potato with 1 tsp (5 mL) olive oil and ¼ tsp (1 mL) ground cinnamon

1½ cups (375 mL) broccoli sautéed in 1 tsp (5 mL) olive oil and 1 tsp (5 mL) minced garlic

Snack

3 tbsp (45 mL) guacamole

½ cup (125 mL) raw cauliflower florets and ½ whole wheat pita, toasted

Breakfast

2 Kitchen Sink Muffins (page 98)

⅔ cup (150 mL) plain 2% Greek yogurt

Lunch

Curry and Harissa Chicken Salad (page 114)

Snack

¼ cup (60 mL) almonds

1 medium orange

Dinner

5 oz (150 g) grilled filet mignon

1½ cups (375 mL) Brussels sprouts roasted in 1 tsp (5 mL) olive oil

1 cup (250 mL) diced potatoes roasted in 1 tsp (5 mL) olive oil

MONDAY

Breakfast

2 whole-grain waffles (20 grams carbohydrate total) with 1 tbsp (15 mL) natural peanut butter, 2 tsp (10 mL) agave nectar or liquid honey and $\frac{1}{2}$ tsp (2 mL) ground cinnamon

Lunch

Classic Tuna Wrap (page 120)

Hummus with Crudités: $\frac{1}{4}$ cup (60 mL) hummus; $\frac{1}{2}$ apple, sliced; $\frac{1}{2}$ cup (125 mL) baby carrots

Snack

$\frac{1}{2}$ cup (125 mL) cottage cheese
$\frac{3}{4}$ cup (175 mL) blueberries

Dinner

Chinese Five-Spice Tempeh (page 136)
Grapefruit Olive Oil Cake (page 220)

TUESDAY

Breakfast

Avocado Toast with a Twist (page 77)

Lunch

1 cup (250 mL) lentil soup
2 cups (500 mL) mixed greens with 1 oz (30 g) goat cheese, crumbled; $\frac{1}{4}$ cup (60 mL) raspberries; 1 tbsp (15 mL) vinaigrette

Snack

Becca's Baked Brie with Apple Dippers (page 206)

Dinner

Hoisin Chicken (page 173)
$\frac{1}{2}$ cup (125 mL) steamed diced butternut squash

Snack

2 cups (500 mL) air-popped popcorn
1 oz (30 g) Cheddar cheese

WEDNESDAY

Breakfast

2/3 cup (150 mL) plain 2% Greek yogurt with Homemade Granola (page 71)

Lunch

Turkey Sandwich: 2 slices sprouted bread sandwich with 1 tbsp (15 mL) Olive Tapenade (page 202) and 4 oz (125 g) turkey breast

1 1/4 cups (300 mL) mixed berries

Snack

Balsamic Avocado (page 204)

Dinner

Mama's Chicken Parmesan (page 166)

1 1/2 cups (375 mL) steamed mixed vegetables (such as Tuscan kale, carrots and broccoli)

THURSDAY

Breakfast

1 cup (250 mL) bran flakes cereal topped with 3/4 cup (175 mL) unsweetened almond milk, 2 tbsp (30 mL) chopped pecans, 1 tsp (5 mL) wheat germ, 1 cup (250 mL) blueberries

Lunch

Grilled Salmon over Chopped Greek Salad (page 109)

Snack

2/3 cup (150 mL) flavored 2% Greek yogurt (such as Key lime or coconut)

Dinner

Herbed Pork Tenderloin with Smashed Potatoes (page 182)

1 cup (250 mL) thinly sliced red bell pepper

Snack

1 higher-fiber, lower-carbohydrate, higher-protein bar (about 5 grams fiber, 15 grams carbohydrate, 7 to 14 grams protein)

FRIDAY

Breakfast

Everyday Breakfast Sandwich
(page 78)

Lunch

Beef Tacos (page 128)
1 cup (250 mL) baby carrots

Snack

2 cups (500 mL) air-popped
popcorn
1/4 cup (60 mL) almonds

Dinner

Pasta and Shrimp with Spicy
Tomato Spinach and Cream Sauce
(page 156)

Snack

2/3 cup (150 mL) plain 2% Greek
yogurt mixed with 1/2 cup
(125 mL) berries and 1 tbsp
(15 mL) wheat germ

SATURDAY

Breakfast

Huevos Rancheros (page 82)

Lunch

Turkey Noodle Soup (page 104)
2 cups (500 mL) nonstarchy
vegetables (such as broccoli,
cauliflower and Brussels sprouts)
roasted with 1 tsp (5 mL) olive oil

Snack

1/2 cup (125 mL) cottage cheese
3/4 cup (175 mL) diced fresh
pineapple

Dinner

Vegetable Tofu Stir-Fry: 3 cups
(750 mL) mixed vegetables (such
as snow peas, carrots and broccoli),
1/2 cup (125 mL) thawed frozen
shelled edamame, 1 cup (250 mL)
cubed firm tofu, 2 tbsp (30 mL)
reduced-sodium teriyaki sauce and
1 tbsp (15 mL) toasted sesame seeds
3/4 cup (175 mL) cooked whole
wheat couscous

Snack

3/4 cup (175 mL) ice cream

References

Accu-Chek. How to test your blood sugar. *Accu-Chek*. Accessed Oct 15, 2016. Available at www.accu-chek.com/us/glucose-monitoring/how-to-check.html.

Alavian SM. Diabetes mellitus and fatty liver disease: Which comes first? *Int J Endocrinol Metab*. 2010; 8 (3): 130–1.

Alexandria V. American Diabetes Association applauds FDA's revised nutrition label rules. May 24, 2016. *American Diabetes Association*. Accessed Jul 10, 2016. Available at www.diabetes.org/newsroom/press-releases/2016/ada-applauds-fda-revised-nutrition-label-rules.html.

American Diabetes Association. About our meal plans. *American Diabetes Association*. Accessed Jun 9, 2016. Available at www.diabetes.org/mfa-recipes/about-our-meal-plans.html.

American Diabetes Association. Adjusting the meal plan. *American Diabetes Association*. Accessed Jun 9, 2016. Available at www.diabetes.org/mfa-recipes/2016-04-adjusting-the-meal-plan.html.

American Diabetes Association. Alcohol. *American Diabetes Association*. Jun 6, 2014. Accessed Jul 2, 2016. Available at www.diabetes.org/food-and-fitness/food/what-can-i-eat/making-healthy-food-choices/alcohol.html.

American Diabetes Association. Dawn phenomenon. *American Diabetes Association*. Updated Jun 7, 2013. Accessed Jun 28, 2016. Available at www.diabetes.org/living-with-diabetes/treatment-and-care/blood-glucose-control/dawn-phenomenon.html.

American Diabetes Association. DKA (ketoacidosis) & ketones. *American Diabetes Association*. Mar 18, 2015. Accessed Jul 1, 2016. Available at www.diabetes.org/living-with-diabetes/complications/ketoacidosis-dka.html.

American Diabetes Association. Nutrition recommendations and interventions for diabetes. *Diabetes Care*. 2008 Jan; 31 (Supplement 1): S61–S78.

American Diabetes Association. Standards of Medical Care in Diabetes — 2016. *Diabetes Care*. 2016; 39 (1): 13–22; 36–8; 39–46; 72–80.

American Heart Association. Cardiovascular disease & diabetes. *American Heart Association*. Updated Mar 23, 2016. Accessed Jun 18, 2016. Available at www.heart.org/HEARTORG/Conditions/Diabetes/WhyDiabetesMatters/Cardiovascular-Disease-Diabetes_UCM_313865_Article.jsp#.WBd-_TtU6t8.

Armstrong MJ, Colberg SR, Sigal RJ. Moving beyond cardio: The value of resistance training, balance training, and other forms of exercise in the management of diabetes. *Diabetes Spectr*. 2015 Jan; 28 (1): 14–23.

Barbara Davis Center for Diabetes. Ketone testing. *University of Colorado*. Accessed Jun 13, 2016. Available at www.ucdenver.edu/academics/colleges/medicalschool/centers/BarbaraDavis/Documents/book-understandingdiabetes/ud05.pdf.

Bhupathiraju SN, Pan A, Manson JE, et al. Changes in coffee intake and subsequent risk of type 2 diabetes: Three large cohorts of US men and women. *Diabetologia*. 2014 Jul; 57 (7): 1346–54.

Bittman M. Butter is back. *The New York Times*. Mar 25, 2014. Accessed Jun 12, 2016. Available at www.nytimes.com/2014/03/26/opinion/bittman-butter-is-back.html?_r=0.

Brown SA, Sharpless JL. Osteoporosis: An under-appreciated complication of diabetes. *Clin Diabetes*. 2004; 22: 10–20.

Bwell Health Promotion. Alcohol and your body. *Brown University*. Accessed Jul 2, 2016. Available at www.brown.edu/campus-life/health/services/promotion/alcohol-other-drugs-alcohol/alcohol-and-your-body.

Caldwell J. Sports drinks: Are they effective in improving athletic performance? *Vanderbilt University*. Apr 21, 1997. Accessed Apr 6, 2014. Available at http://healthpsych.psy.vanderbilt.edu/HealthPsych/gatorade.htm.

Carley DW, Farabi SS. Physiology of sleep. *Diabetes Spectr*. 2016 Feb; 29 (1): 5–9.

Case S. Are spices safe for a gluten-free diet? *Allergic Living*. Accessed Jul 2, 2016. Available at http://allergicliving.com/2014/07/02/are-spices-safe-for-a-gluten-free-diet.

Castaneda C, Layne JE, Munoz-Orians L, et al. A randomized controlled trial of resistance exercise training to improve glycemic control in older adults with type 2 diabetes. *Diabetes Care*. 2002 Dec; 25 (12): 2335–41.

Celiac Disease Foundation. Celiac disease and diabetes. *Celiac Disease Foundation*. Accessed Jul 2, 2016. Available at https://celiac.org/celiac-disease/understanding-celiac-disease-2/celiac-disease-and-comorbid-conditions/cd-and-diabetes.

Centers for Disease Control and Prevention. Diabetes latest. *Centers for Disease Control and Prevention*. Updated Jun 17, 2014. Accessed Jun 9, 2016. Available at www.cdc.gov/Features/DiabetesFactSheet.

Chen JT, Kotani K. Association between coffee consumption and an oxidative stress marker in women. *Wien Klin Wochenschr*. 2015 Jul; 127 (13–14): 567–9.

Cipullo L. 5 Strategies for balancing blood sugar during the holidays. *Diabetic Connect*. Apr 9, 2016. Accessed Jun 28, 2016. Available at www.diabetic connect.com/diabetes-information-articles/ general/2299-a-sweet-strategy-for-balancing-blood-sugar.

Cipullo L. Why you crave! *Laura Cipullo*. Jun 7, 2016. Accessed Jun 26, 2016. Available at www.lauracipullo.com.

Cipullo L, Editors of Women's Health. *The Women's Health Body Clock Diet: The 6-Week Plan to Reboot Your Metabolism and Lose Weight Naturally*. New York: Rodale Books, 2015.

Cleveland Clinic Staff. Heart health benefits of chocolate. *Cleveland Clinic*. Jan 2012. Accessed Oct 21, 2016. Available at http:// my.clevelandclinic.org/services/heart/prevention/ nutrition/food-choices/benefits-of-chocolate.

Cohen S. 5 reasons to take astaxanthin every day. *Huffington Post*. Feb 28, 2013. Accessed Oct 30, 2016. Available at www.huffingtonpost.com/suzy-cohen-rph/astaxanthin_b_2750910.html.

Colberg SR, Sigal RJ, Fernhall B, et al. Exercise and type 2 diabetes: The American College of Sports Medicine and the American Diabetes Association: Joint position statement executive summary. *Diabetes Care*. 2010 Dec; 33 (12): 2692–6.

Cowan M. Are beets good for people with diabetes? *Medical News Today*. Accessed Oct 21, 2016. Available at www.medicalnewstoday.com/ articles/311343.php#are_beets_good_for_people_ with_diabetes.

Cryer P. Hypoglycemia during therapy of diabetes. May 28, 2015. In: De Groot LJ, Beck-Peccoz P, Chrousos G, et al; editors. *Endotext* [Internet]. South Dartmouth (MA): MDText.com, Inc.; 2000–.

CTV News Staff. Maple syrup could protect against Alzheimer's, research suggests. *CTV News*. Mar 19, 2016. Accessed Oct 21, 2016. Available at www. ctvnews.ca/health/maple-syrup-could-protect-against-alzheimer-s-research-suggests-1.2824329.

Dalgård C, Petersen MS, Weihe P, et al. Vitamin D status in relation to glucose metabolism and type 2 diabetes in septuagenarians. *Diabetes Care*. 2011 Jun; 34 (6): 1284–8.

Daniluk J. 4 health benefits of limes. *Chatelaine* magazine. Jul 30, 2014. Accessed Oct 21, 2016. Available at www.chatelaine.com/health/diet/ health-benefits-of-limes.

De Lorenzo A, Del Gobbo V, Premrov MG, et al. Normal-weight obese syndrome: Early inflammation? *Am J Clin Nutr*. 2007 Jan; 85 (1): 40–5.

de Lorgeril M, Salen P, Martin JL, et al. Mediterranean diet, traditional risk factors, and the rate of cardiovascular complications after myocardial infarction: Final report of the Lyon Diet Heart Study. *Circulation*. 1999 Feb 16; 99 (6): 779–85.

de Roos N, Schouten E, Katan M. Consumption of a solid fat rich in lauric acid results in a more favorable serum lipid profile in healthy men and women than consumption of a solid fat rich in trans-fatty acids. *J Nutr*. 2001 Feb; 131 (2): 242–5.

Delahanty LM. Making a meaningful difference: Learning from people, practice and research. *Diabetes Spectr*. 2016 Feb; 29 (1): 58–64.

Delahanty LM, Meigs JB, Hayden D, et al. Psychological and behavioral correlates of baseline BMI in the diabetes prevention program (DPP). *Diabetes Care*. 2002 Nov; 25 (11): 1992–8.

Depner CM, Traber MG, Bobe G, et al. A metabolomic analysis of omega-3 fatty acid-mediated attenuation of Western diet–induced nonalcoholic steatohepatitis in LDLR-/- mice. *PLoS One*. 2013 Dec 17; 8 (12): e83756.

Devon LJ. Mindfulness training improves diabetes symptoms and blood sugar levels. *Natural News*. Aug 25, 2014. Accessed Oct 31, 2016. Available at www.naturalnews.com/046585_mindfulness_ diabetes_symptoms_blood_sugar_levels.html.

Diabetes Prevention Program Research Group, Knowler WC, Fowler SE, et al. 10-year follow-up of diabetes incidence and weight loss in the Diabetes Prevention Program Outcomes Study. *Lancet*. 2009 Nov 14; 374 (9702): 1677–86.

DiNardo M. Mindfulness training benefits U.S. veterans with diabetes. *Newswise*. Aug 4, 2014. Accessed Oct 31, 2016. Available at www. newswise.com/articles/mindfulness-training-benefits-u-s-veterans-with-diabetes.

Dinsmoor R. Counterregulatory hormones. *Diabetes Self-Management*. Mar 27, 2014. Accessed Oct 31, 2016. Available at www.diabetesselfmanagement .com/diabetes-resources/definitions/ counterregulatory-hormones.

Dinsmoor R. Type 1.5 diabetes. *Diabetes Self-Management*. Apr 9, 2014. Accessed Jun 20, 2016. Available at www.diabetesselfmanagement.com/ diabetes-resources/definitions/type-1-5-diabetes.

Duggan C, de Dieu Tapsoba J, Mason C, et al. Effect of vitamin D_3 supplementation in combination with weight loss on inflammatory biomarkers in postmenopausal women: A randomized controlled study. *Cancer Prev Res (Phila)*. 2015 Jul; 8 (7): 628–35.

Estruch R, Martínez-González MA, Corella D, et al. Effect of a high-fat Mediterranean diet on body-weight and waist circumference: A prespecified secondary outcomes analysis of the PREDIMED randomised controlled trial. *Lancet Diabetes Endocrinol*. 2016 Aug; 4 (8): 666–76.

Farabi S. Type 1 diabetes and sleep. *Diabetes Spectr*. 2016 Feb; 29 (1): 10–3.

Franz MJ, Powers MA, Leontos C, et al. The evidence for medical nutrition therapy for type 1 and type 2 diabetes in adults. *J Am Diet Assoc*. 2010 Dec; 110 (12): 1852–89.

Friis AM, Consedine NS, Johnson MH. Does kindness matter? Diabetes, depression, and self-compassion: A selective review and research agenda. *Diabetes Spectr.* 2015 Nov; 28 (4): 252–7.

Fruits and Veggies More Matters Staff. Parsnips: Nutrition, selection, storage. *Fruits and Veggies More Matters.* Accessed Oct 21, 2016. Available at www.fruitsandveggiesmorematters.org/parsnips.

Fukuchi Y, Hiramitsu M, Okada M, et al. Lemon polyphenols suppress diet-induced obesity by up-regulation of MRNA levels of the enzymes involved in beta-oxidation in mouse white adipose tissue. *J Clin Biochem Nutr.* 2008 Nov; 43 (3): 201–9.

The George Washington University: Health Promotion and Prevention Services. Alcohol absorption. *The George Washington University.* Accessed Jul 2, 2016. Available at https://prevention.gwu.edu/alcohol-absorption.

Gilbert MP, Pratley RE. The impact of diabetes and diabetes medications on bone health. *Endocr Rev.* 2015 Apr; 36 (2): 194–213.

Glycemic Research Institute. The diabetic exchange list (exchange diet). *Glycemic Research Institute.* Accessed Jul 10, 2016. Available at http://glycemic.com/diabeticexchange/the diabetic exchange list.pdf.

Grace Communications Foundation. Do you have to eat 100% local, sustainable, and organic? *Grace Communications Foundation.* Accessed Jun 26, 2016. Available at www.sustainabletable.org/568/do-you-have-to-eat-100-local-sustainable-and-organic.

Greenberg JA, Boozer CN, Geliebter A. Coffee, diabetes, and weight control. *Am J Clin Nutr.* 2006 Oct; 84 (4): 682–93.

Hamasaki H. Daily physical activity and type 2 diabetes: A review. *World J Diabetes.* 2016 Jun 25; 7 (12): 243–51.

Hamman RF, Wing RR, Edelstein SL, et al. Effect of weight loss with lifestyle intervention on risk of diabetes. *Diabetes Care.* 2006 Sep; 29 (9): 2102–7.

Harvard T.H. Chan School of Public Health. Added sugar in the diet. *Harvard T.H. Chan School of Public Health.* Accessed Jul 10, 2016. Available at www.hsph.harvard.edu/nutritionsource/carbohydrates/added-sugar-in-the-diet.

Heart Foundation. Eggs. *Heart Foundation.* Accessed Oct 21, 2016. Available at www.heartfoundation.org.au/healthy-eating/food-and-nutrition/protein-foods/eggs.

Heinonen OP, Albanes D; Alpha-Tocopherol, Beta Carotene Cancer Prevention Study Group. The effect of vitamin E and beta carotene on the incidence of lung cancer and other cancers in male smokers. *N Engl J Med.* 1994 Apr 14; 330 (15): 102935.

Hernandez TL. Carbohydrate content in the GDM diet: Two views: View 1: Nutrition therapy in gestational diabetes: The case for complex carbohydrates. *Diabetes Spectr.* 2016 May; 29 (2): 82–8.

Hu FB, Stampfer MJ, Manson JE, et al. Dietary fat intake and the risk of coronary heart disease in women. *N Engl J Med.* 1997 Nov 20; 337 (21): 1491–9.

Ipatenco S. Are pinto beans healthy? *Healthy Eating.* Accessed Oct 21, 2016. Available at http://healthyeating.sfgate.com/pinto-beans-healthy-3779.html.

Ipatenco S. What are the benefits of eating green bell peppers? *Healthy Eating.* Accessed Oct 21, 2016. Available at http://healthyeating.sfgate.com/benefits-eating-green-bell-peppers-4245.html.

Jeffrey K. How to hydrate before, during, and after a workout. *Active.com.* Accessed Apr 6, 2014. Available at www.active.com/nutrition/articles/how-to-hydrate-before-during-and-after-a-workout.

Jiang Y, Wu SH, Shu XO, et al. Cruciferous vegetable intake is inversely correlated with circulating levels of proinflammatory markers in women. *J Acad Nutr Diet.* 2014 May; 114 (5): 700–8.e2.

Johansson E, Hussain A, Kuktaite R, et al. Contribution of organically grown crops to human health. *Int J Environ Res Public Health.* 2014 Apr 8; 11 (4): 3870–93.

Johnson PM, Kenny PJ. Dopamine D2 receptors in addiction-like reward dysfunction and compulsive eating in obese rats. *Nat Neurosci.* 2010 May; 13 (5): 635–41.

Joshi AN, Bhatt AD. Type 1.5 diabetes mellitus. *J MGIMS.* Sep 2008; 13 (2): 25–8.

Joshi AS, Varthakavi PK, Bhagwat NM, et al. Response to review article "Type 1 diabetes and osteoporosis: Review of literature." *Indian J Endocrinol Metab.* 2014 Jul; 18 (4): 589–90.

Joslin Diabetes Center. Can I eat as many sugar-free foods as I want? *Joslin Diabetes Center.* Accessed Jun 26, 2016. Available at www.joslin.org/info/can_i_eat_as_many_sugar_free_foods_as_i_want.html.

Joslin Diabetes Center. Diabetes and scheduling: Starting a routine. *Joslin Diabetes Center.* Accessed Jun 13, 2016. Available at www.joslin.org/info/diabetes_and_scheduling_starting_a_routine.html.

Joslin Diabetes Center. Why did I gain weight when I started taking insulin? *Joslin Diabetes Center.* Accessed Jun 28, 2016. Available at www.joslin.org/info/why_did_i_gain_weight_when_i_started_taking_insulin.html.

Juneja R, Palmer JP. Type $1\frac{1}{2}$ diabetes: Myth or reality? *Autoimmunity.* 1999; 29 (1): 65–83.

Kratina K. Orthorexia nervosa. *National Eating Disorders.* Accessed Jun 22, 2016. Available at www.nationaleatingdisorders.org/orthorexia-nervosa.

Kris-Etherton PM. AHA science advisory: Monounsaturated fatty acids and risk of cardiovascular disease. *J Nutr.* 1999 Dec; 129 (12): 2280–4.

Liang N, Kitts DD. Antioxidant property of coffee components: Assessment of methods that define mechanisms of action. *Molecules.* 2014 Nov 19; 19 (11): 19180–208.

Lipscombe LL, Jamal SA, Booth GL, et al. The risk of hip fractures in older individuals with diabetes: A population-based study. *Diabetes Care.* 2007 Apr; 30 (4): 835–41.

Loucks EB, Gilman SE, Britton WB, et al. Associations of mindfulness with glucose regulation and diabetes. *Am J Health Behav.* 2016 Mar; 40 (2): 258–67.

Martinez E. Health benefits of black-eyed peas. *Livestrong.* Updated Apr 15, 2015. Accessed Oct 21, 2016. Available at www.livestrong.com/article/414892-health-benefits-of-black-eyed-peas.

Mayo Clinic Staff. Fast fix: Acorn squash with apples. *Mayo Clinic.* Dec 2, 2015. Accessed Oct 21, 2016. Available at www.mayoclinic.org/healthy-lifestyle/nutrition-and-healthy-eating/in-depth/health-tip/art-20049236.

Mayo Clinic Staff. Folate. *Mayo Clinic.* Feb 1, 2014. Accessed Oct 21, 2016. Available at www.mayoclinic.org/drugs-supplements/folate/background/hrb-20059475.

Mayo Clinic Staff. Meatless meals: The benefits of eating less meat. *Mayo Clinic.* Aug 19, 2014. Accessed Jul 12, 2016. Available at www.mayoclinic.org/healthy-lifestyle/nutrition-and-healthy-eating/in-depth/meatless-meals/art-20048193?pg=1.

Mayo Clinic Staff. Slide show: 10 great health foods. *Mayo Clinic.* Mar 25, 2016. Accessed Oct 21, 2016. Available at www.mayoclinic.org/healthy-lifestyle/nutrition-and-healthy-eating/multimedia/health-foods/sls-20076653.

Mayo Clinic Staff. Test ID: DGLDN; Gliadin (deamidated) antibodies evaluation, IgG and IgA, serum. *Mayo Medical Laboratories.* Accessed Jun 25, 2016. Available at www.mayomedicallaboratories.com/test-catalog/Clinical+and+Interpretive/89031.

Mayo Clinic Staff. Weight loss: Feel full on fewer calories. *Mayo Clinic.* Mar 4, 2014. Accessed Oct 21, 2016. Available at www.mayoclinic.org/healthy-lifestyle/weight-loss/in-depth/weight-loss/art-20044318.

McCulloch M. Saturated fat: Not so bad or just bad science? *Today's Dietitian.* 2014 Nov; 16 (11): 32.

Medline Plus. Ketones urine test. *U.S. National Library of Medicine.* Updated Nov 19, 2015. Accessed Jul 2, 2016. Available at https://medlineplus.gov/ency/article/003585.htm.

Medtronic. Continuous glucose monitoring. *Medtronic MiniMed.* Accessed Jun 28, 2016. Available at www.medtronicdiabetes.com/treatments/continuous-glucose-monitoring.

National Cancer Institute. Prostate cancer, nutrition, and dietary supplements (PDQ)-health profession version. *U.S. Department of Health and Human Services.* Updated Oct 21, 2016. Accessed Nov 21, 2016. Available at www.cancer.gov/about-cancer/treatment/cam/hp/prostate-supplements-pdq.

National Institute of Arthritis and Musculoskeletal and Skin Diseases. Calcium and vitamin D: Important at every age. *National Institutes of Health.* May 2015. Accessed Jul 2, 2016. Available at www.niams.nih.gov/Health%5FInfo/Bone/Bone%5FHealth/Nutrition.

National Institute of Diabetes and Digestive and Kidney Diseases. Diagnosis of celiac disease. *U.S. Department of Health & Human Services.* Jun 2016. Accessed Jun 22, 2016. Available at www.niddk.nih.gov/health-information/health-topics/digestive-diseases/celiac-disease/Pages/diagnosis.aspx.

National Institute of Diabetes and Digestive and Kidney Diseases. Eating, diet and nutrition for celiac disease. *U.S. Department of Health & Human Services.* Jun 2016. Accessed Jun 22, 2016. Available at www.niddk.nih.gov/health-information/health-topics/digestive-diseases/celiac-disease/pages/eating-diet-nutrition.aspx.

National Institutes of Health. Folate. *U.S. Department of Health & Human Services.* Updated Apr 20, 2016. Accessed Oct 21, 2016. Available at https://ods.od.nih.gov/factsheets/Folate-HealthProfessional.

National Institutes of Health. Garlic. *U.S. Department of Health & Human Services.* Updated Sep 2016. Accessed Oct 21, 2016. Available at https://nccih.nih.gov/health/garlic/ataglance.htm.

National Institutes of Health: Office of Dietary Supplements. Vitamin D: Fact sheet for health professionals. *U.S. Department of Health & Human Services.* Feb 11, 2016. Accessed Jul 2, 2016. Available at http://ods.od.nih.gov/factsheets/VitaminD-HealthProfessional.

Nestel P, Cehun M, Chronopoulos A. Effects of long-term consumption and single meals of chickpeas on plasma glucose, insulin, and triacylglycerol concentrations. *Am J Clin Nutr.* 2004 Mar; 79 (3): 390–5.

Nordqvist C. Garlic: Health benefits, therapeutic benefits. *Medical News Today.* Sep 15, 2015. Accessed Oct 21, 2016. Available at www.medicalnewstoday.com/articles/265853.php.

Nordqvist J. Apples: Health benefits, facts, research. *Medical News Today.* Jan 12, 2016. Accessed Oct 21, 2016. Available at www.medicalnewstoday.com/articles/267290.php.

Nordqvist J. Oats: Health benefits, facts, research. *Medical News Today*. Jan 19, 2016. Accessed Oct 21, 2016. Available at www.medicalnewstoday.com/articles/270680.php.

Oaklander M. Which is healthier: Wild salmon vs farmed salmon. *Prevention.com*. Jan 28, 2013. Accessed Jul 10, 2016. Available at www.prevention.com/content/which-healthier-wild-salmon-vs-farmed-salmon.

Oelke EA, Putnam DH, Teynor TM, et al. Quinoa. *Alternative Field Crops Manual; University of Wisconsin-Extension and University of Minnesota*. Feb 1992. Accessed Jul 12, 2016. Available at www.hort.purdue.edu/newcrop/afcm/quinoa.html.

Ooi CP, Loke SC. Sweet potato for type 2 diabetes mellitus. *Cochrane Database Syst Rev*. 2013 Sep 3; (9): CD009128.

Organic Facts Staff. Health benefits of dates. *Organic Facts*. Accessed Oct 21, 2016. Available at www.organicfacts.net/health-benefits/fruit/health-benefits-of-dates.html.

Pan XR, Li GW, Hu YH, et al. Effects of diet and exercise in preventing NIDDM in people with impaired glucose tolerance: The Da Qing IGT and Diabetes Study. *Diabetes Care*. 1997 Apr; 20 (4): 537–44.

Patel S, Goyal A. Recent developments in mushrooms as anti-cancer therapeutics: A review. 3 *Biotech*. 2012; 2 (1): 1–15.

Pepino MY, Tiemann CD, Patterson BW, et al. Sucralose affects glycemic and hormonal responses to an oral glucose load. *Diabetes Care*. 2013 Sep; 36 (9): 2530–5.

Powell A. The entire egg. *Harvard Gazette*. Feb 24, 2015. Accessed Jul 12, 2016. Available at http://news.harvard.edu/gazette/story/2015/02/the-entire-egg.

Rains C, Bryson HM. Topical capsaicin: A review of its pharmacological properties and therapeutic potential in post-herpetic neuralgia, diabetic neuropathy and osteoarthritis. *Drugs Aging*. 1995 Oct; 7 (4): 317–28.

Ros E. Health benefits of nut consumption. *Nutrients*. 2010 Jul; 2 (7): 652–82.

Rosenzweig S, Reibel DK, Greeson JM, et al. Mindfulness-based stress reduction is associated with improved glycemic control in type 2 diabetes mellitus: A pilot study. *Altern Ther Health Med*. 2007 Sep–Oct; 13 (5): 36–8.

Schwarzenberg SJ, Brunzell C. Type 1 diabetes and celiac disease: Overview and medical nutrition therapy. *Diabetes Spectrum*. 2002 Jul; 15 (3): 197–201.

Spero D. The mystery of coffee and diabetes. *Diabetes Self-Management*. Mar 2, 2011. Accessed Jun 26, 2016. Available at www.diabetesselfmanagement.com/blog/the-mystery-of-coffee-and-diabetes.

Spritzler F. A low-carbohydrate, whole-foods approach to managing diabetes and prediabetes. *Diabetes Spectrum*. 2012 Nov; 25 (4): 238–43.

Stull AJ, Cash KC, Johnson WD, et al. Bioactives in blueberries improve insulin sensitivity in obese, insulin-resistant men and women. *J Nutr*. 2010 Oct; 140 (10): 1764–8.

Sugar Association. Labeling terms. *The Sugar Association*. Accessed Jun 26, 2016. Available at www.sugar.org/sugar-basics-2/food-labeling/labeling-terms.

Swalin R. 6 things you should know about zucchini. *Health.com*. Aug 8, 2014. Accessed Oct 21, 2016. Available at http://news.health.com/2014/08/08/6-things-you-should-know-about-zucchini.

Tay J, Luscombe-Marsh ND, Thompson CH, et al. Comparison of low- and high-carbohydrate diets for type 2 diabetes management: A randomized trial. *Am J Clin Nutr*. 2015 Oct; 102 (4): 780–90.

University of California, San Diego. Blood sugar & other hormones. *Diabetes Education Online*. Accessed Jun 28, 2016. Available at https://dtc.ucsf.edu/types-of-diabetes/type2/understanding-type-2-diabetes/how-the-body-processes-sugar/blood-sugar-other-hormones.

University of California, San Diego. Diabetes and exercise. *Diabetes Education Online*. Accessed Jun 9, 2016. Available at https://dtc.ucsf.edu/learning-library/videos/videos-2/diabetes-and-exercise.

U.S. Department of Agriculture. Sustainable agriculture: Definitions and terms. *United States Department of Agriculture: National Agricultural Library*. Sep 1999. Updated Aug 2007. Accessed Jun 26, 2016. Available at www.nal.usda.gov/afsic/sustainable-agriculture-definitions-and-terms.

U.S. Department of Agriculture. USDA Organic. *U.S. Department of Agriculture*. Jun 2016. Accessed Jul 2, 2016. Available at www.usda.gov/wps/portal/usda/usdahome?contentid=organic-agriculture.html.

U.S. Food and Drug Administration. Final determination regarding partially hydrogenated oils (removing trans fat). *U.S. Food and Drug Administration*. Updated Oct 7, 2016. Accessed Dec 4, 2016. Available at www.fda.gov/Food/IngredientsPackagingLabeling/FoodAdditivesIngredients/ucm449162.htm.

U.S. Food and Drug Administration. Gluten and food labeling. *U.S. Food and Drug Administration*. Updated May 2, 2016. Accessed Jun 22, 2016. Available at www.fda.gov/food/guidanceregulation/guidancedocumentsregulatoryinformation/allergens/ucm367654.htm

U.S. Food and Drug Administration. What you need to know about mercury in fish and shellfish (brochure). *U.S. Food and Drug Administration*. Mar 2004. Accessed Jul 10, 2016. Available at www.fda.gov/food/resourcesforyou/consumers/ucm110591.htm.

van Dijk AE, Olthof MR, Meeuse JC, et al. Acute effects of decaffeinated coffee and the major coffee components chlorogenic acid and trigonelline on glucose tolerance. *Diabetes Care.* 2009 Jun; 32 (6): 1023–5.

Van Gaal L, Scheen A. Weight management in type 2 diabetes: Current and emerging approaches to treatment. *Diabetes Care.* 2015 Jun; 38 (6): 1161–72.

Vetter C, Devore EE, Ramin CA, et al. Mismatch of sleep and work timing and risk of type 2 diabetes. *Diabetes Care.* 2015 Sep; 38 (9): 1707–13.

Virtanen JK, Mursu J, Voutilainen S, et al. Serum omega-3 polyunsaturated fatty acids and risk of incident type 2 diabetes in men: The Kuopio Ischemic Heart Disease Risk Factor study. *Diabetes Care.* 2014; 37 (1): 189–96.

Ware M. Bananas: Health benefits, facts, research. *Medical News Today.* Jan 11, 2016. Accessed Oct 21, 2016. Available at www.medicalnewstoday.com/articles/271157.php.

Ware M. Cabbage: Health benefits, facts, research. *Medical News Today.* Oct 24, 2016. Accessed Dec 2, 2016. Available at www.medicalnewstoday.com/articles/284823.php.

Ware M. Cilantro: Health benefits, facts, research. *Medical News Today.* Sep 1, 2016. Accessed Oct 21, 2016. Available at www.medicalnewstoday.com/articles/277627.php.

Ware M. Cucumbers: Health benefits, facts, research. *Medical News Today.* Jul 6, 2016. Accessed Oct 21, 2016. Available at www.medicalnewstoday.com/articles/283006.php.

Ware M. Parsley: Health benefits, facts, research. *Medical News Today.* Nov 24, 2016. Accessed Oct 21, 2016. Available at www.medicalnewstoday.com/articles/284490.php.

Ware M. Peaches: Health benefits, facts, research. *Medical News Today.* Feb 9, 2016. Accessed Oct 21, 2016. Available at www.medicalnewstoday.com/articles/274620.php.

Ware M. Pineapple: Health benefits, recipes, health risks. *Medical News Today.* Sep 10, 2015. Accessed Oct 21, 2016. Available at www.medicalnewstoday.com/articles/276903.php.

Ware M. Spinach: Health benefits, uses, precautions. *Medical News Today.* Sep 13, 2015 Accessed Oct 21, 2016. Available at www.medicalnewstoday.com/articles/270609.php.

Ware M. Watermelon: Health benefits and nutritional information. *Medical News Today.* Sep 13, 2015. Accessed Oct 21, 2016. Available at www.medicalnewstoday.com/articles/266886.php.

Whitebird RR, Kreitzer MJ, O'Connor PJ. Mindfulness-based stress reduction and diabetes. *Diabetes Spectr.* 2009 Sep 21; 22 (4): 226–30.

Whitley HP, Yong EV, Rasinen C. Selecting an A1c point-of-care. *Diabetes Spectr.* 2015 Aug; 28 (3): 201–8.

Wilson DR. Arugula: Health benefits, facts, research. *Medical News Today.* Aug 25, 2016. Accessed Oct 21, 2016. Available at www.medicalnewstoday.com/articles/282769.php.

Yancy WS Jr, Foy M, Chalecki AM, et al. A low-carbohydrate, ketogenic diet to treat type 2 diabetes. *Nutr Metab (Lond).* 2005 Dec 1; 2: 34.

Zakhari S. Overview: How is alcohol metabolized by the body? *Alcohol Res Health.* 2006; 29 (4): 245–54.

Zeratsky K. Go nuts for good health. *Mayo Clinic.* Feb 20, 2014. Accessed Oct 21, 2016. Available at www.mayoclinic.org/healthy-lifestyle/nutrition-and-healthy-eating/expert-blog/nuts-and-health/bgp-20087724.

Zeratsky K. I've heard that canned pumpkin is healthier than fresh pumpkin. Is that true? *Mayo Clinic.* Nov 6, 2014. Accessed Oct 21, 2016. Available at www.mayoclinic.org/healthy-lifestyle/nutrition-and-healthy-eating/expert-answers/pumpkin/faq-20058106.

Zeratsky K. What are MUFAs, and should I include them in my diet? *Mayo Clinic.* Feb 19, 2015. Accessed Oct 21, 2016. Available at www.mayoclinic.org/healthy-lifestyle/nutrition-and-healthy-eating/expert-answers/mufas/faq-20057775.

Library and Archives Canada Cataloguing in Publication

Cipullo, Laura, author
     Everyday diabetes meals : cooking for one or two / Laura Cipullo, RD, CDE, CEDRD, CDN & Lisa Mikus, RD, CNSC, CDN.

Includes index.
ISBN 978-0-7788-0566-3 (softcover)

     1. Diabetes—Diet therapy—Recipes. 2. Cooking for one. 3. Cooking for two. 4. Cookbooks.
I. Mikus, Lisa, 1988–, author II. Title.

RC662.C583 2017   641.5'6314   C2016-907744-6

Index